THE STATE IN NORTH AFRICA

COMPARATIVE POLITICS
AND INTERNATIONAL STUDIES SERIES

Series editors, Christophe Jaffrelot and Alain Dieckhoff
Series managing editor, Miriam Perier

The series consists of original manuscripts and translations of note-worthy manuscripts and publications in the social sciences emanating from the foremost French researchers.

The focus of the series is the transformation of politics and society by transnational and domestic factors—globalisation, migration and religion. States are more permeable to external influence than ever before and this phenomenon is accelerating processes of social and political change the world over. In seeking to understand and interpret these transformations, this series gives priority to social trends from below as much as to the interventions of state and nonstate actors.

LUIS MARTINEZ

The State in North Africa

After the Arab Uprisings

Translated by
Cynthia Schoch

HURST & COMPANY, LONDON

This English language edition first published in the United Kingdom in 2020 by
C. Hurst & Co. (Publishers) Ltd.,
41 Great Russell Street, London, WC1B 3PL
© Luis Martinez, 2020
English language translation © Cynthia Schoch, 2020
All rights reserved.
Printed in India

The right of Luis Martinez to be identified as the author of
this publication is asserted by him in accordance with the
Copyright, Designs and Patents Act, 1988.

The right of Cynthia Schoch to be identified as the translator
of this publication is asserted by her in accordance with the
Copyright, Designs and Patents Act, 1988.

A Cataloguing-in-Publication data record for this book
is available from the British Library.

ISBN: 9781787382961

This book is printed using paper from registered sustainable
and managed sources.

www.hurstpublishers.com

For Neyla

CONTENTS

ACKNOWLEDGMENTS

My gratitude goes to the Center for International Studies (CERI Sciences Po) and its director Alain Dieckhoff for their constant support of my research. I would also like to thank Christophe Jaffrelot for his critical reading of the first version of this manuscript. I am also grateful to the various institutions of research and expertise, both in France and elsewhere, that have facilitated my research. I would also like to thank the students, colleagues and experts—both sides of the Mediterranean—who have agreed to discuss and debate on the transformations of the region over the last few years. A very big thanks goes also to Miriam Perier for her remarkable support and to Dorian Ryser for his precious help. Finally, I would like to give a warm thanks to my publisher, Michael Dwyer for his constant interest in my work and to the Hurst team for their formidable professionalism. Last but not least, I would like to thank my talented translator, Cynthia Schoch.

LIST OF ABBREVIATIONS

AIS	Islamic Salvation Army
AMU	Arab Maghreb Union
ANDI	National Investment Agency
ANSEJ	National Agency for Youth Employment Support
AQIM	al-Qaeda in the Islamic Maghreb
BAT	Tunisian Antiterrorism Brigade
CCDH	Advisory Council on Human Rights
CGEM	Moroccan business federation
COMESSA	Community of Sahel and Saharan States
CSO	civil society organization
DSE	Directorate of State Security
EEC	European Economic Community
ENA	North African Star
ENP	European Neighbourhood Policy
EU	European Union
FIS	Islamic Salvation Front
FLN	National Liberation Front
GIA	Armed Islamic Group
GNA	Government of National Accord
GNC	General National Congress
GSPC	Salafist Group for Preaching and Combat
IER	Fairness and Reconciliation Commission
IMF	International Monetary Fund
Ircam	Royal Institute for Amazigh Culture
IS	Islamic State

LIST OF ABBREVIATIONS

ISGS	Islamic State in the Greater Sahara
ISIS	Islamic State of Iraq and Syria
JDP (PJD)	Justice and Development Party
LIFG	Libyan Islamic Fighting Group
LIMC	Libyan Islamic Movement for Change
LNA	Libyan National Army
MNLA	National Movement for the Liberation of Azawad
MOJWA	Movement for Oneness and Jihad in West Africa
MSP	Movement of the Society for Peace
NATO	North Atlantic Treaty Organization
NGO	non-governmental organization
NOC	National Oil Corporation
NTC	National Transitional Council
OAU	Organization of African Unity
OCP	Office Chérifien des Phosphates
OCRS	Common Organization of Saharan Regions
ONA	Omnium Nord-Africain
PSU	United Socialist Party
RND	National Rally for Democracy
RNI	National Rally of Independents
SADR	Sahrawi Arab Democratic Republic
SNI	National Investment Corporation
SSR	security sector reform
UDMA	Democratic Union of the Algerian Manifesto
UGTA	Algerian General Workers' Union
UGTT	Tunisian General Workers' Union
UN	United Nations
UNDP	United Nations Development Programme
UNSMIL	United Nations Support Mission in Libya
US	United States
USFP	Socialist Union of Popular Forces
USGT	Special Unit of Tunisian Guards
WTO	World Trade Organization

LIST OF FIGURES

INTRODUCTION

FROM COLONIAL RULE TO THE WAR ON TERROR

The disintegration of the state in Libya has stirred up a host of questions about nation-states in North Africa. The issue of national cohesion in North African countries is an old one, having risen almost immediately after each nation gained independence. In the summer of 1962, as the various protagonists were vying for power in Algiers, the spectre of "Congolization" in Algeria loomed.[1] In Morocco, under Hassan II's rule in the 1960s, several political figures and observers pointed out that "the apparent calm and relative ease of the transition should not let us forget that independence was a revolution and that a potentially revolutionary situation has prevailed in the country for the past ten years or so."[2] The political regimes that came on the heels of colonial rule did their utmost to prove such pessimistic prognoses wrong. From the 1970s, the political regimes of North Africa, under the leadership of charismatic figures such as Habib Bourguiba and Muammar Qadhafi and, to a lesser extent, Houari Boumediene and Hassan II[3] projected an image of strength and stability that reinforced an optimistic view of their evolution. Starting in the 1980s and especially in the 1990s, however, North Africa's failure to develop was patent: riots broke out throughout the entire region, a sign of the malaise afflicting the younger generation.[4] From the 1980s, North Africa was viewed as a powder keg. It claimed its first victims during the civil war that exploded in Algeria (1991–1999).[5]

1

All countries in the region, with or without hydrocarbon wealth, are faced with a large unemployed young population, a segment of which has advanced degrees, who bear the brunt of the failure of the region's economic development. While poverty diminished considerably, the inherent instability of unemployment and the shortcomings of the welfare state remained of great concern. Between 1970 and 2000, North Africa was faced with a population boom that cancelled out an economic growth insufficient to integrate newcomers in the job market. The factors responsible for this failure are well known: poor governance, corruption, economies dependent on volatile sectors such as hydrocarbons and tourism, misguided economic development models, and a weak private sector.[6] During the 1964–2010 period, the average annual growth rate was 1.40% for Algeria, 2.21% for Morocco, and 3.25% for Tunisia; it was 5.63% for South Korea.[7] Policy choices have once again raised the question of the general interest, the source of many criticisms directed at the state.[8] Among the grievances expressed is that public policy neglected to take into account the general interest.[9] The state is excoriated for an infinite number of reasons. It is accused of all ills and hardships, and crystallizes all the people's resentment and frustration. Its actions are consistently perceived as running counter to their interest or their well-being. Far from ensuring the general interest, the state has been accused of protecting and enriching "clans" that control its workings and its resources. Since the countries gained independence (Libya in 1951, Morocco and Tunisia in 1956, Algeria in 1962), the general interest has boiled down to guaranteeing law and order and the exploitation of natural resources (oil, natural gas and phosphates).

One explanation for these criticisms can be found in Frederick Cooper's work. He emphasizes that the impasse in which many developing countries found themselves has roots in the colonial economy. He has shown that the colonial economy fostered a type of state whose function was to ensure the extraction of resources and to produce order, not to guarantee public services in the name of the general interest.[10] Acemoglu also advances the hypothesis with regard to sub-Saharan Africa that the colonial period created structures that crushed endogenous reform: "Colonialism didn't just freeze Africa and remove the possibility for endogenous reform, it created structures which have

subsequently inhibited economic growth ... The colonial period created other legacies which may have greatly impeded African prosperity.
First, the organization of colonial states, though it typically built on
absolutist structures, often intensified these structures."[11] The legacy of
the colonial state in North Africa is expressed through post-colonial
state design, which has maintained, within the framework of an authoritarian state, the functions of guaranteeing the extraction of resources
and keeping law and order. Keeping order was an imperative from the
start of independence, but from the 1980s and 1990s the scale of protest action put the countries of North Africa on different trajectories.

Chadli Bendjedid's arrival at the head of the Algerian state in 1979
brought an end to social harmony. The developmentalist project implemented under Houari Boumediene fell apart after his death on 27
December 1978. Despite emigration, mass unemployment continued.
Algerian society sank into the throes of resentment due to widening
inequality.[12] The state, which according to the official rhetoric came
into being on the back of a million and a half martyrs of the revolution,
had become an instrument for the enrichment of a minority who cap-
tured the fruits of the war of independence.[13] Oil wealth became an
illusion for the majority, who denounced corruption and the misappropriation of public funds. Throughout the entire 1980s, Algeria was
rocked by revolts culminating in the October 1988 riots in Algiers that
destabilized the government. The bloody crackdown on protesters
restored order, but it led to a breakdown in relations between the
army, the National Liberation Front (FLN) and the youth. The Islamic
Salvation Front (FIS) handily exploited the feeling of abandonment
common among young people and offered them a new utopia through
its project for a just and righteous Islamic state. The party's strong
score in the 1990 municipal elections and the legislative elections in
1991 sowed panic among the nationalist elites who had ruled the country since independence. The army stepped in, put President Chadli
Bendjedid under house arrest, cancelled the electoral process, dis-
solved the FIS and arrested thousands of Islamist activists, who were
then deported to camps in the Sahara.[14]

Algeria sank into a deadly civil war between the Islamists and the
military (200,000 casualties; 1.5 million internally displaced persons)
that did not end until 1999. The army, victorious, took stock of the

damage done to the country. Its youth was faced with countless existential woes (social, emotional and sexual deprivation) and its economy was so atrophied that it was incapable of producing wealth. The advent of the Bouteflika presidency in 1999 was accompanied by a plan for national reconciliation: on 16 September 1999, the Civil Concord Law was approved by referendum. It contained amnesty provisions for people involved in supporting the Islamist fighters. In August 2005, a national reconciliation referendum provided for the end of legal action against Islamists who laid down arms. While the referendum offered a chance for the state to improve the authorities' image, it did not bring true national reconciliation due to the lack of a truth and justice commission that would have addressed the question of the "disappeared", for example, as some critical observers have noted.[15] The government took advantage of rising oil prices between 2003 and 2013 to devote half of the revenues from hydrocarbon exports (770 billion dinars, or 13% of GDP) to social transfers to correct the devastating effects of the previous drop in oil prices (1986–2001).

In Libya, in the early 1970s, nationalization of the hydrocarbon sector provided Qadhafi's revolutionary regime with the financial windfall needed to achieve his political ambitions. Oil became the "fuel of the revolution".[16] Some of the hydrocarbon revenue was invested in civil infrastructure, thus greatly improving the population's living standards. The oil rent fostered the development of clientelism by forcing the population to negotiate with the revolutionary organizations for access to goods and services without obeying blindly or reassuring the regime of its allegiance. In 1979, only ten years after the revolution of 1969, Qadhafi's Libya had to face widespread dissent: "The head of state can no longer trust anyone but members of his tribe, and army officers have apparently been replaced by men from Sirte."[17] An economy of plunder that benefited those close to the regime[18] thus rapidly developed in a context featuring both political violence and international sanctions imposed between 1991 and 1998. Struggling for survival under the embargo as the result of attempted coups by the army and an Islamist insurgency, the regime tightened political controls. In 1998, the creation of popular and social "commands", or structures made up of tribal leaders, notables and high-ranking military officers, was part of a bid to strengthen its authority.

Overcoming the three challenges it faced—armed Islamist dissidence, international sanctions and attempted coups—the Libyan regime managed to survive and seized the twin opportunities offered by the 9/11 attacks and the US-led invasion of Iraq in 2003. An accomplished tactician, Muammar Qadhafi signed up Libya to "the global war on terror" and fashioned an image of the new Libya as a kind of oil Eldorado in the Mediterranean.[19] These changes aroused concern among regime dignitaries. To reassure them, Qadhafi delivered a combative speech on the 37th anniversary of the revolution: "Be prepared at any moment to crush the enemies within who try to impede the people's progress ..."[20] It should be remembered that on 17 February 2006, in front of the Italian consulate, demonstrators led by the Revolutionary Committees began chanting anti-Italian slogans, protesting against the provocation of an Italian minister who had worn a T-shirt reproducing a caricature of the Prophet. Soon, anti-Qadhafi slogans were also heard and the beleaguered police force fired on the crowd, leaving 11 dead and 60 wounded.[21] Following the incident, the regime's leading figures all travelled to Benghazi to calm the situation. In a gesture of appeasement, the interior minister was dismissed and a number of Muslim Brothers from the region who had been jailed since 1998 were released. In September 2009, the regime celebrated the 40th anniversary of the revolution with great fanfare, but beneath its semblance of triumph, dissension was on the rise.

In Morocco during the 1960s, the monarchy under Hassan II's rule was confronted with political opposition initially led by Mehdi Ben Barka, denouncing "a theocratic, feudal regime aiming to resuscitate Moroccan society's medieval structures."[22] The revival of traditions set in motion in the wake of independence, granted in 1956, contributed to consolidating the innovative transformation of the sultanate into a monarchy and the sultan into a king. The king's role was reinforced in the 1962 constitution, angering the socialist opposition movements as much as Islamist opponents such as Sheikh Yassine.[23] Ben Barka's abduction in Paris in 1965 and his subsequent disappearance radicalized his sympathizers.[24] After the March 1965 riots, Hassan II decided in July to dissolve the parliament elected in 1963. The new constitution of 1970 did not alleviate tensions; on the contrary. In 1971, the enemy was no longer political opponents, be they socialists or Islamists, but the army. An attempt to assassinate Hassan II at his palace in Skhirat failed; in 1972, General Oufkir organized a coup by having the King's Boeing 727 attacked by two F-5 jets which tried to shoot it down. These assassination attempts brought on "the dark years"[25] in Morocco during which merciless crackdowns targeted opponents of the monarchy and arbitrary justice was meted out. The withdrawal of Spanish troops from Western Sahara in 1975 gave the monarchy—and Mauritania, until that country renounced any claim on the territory in 1979—the chance, after annexing Western Sahara, to portray itself as defending the Moroccan nation in the face of the regional ambitions of its rival and neighbour, Algeria.[26] From 1975 to 1991, from annexation to ceasefire, Morocco maintained an army, 130,000–160,000 strong, in the Sahara, thereby crippling its economic development. In the 1980s, a serious economic crisis forced Morocco to accept an International Monetary Fund (IMF) structural adjustment plan. Riots broke out in 1981 and 1984 in the working-class neighbourhoods of the major cities such as Casablanca.[27] Weakened, the monarchy found the backing it needed in rural areas, restoring the power of local elites who in exchange guaranteed it their support.[28] Until the end of his reign, King Hassan II strove to maintain this balance. The gradual adhesion of opposition forces (nationalist, socialist, military and, later, Islamist) to the monarchy consolidated that institution's grip on a devitalized political sphere,[29] but this successful political cooptation still did not meet the demands for social justice expressed during the Arab Spring.

In Tunisia, Habib Bourguiba set up a regime advocating the modernization of the state and society. With a growth rate of 8% between 1970 and 1980 and with 30% of the state's budget devoted to education, Tunisia, despite its modest economic resources, set an example. Promoting a personal status code in 1956 that granted women the right to vote and stand for election, that made it mandatory for them to give their consent to marriage and abolished polygamy, Bourguiba broke with tradition and put the Tunisian state on the road to modernity. Convinced that it was the politicians' duty to adapt and make religion evolve with the times, he had no qualms about offending the clerics with his words and deeds. His legacy is not above reproach, as the chapters on Habib Bourguiba in Michel Camau and Vincent Geisser's edited volume point out,[30] in particular his determination to eradicate the "Islamist poison". In November 1987, Ben Ali's "surgical coup" put an end to the Bourguiba regime and ushered in a new era for Tunisia. "Under President Ben Ali's influence, Tunisia firmly embarked on the path to democratizing politics, achieving social progress and liberalizing its economy."[31] Such optimism was rooted in concerns raised in the later years of Bourguiba's presidency, but also by the situation that reigned in the Maghreb at the time. At the start of the 1990s, Algeria was slowly but surely descending into civil war, Libya was entering a cycle of international sanctions due to its support for terrorism, and Morocco was suffering the consequences of its war against the Polisario in Western Sahara and the excesses of absolute monarchy. In such a context, Ben Ali's policies seemed to indicate a path of renewal for a Maghreb entrenched in authoritarian and corrupt regimes. His initial decisions hinted that Tunisia was going to move toward greater political liberalism, but the regime eventually turned into a police state. Tunisia's securitarianism did not harm the image of a country considered by international institutions their "best pupil" in Maghreb, and this remained true until rebellion broke out.

From this perspective, the 2010 revolts represent a profound re-examination of these countries' trajectories.[32] Demands for good governance and the fight against social and territorial injustice underscore how, over a half-century after acquiring independence, the populace expected their governments to carry out policies that did more than just ensure oil, natural gas and phosphate exports or pander to the needs of tourists. These revolts, the first social revolutions of the post-independence era, called for a reconfiguration of the state. From Morocco to Libya, protesters' demands illustrated a desire to see states that were fairer and that produced greater national and territorial solidarity. Paradoxically, Libya, the richest of these countries in proportion to its population, was affected by the most violent of revolutions. In fact, social injustice was compounded by territorial injustice which threatened these countries' national cohesion. These revolts and revolutions broke out unexpectedly in an economic context of growth and prosperity after two decades of recession. Political leaders in North Africa were convinced that the hardest times were behind them and that demonstrators and Islamists were resigned to accepting the consolidation of these autocratic states: a police state in Tunisia, military in Algeria, paramilitary in Libya.

Consequently, when the revolts flared up, the countries' rulers were entirely taken by surprise, so imbued with confidence were they by the economic growth of the first decade of the 2000s. According to the IMF, Tunisia for instance showed a growth rate of almost 4.5% on average during the 2000–2010 period.[33] The average annual GDP per capita growth rate (PPP) was 4% in Libya, 4% in Algeria and 5.5% in Morocco. In 2010, on the eve of these revolts, Libya had a growth rate of 10%. The revolts thus occurred after a decade of sustained economic growth. They differed from the hunger riots of the 1980s: demonstrators were not demanding price subsidies, but a new form of governance based instead on justice and solidarity. The population aspired to a better standard of living. Geographer Laurent Davezies points out that "economic takeoff is necessarily painful, even politically dangerous, in terms of territorial inequality."[34] In short, it was during the most prosperous economic period that, in the name of economic solidarity, revolts broke out in the most deprived areas—Cyrenaica, southern Tunisia, the Rif in Morocco, and the Algerian Sahara. One goal they all had in common was to force their governments to better address these social and territorial inequalities. Davezies states that "in general, and without dramatizing, it should be kept in mind that most revolts, revolutions and secessions in the past were detonated by fiscal factors."[35] In North Africa, unlike "most revolts", it was not the tax burden that was responsible. Tax revenue from income, corporate and other sources represented 16% of GDP in Algeria and 23% of GDP in Morocco and in Tunisia.[36]

On the other hand, demands in the name of dignity, respect and good governance found resonance because of social and especially territorial injustices. Asymmetric development in these countries[37] intensified territorial fractures that were characterized by strong historical identities. Cyrenaica in Libya, southern Tunisia, southern Algeria and the Moroccan Rif have not sufficiently benefited from national mechanisms of social and economic solidarity. In fact, the revolts broke out in a context of economic growth conducive to kindling social demands and expectations of the state. Davezies claims that "once the takeoff stage has passed, emerging countries will implement adjustment mechanisms that will enable them better to share their growth among territories and move closer to the Western model of territorial cohesion."[38] In North Africa, indeed, the weakness of such mechanisms is one reason that the social and territorial revolts began in 2010 in Tunisia in one of the poorest areas of the country, the centre-west.[39] The same causes have been evident in the Moroccan Rif since 2016. These territorial revolts explain the process of territorial fragmentation at work in the countries of North Africa, despite considerable efforts and investments made by their governments to preserve a semblance of national cohesion and territorial unity. Historically, the nations of North Africa found ties that brought them together in protest against colonial oppression: in post-colonial states, what ties still unite individuals, groups and communities? What continues to hold these nation-states together? If the general interest is not the focal point of state action, how can ties of loyalty be preserved? The Algerian civil war (1991–1999) revealed the ideological and social fractures running through society; the Libyan civil war illustrates the fragmentation of its territory; while revolts in the Rif and southern Tunisia highlight the feeling of marginalization common in these territories and the risks it carries for the central government.

Yet it must be recognized that since independence, the state in these countries has managed, despite situations of violence—riots, revolt, insurgency, civil war—to deploy resources to reinforce its authority and strengthen social ties through government programmes. Since independence, many policies have been enacted with a view to promoting and reinforcing national cohesion. The authorities have endeavoured to produce "the instruments"[40] to govern societies they fear. In 2011, the overthrow of Ben Ali and the implosion of Libya triggered a re-examination of the state in the region. The model of the strong state and its "social pact",[41] one that defines political identity and is the guarantor of society, came to be hotly disputed because of territorial injustices.

Until the Arab revolts, the process of state consolidation in North Africa was believed to be completed, and territory and border control came under state sovereignty. The governments of North Africa discovered with dismay that they were facing challenges that undermined this long task of territorial unification as well as the cultural and administrative harmonization undertaken in the wake of their independence.[42] Border control problems, until then confined to the dispute between

Algeria and Morocco over Western Sahara, extended to the rest of the region. From Tunisia to Mali, border control has become a vital issue for countries exposed to the movement of jihadi groups and criminal organizations. To address these changes,[43] new approaches are emerging to understand state reconfiguration in the region in the framework of a "contemporary sociology of the state deeply infused with issues of globalization that challenge the classical approach to the state in its relationship to nation and territory."[44]

Jihadi groups affiliated with AQIM (al-Qaeda in the Islamic Maghreb) or the Islamic State group (ISIS or Daesh) are actors in the deconstruction of the nation-state that was shaped during the colonial period and handed down to the nationalists, who worked to strengthen it. Of all the social and political forces opposing political regimes formed since independence, no other has an ideological arsenal as diametrically opposite to that of the nationalists. Jihadi groups fit within the traditional figures that have marked the colonial history of the Maghreb, rebels who contest not only authority but the very political system in which it is deployed. Jihadis have taken over the long task of deconstructing the state's legitimacy initiated by Salafi movements in the 1980s. For today's heirs of the strong state model, jihadi violence is there to remind them that seeds of chaos and violence remain within society and threaten the very existence of the nation-state. In the early twenty-first century, the challenge facing states in the region is how to sustain crumbling nations that jeopardize people's very security. The "decomposition of the national fabric", a process noted by Burhan Ghalioun,[45] has been accelerating since the Arab revolts, reviving fears that chaos will take hold, countries will descend into violence, and the state will collapse, following the examples of Libya, Syria,[46] Yemen[47] and Iraq.[48] The view that the end of authoritarianism will produce democracy as an outcome has, with the exception of Tunisia, proved to be illusory.[49]

Demands for Democracy

Following independence, trade union and political representatives in these countries demanded the institution of a political order based on a democratic regime.[50] Their struggle resonated with heads of state and of government who took the fate of these new countries in hand. However, nationalist sentiment quickly pushed democratic demands to the side as it intensified a vision of society based on a strong state and a united society. During this period, neither the "people" nor civil society was thought to have the maturity required to set up a democratic regime. Reactivating representations projected under colonial rule, the new leaders endeavoured to "re-educate" the people, to civilize them so as to adapt the populace to the post-colonial era.

Yet, the question of democracy was present in leaders' speeches as a possible horizon right at independence.[51] After independence, however, post-colonial states did not view democracy as a priority compared to the challenges of underdevelopment, the building of strong states or the recovery of a lost identity. The establishment of authoritarian political systems seemed to be a necessary path toward bringing societies not yet described as civil up to speed in the context of the "democracy of bread".[52] Charismatic figures (Boumediene, Bourguiba, Qadhafi, Hassan II) embodied the young states striving for change. But they also masked the profound upheavals taking place in these societies: demographic revolution, lack of legitimacy of political institutions, and economic failure of development models. As these emblematic figures disappeared one by one, the vulnerability of their regimes in the face of social revolt became apparent. With the collapse of the nationalist project in the 1980s,[53] security became the fundamental issue around which the countries of North Africa deployed their resources. Citizens had to be protected against the trauma of civil war.

Throughout the entire first decade of the 2000s, human rights activists called attention to the political regression closing in on the region. The countries of North Africa were unable to foster a way of living together that could achieve "conviviality". "Why do millions of people live in deplorable conditions without killing each other?" Arjun Appadurai asked with regard to Mumbai.[54] There was no rebuilding of the state such as that undertaken by the Bolivian and Ecuadorian governments seeking to foster well-being in the framework of a pluri-national state.[55] The continuation of national policies established in the wake of independence ran out of steam in North Africa's post-colonial states. More than a half-century after independence, territories fractured under the pressure of regional identity claims, and the national community tore itself apart over the issue of the function of Islam in society. Furthermore, unlike the countries of Eastern and Central Europe, the countries of the Maghreb measure their isolation against a European Union unwilling to enlarge so as to include them, and an atomized region in which regional powers attempt to restore state sovereignty by desperately inadequate means. Despite their being involved in the European Neighbourhood Policy, North African states are not yet engaged in a strategic partnership with the European Union.[56]

This book describes how the states of North Africa are reconfiguring themselves and how they are developing public policies to "hold together" despite revolts, insurrections and revolutions that threaten to bring about their collapse. It analyses government implementation of policies combating a society considered "archaic and backward", and how policies to manage social violence are devised. Lastly, the book shows that the fight against jihadi groups has contributed to developing border control policies. It also points out how the fight against terrorism helps to rebuild the political and social ties essential to preserving national cohesion.[57]

Chapter One analyses the trials and tribulations of the nation-building process. It emphasizes the extent to which national cohesion was, right from independence, a major concern for the countries' rulers, whose ambition was to build strong states capable of controlling their populations. Chapter Two highlights the limits of the authoritarian systems set up by these governments in the face of social transformations and political change. Demands for better governance and greater social justice clashed with state practices designed to produce security. Revolts and riots structure relations between society and states, which each time manage to restore order. The ability of these states to keep a lid on unrest caused them to be perceived and analysed as "robust". The unexpected and unforeseeable outbreak of the Arab revolts represents a huge challenge for the countries of North Africa.

Chapter Three analyses how the collapse of Ben Ali's regime brought insecurity and stoked fears of seeing Tunisia sink into civil war. The establishment of a new political regime and the restoration of constitutional rule are the result of a historic democratic compromise. Even if its political institutions have been strengthened, the difficulty the authorities face in restoring security posed by the threat of terrorism and in reviving the economy is reflected in recurrent social uprisings that weaken Tunisia's young democracy.

Chapter Four analyses state collapse in Libya after the war to bring down the Qadhafi regime. Unlike Tunisia, Libya has been unable to achieve a democratic compromise. On the contrary, the demise of Qadhafi's regime brought to light the historical rifts in the Libyan state. Its implosion into several different regional and tribal entities indicates the weakness of social ties. Under the Qadhafi regime, the state was continually undermined by the tribes and militias. The state's underdeveloped resources were never used to produce national cohesion and territorial unity.

By contrast, Chapter Five demonstrates how reforms implemented by the monarchy in Morocco defused social and political demands expressed by various protest movements. Throughout the monarchy's long experience in its fight against political opposition, it has gained immeasurable skill in handling movements of dissent. From the 20 February Movement to the Hirak Movement, the state has deployed the full range of its resources to manage and control revolts likely to destabilize the monarchy.

Chapter Six analyses how Algeria, considered a country on the edge of a precipice, has been able to overcome the threats it faces. From civil war in the 1990s to the Arab revolts and AQIM terrorism, the state, owing to its oil revenue, has managed to develop instruments that have contributed immensely to the country's stability. Questions are raised, however, as to the durability of a system whose stability depends on the international oil market.

Chapter Seven shows how jihadi groups have taken advantage of the Arab revolts that are undermining political regimes, giving them a chance to take revenge. Many groups took refuge in the sanctuary offered by post-Qadhafi Libya, re-formed there, and set out to destroy the nation-state and replace it with an Islamic state. Jihadi networks straddle national borders to such an extent that the fight against jihadi groups has become a regional and international imperative.

Chapter Eight analyses this security disaster and the region's disintegration. The collapse of the state in Libya as well as the development of jihadi groups in North Africa and in the Sahel is eroding the state in

North Africa. These countries are being pressured by the European Union to retake control of their borders and stem migration flows. Security policies are draining part of these states' meagre resources to the detriment of economic and social development.

Chapters Seven and Eight expand on Chapter Two, in which I examine the social transformations and political mutations that preceded the Arab uprisings and show that reconfigurations of the state are partly a response to such changes. Civil society expresses demands for a more just and more inclusive state. The Arab revolts weakened the repressive apparatuses and opened new opportunities for jihadi groups. Chapters Seven and Eight show why and how it is difficult for North African states to meet civil society's claims while addressing the problem of jihadi violence.

The Conclusion highlights the need to rebuild a sense of belonging and loyalty to the state. Maghreb leaders understand the vulnerability of their political communities and the inadequacy of state instruments to sustain the nation in all its diversity and plurality.

1

THE TRIALS AND TRIBULATIONS
OF NATION-BUILDING

The fight for independence helped to develop a national consciousness and, though not without some resistance, united territories around new states. In Tunisia, Bourguiba undertook "authoritarian modernization" in the name of the legitimacy that the title "Supreme Combatant" conferred upon him.[1] Reform of the educational system and religious institutions forged post-colonial Tunisia's new identity. In Algeria and in Morocco, the authorities channelled the development of nationalism and handled negotiations through various forms of social mobilization.[2] Given the low level of state sovereignty over certain parts of the territory, Algeria's military authorities and the royal authorities in Morocco strove to reinforce a sense of national belonging with a discourse merging the state into the nation.[3] In Libya, the Idris monarchy (1951– 1969) institutionalized territorial fragmentation and the multiplicity of national identities by establishing a decentralized federal government that fostered the preservation of bonds to one's immediate community.[4] In the 1960s, the ability of North African countries to implement measures that would ensure the peaceful cohabitation of all its citizens came into question. Once the colonial state was overthrown, post-colonial states had the duty to pursue the building of the nation-state, but with limited means and ability. The challenge was in essence: "How to unify the culture of citizens of a nation-state and thereby delineate

15

the space of national identity and mark out the political territory over which the state exercises its authority?"[5]

Nation-states, as Arjun Appadurai points out, face huge difficulties in carrying out the task of producing "the people": "the nation-state is by no means the only game in town as far as translocal loyalties are concerned."[6] How can loyalty among members of the national community be produced? Regional locales of protest are many and periodic rebellions each time produce negotiations and compromise with the state over cultural and linguistic pluralism, the function of Islam in society, bad governance and social injustice. In fact, since independence, contestation of the state has been a permanent factor; it is part of the citizenship process in North Africa. After the massive waves of legal migration in the 1960s and 1970s, the path of exile diminished considerably. Since the 1980s and 1990s, rioting and violent protest have structured relations with the authorities. Expectations of the state have continually grown even as governments maintain practices and an ethic reminiscent of colonial rule.

Reconfiguring the State

How have the instruments of state been deployed to control, manage and administer the many forms of opposition and resistance to its development? From the period of independence until the Arab revolts of 2011, the countries of North Africa implemented educational, religious, economic and security policies aimed at winning over the populace after having conquered spaces and territories. States applied the policies necessary to strengthen their sovereignty and protect their territory. These policies fit within the framework of developing a "security state", a state in which rights were constantly violated on the often justified pretext of internal and external threats. In fact, the states of North Africa inherited territories where the homogenization process had not been completed, and the nationalists exploited regional rivalries between Morocco and Algeria to promote a sense of national identity and produce the "cultural homogenization" that would guarantee national cohesion.[7] In a compelling article, Victor T. Le Vine analysed the inability of certain African states—especially those established after the Second World War, such as Libya, Tanzania, Rwanda, Burundi,

Somalia, and Cameroon—to move from "juridical states towards empirical statehood". The fact that these states were not buttressed by "coherent communities of support and identity or, in short, by national citizenries ... has resulted in the disintegration of the state ..., civil war or other political disasters".[8] Analysis of the process of nation-building, defined as "the creation of a sense of a common political belonging", proves essential for understanding, for instance, why the Libyan state disintegrated and the Tunisian state did not after the Arab revolts of 2011.

Following independence, the great majority of the population in North African countries were living in poverty. Illiteracy was widespread; people deserted the countryside owing to the collapse of the colonial agricultural system. Hundreds of thousands of adults converged on the cities in the hope of finding a job and earning a living. What was to be done with these unemployed farmers and day labourers who then made up the country? Freed from the colonial system, they yearned for dignity and fairness. How were social disparities to be managed? Or the diversity of aspirations? The pluralism of ideas? The struggle for political power? The nationalists dreamed of establishing a strong, centralized state, administered and endowed with all the necessary instruments to conduct a regional development policy. In continuity with the colonial state, they devised administrative plans to conquer lost or abandoned spaces. More than the peoples inhabiting them, the regions were what concerned the authorities. They feared that the territories handed down from colonial rule would implode under the constant battering of regionalism. The sense of belonging to the nation-state remained tenuous: its legitimacy was being tested, its ability to act in the name of common interest was challenged. For nationalist leaders, time was a precious resource. They knew they had to provide these "backward people"[9] with the benefits they had promised them.

Certainly, leaders in both Tunisia and Morocco clearly expressed their support for the democratic ideal, without, however, undertaking the reforms necessary to set up such a regime. As Michel Camau points out, right from independence, democracy was on the horizon of the region's leaders. Habib Bourguiba contemplated installing a constitutional and democratic regime. In Morocco, Mohammed V planned to organize the country on the basis of a constitutional monarchy. But this democratic ideal was very soon overtaken by a more material view of democracy: "if one considers that democracy means clothing, educating and promoting, it is immediately clear that any collective agreement imposes on the state the obligation sometimes to delve into so-called private affairs."[10] Given the challenges of economic development, these leaders did not make democracy a priority.[11]

Such a simplistic view of democracy aroused criticism from the socialist opposition led by Ben Barka, who accused Moroccan political parties of "collaborating with the throne". "We are the party of the urban and rural toiling masses par excellence, an unwavering alliance of workers, farmers and the revolutionary intelligentsia ... We are therefore the party of the Moroccan people, excluding the exploiting classes, the feudal landowners and parasitic bourgeoisie, allies and pillars of neocolonialism."[12] During the 1960s, the debate was settled and democracy gave way to authoritarian regimes, held up as the only type that could foster political and economic development.

The establishment of authoritarian political systems was advertised as the necessary path to improving societies that were not yet considered civil.[13] The single party, or political parties under control, held sway; they were not the expression or representation of political forces but more instruments for "organizing the people".[14]

Cohesion First

Once independence was achieved, the ruling elites of the new states set up autocratic political regimes. Rulers in Maghreb considered that while democracy remained an ideal to strive for, the conditions for developing it were not fulfilled at the end of the colonial period. They espoused the analysis of Charles Issawi, who insisted that in the 1950s economic and social conditions were not conducive to bringing about democracy. Only a sweeping economic and social transformation would strengthen society enough to enable it to bear the weight of a modern state. Characterized by its agricultural economy and its lack of a middle class, the Arab world lacked the prerequisites for democratization—education, urbanization, linguistic and religious homogeneity, economic development—and, especially, it suffered from the failings of its wealth distribution and the absence of a private sector.[15]

Contrary to the reformist current that developed in the shadow of the Ottoman Empire, nationalists endeavoured to build a strong state without worrying about the weakness of the society that was to uphold it. They inherited the post-colonial state administration as well as "practices and a situation that obeyed their own logic, that of the French Jacobin state".[16] They were prepared to pursue the long, arduous task of unifying the territory that had begun with colonization in the nineteenth century. The primary tasks to be undertaken to consolidate the state were the strengthening of a central administration and the establishment of recognized borders, even if that meant maintaining "institutional colonization" in Algeria after 1963, as Amar Mohand-Amer points out, given that the country could not be "left without law" after independence.[17]

The political authorities in place since independence were clearly convinced, as Bourguiba claimed, that "only a strong state can guarantee security, well-being and infuse the notions of progress and civilization with real content ... For people's lives to improve and for them to prosper, they must live under the shelter of a just and strong rule."[18] The political and legal framework in which the nationalist elites designed their plans for development was one of a legal-rational state that hewed to the modern model. Modernity was viewed as Jacobinism, a centralized state that combats regionalism. By placing development of the nation-state at the centre of their actions, nationalist leaders marginalized the reformists working to bring about justice and freedom under the rule of law.[19]

Throughout the nineteenth century, proponents of reform, influenced more by "frequent travels to Europe and relations with consuls and tradesmen" than by Enlightenment philosophy,[20] emphasized the importance of political reform based on justice and freedom, these values being significant in Islam but non-existent in Ottoman governance of its provinces in North Africa: "the inhabitants of Algeria, who made up the majority of the population, were fed up with the Turks' tyranny."[21] The key idea developed by the reformist current was that tyranny weakened "love for one's country" and destroyed national cohesion. Under the Ottoman Empire, Maghreban reformists idealized European state administration and organization and planned to assimilate its instruments of power. The most famous of them, Kheireddine, wrote, "Development of the Oumrane [human development], wealth and military power in the Muslim umma was once based on justice, cohesion, solidarity between the provinces and focus on the sciences, arts and trades."[22] In short, for Muslims, well-being was based on good governance. The reformers conveyed "a new political culture" that had the appearance of an embryonic liberal philosophy. Its vocabulary—nation, justice, equality—would be usurped by the nationalists a few decades later in the context of the revolutionary independence movement. Of the reformist current, the nationalists retained only its language and discarded the liberal spirit in which a thinker such as Ahmed ben Dhiaf imagined his project: "opinion is free," he affirmed, and "the Constitution has made it possible to civilize the country."[23] Before the era of nationalism, good governance and the rule of law were the ideals held dear by reformist thinkers in the Maghreb.

Colonization of the Maghreb destroyed the European ideal-type and placed the reformists in a historical impasse. Instead of justice and equality, much-admired Europe exported to Maghreb its military might, its fierce nationalism and the arbitrary exercise of power. In religious matters, the French republic, so proud of its 1905 law establishing the separation of church and state, promulgated a decree on 27 September 1907 introducing an exception, making the law of separation ineffective in Algeria.[24] From a societal standpoint, the work of reformers was devalued in favour of an essentialist vision of society. In contrast to indigenous Muslim reformers, as Julia Clancy-Smith points out, "the new race of French Algerians vigorously promoted another vision of Islam and the Arab woman. They proclaimed the existence of an invincible Islamic legal system and unchanging indigenous *mentalité* toward women and sexuality."[25] The contradictions of colonial policy fostered the rise of national movements that would prove fatal to the democratic ideal. By projecting on the liberated society the same prejudices that colonial rule had of the natives, the nationalists manufactured the narrative of a society they imagined to be monolithic and unanimous in its beliefs. Once the colonial state was ousted, the independent state took on all the trappings of its enemy. In Morocco, "the old sultanate regime" was modernized and took on the guise of an absolute monarchy; in Tunisia, development of the state was associated with security, well-being, progress and civilization; in Algeria, the state was the lever of the revolution. Only in Libya was the state the enemy of society, and Qadhafi's revolution aimed to tear it down.

Nationalists viewed diversity as a source of discord and chaos, adopting a belief that prevailed in Europe until the seventeenth century. According to Giovanni Sartori, "unanimity was regarded as the necessary foundation of any government".[26] The colonial state did its utmost to divide and conquer, and the nationalists imposed a unanimity of belief all the better to establish their rule. With nuances and to varying degrees, the nationalist political imaginary was suffused with a rejection of Western democracy. The post-colonial states emerged after a long struggle for freedom. The liberal reformist current was marginalized after the Second World War to make way for nationalist movements that placed "the strong state" at the top of their political agenda. Once independence had been won, political freedoms, civil society and the right of free speech were pushed into the background. On the strength of the legitimacy they had earned in the fight for independence, nationalists planned to shape society through the lens of their beliefs. If the colonial state sought to "civilize the natives", the post-colonial state aimed to refashion what it viewed as "archaic" mentalities. Reform only returned to the fore in 2011 owing to the Arab Spring, which brought back demands for the rule of law, respect for civil liberties and dignity.

Fear of the People: "Reshaping Mentalities"

Imbued with progressive ideologies, nationalist leaders devised policies to subjugate the individual through authoritarian, police, military and paramilitary regimes. Right from independence, constructions and representations of the national community were characterized by a fear of the people, deemed to be "archaic and backward". The progressive and hegemonic ideologies of the 1960s and 1970s (socialist, communist, third-worldist) saw flaws in individual behaviours that were analysed as being part of the colonial or feudal legacy, which it fell to the post-colonial nation-state to demolish. For the nationalist elites, the societies that came under their rule contained the seeds of chaos and violence; the territories they had to administer were potentially resistant to the Jacobin and Nasserian vision of the state: Riffians, Kabyle,

Amazigh and Tuareg personified rebellion against the central state in gestation, from Morocco to Libya.[27] Rejection of pluralism was rooted in the fear of differences, conflicts and oppositions.

On the basis of the notion that "the modern state makes the nation",[28] nationalist leaders considered they had to rid the people of its many "historical shortcomings". A "campaign against bad instincts" was begun in Tunisia under Bourguiba as part of the "moral reconstruction" effort. Yâdh ben Achour identified some of these instincts affecting the Tunisian people as a "strong propensity for anarchy; [a] clan spirit, [an] inability to abide by rules and consent and the minorities' unabashed recourse to violence".[29] Soukaine Bouraoui recalls how Habib Bourguiba wished to combat the Tunisians' "backward, archaic, lazy and vulgar mentalities".[30] Clement Henry Moore points out that for Bourguiba "education was necessary to change 'backward' mentalities".[31]

In Algeria, the agrarian revolution was in jeopardy if "it did not manage to modify the peasant mentality and destroy all archaic structures of thought, action, and worldview".[32] The construction of socialist villages was meant to "ensure a transition between the 'archaic' rural world and the city where decisions were made and new emancipating models were experienced". While peasants represented a threat to the agrarian revolution, the country itself was paralysed by the condition of women. "Liberate your women," Ben Bella ordered, "so that they can take up their responsibilities; by leaving women prisoners, it is half of our people, half of our country that is paralysed; don't think that the veil will protect them. The Revolution will protect them."[33] For the "modernist elite trained in the Western fashion",[34] the Muslim faith bore the weight of values specific to an ancient rural civilization characterized by reactionary traditions. Adapting Islam to the revolution, to socialism and to progress involved purging the official ulamas' discourse of the "traditional", "archaic" dimension of religion. Mohammed Arkoun wonders if such expurgation did not pave the way for the "apologetic literature" that fuels the Islamist imaginary:

> Where are the magic practices, the very ancient rituals, that surround the important moments in life … Where are the local pilgrimages, the saint worship, the messianic expectations, the behaviours inseparably connected with *baraka* and honour? This exuberant world of fantasy-breeding symbols, metaphors, invisible beings, supernatural forces, and

propitiatory acts continues to be widely represented not only in rural areas, but in cities more than ever linked to the common culture in which archaic Islamic practices and traditions mingle. And yet, none of this appears in the expurgated, rationalistic, scientistic but rarely scientific discourse of the official ulama.[35]

In the aftermath of independence, North Africa's political leaders remained influenced by representations of societies designed under the colonial powers. They borrowed the term "archaic mentality" from the colonial lexicon and did not hesitate to claim it was the primary obstacle to implementing reform. The political answer to this colonial anthropological interpretation of societies was single-party rule or submission to a hegemonic political authority. From Morocco to Libya the issue of the people's representation was raised. Until independence, underground or tolerated political parties alike were divided as to how to combat colonial domination. While some favoured a peaceful, negotiated and step-by-step process, others believed independence could only be achieved through armed revolution. After independence was won, the divide revolved around popular representation. Two conceptions were at odds: the first, the revolutionary socialist trend in vogue at the time, believed a single party could best represent the people; the second, more liberal, introduced a multiparty system.

Thus Algeria under Ben Bella (1962–1965), and then Boumediene (1965–1978), granted the monopoly on representation to the National Liberation Front (FLN). Decree no. 63–297 issued on 14 August 1963 banned all political associations other than the FLN. This was confirmed by Article 23 of the 10 September 1963 constitution: the FLN was the vanguard, single party in Algeria. The project for a pluralist and democratic post-colonial Algeria embodied by the Democratic Union of the Algerian Manifesto (UDMA) withered away, replaced by a unanimist conception of the social and political body. Instead of building legitimate and representative political institutions, Algeria's new leaders, swept up in the wind of revolution, would shape a social and political body in the image of their ideology.[36] The dominant vision was one of a society imagined as divided and dangerous because it was in a state of constant struggle. Pluralism was frightening; it embodied division and weakness, as Bourguiba claimed regarding Tunisia: "In the current phase of our revolution, it has become clear to us as to yourselves that party

pluralism, which tends to produce infighting, one-upmanship, dema-
gogy and sabotage, would be a luxury that would render impossible the
necessary mobilization of an entire people. It would harm the austerity,
work and discipline without which we will never be able to achieve our
objectives."[37] The country needed a strong, united party working
toward the consolidation of the state.

In Morocco, from the Istiqlal party to Ben Barka, criticism intensified after the 1962 constitution.[38] For socialist opponents of the monarchy, Hassan II was turning the kingdom into "an archaistic, precolonial absolute monarchy". Like Ben Bella in Algeria, Ben Barka hoped
his revolution would put an end to "archaism" and "feudalism". His
political group demanded the right to represent the country's life-
blood, those who would bring about change, but Istiqlal, a popular and
nationalist party, also claimed a monopoly on the people's representation, emphasizing the major role it had played in the fight for independence. However, Istiqlal's criticism of the 1962 constitution pertained
instead to the dangers it held in store for the monarchy. Its leader, Allal
al-Fassi, notably said, "I would also like to remind His Majesty of
threats that a contempt for democracy have posed, first in the Ottoman
Empire, then in Iraq and in Egypt."[39]

> We are saying that Istiqlal never sought to establish itself as a single
> party, because Morocco has always seen several parties coexist. But
> Istiqlal in fact represented the overwhelming majority of the people
> and was even the only party able to lead the resistance and armed
> struggle at a time when those who claim to be nationalists today were
> often visitors to the General Residence and advocated keeping the
> French judiciary system in Morocco.[40]

The desire to "reshape mentalities" and change "the peasant outlook"
faded: on the crest of its development, the state was in a position to
handle conflicts and tensions running through society.[41] Energy
resources (oil, natural gas and phosphates) and economic policy (agriculture and tourism) ensured the North African states of substantial
means that were allocated to keeping law and order. In the 1980s, the
authorities were still afraid of the populace, not because of its "historical shortcomings" or its "archaism" but because of the ever-increasing
youth of the population: people under 30 made up 70% of the population and, like their elders, they developed a keen interest in a new

ideology: Islamism. In a decolonized world, nationalism lost its power and its fervour: the struggle was no longer over territory but over identity, and the Islamist ideology forcefully expressed the new struggle to be led against the West. In Islamist ideology, nationalist leaders in North Africa lost their aura as genuine champions of the people and instead appeared as allies of the Western powers. In their determination to consolidate the state, nationalist leaders neglected religion as a binding factor. Arab nationalism, the strong state, and democracy were discarded in favour of Islamic solidarity, restoration of the caliphate, and the establishment of an Islamic state and application of the sharia. In the space of a few years, the nationalists' colossal effort to "catch up to the West", "modernize tradition", and "close the economic gap" was swept away by an ideological revolution that shook up their societies and shattered the socialist, progressive, third-worldist illusions that fuelled post-colonial debates. Beginning in the 1980s, Algeria and Libya, the regional champions of socialism, were faced with violent armed insurgencies claiming to wage jihad against "apostate regimes". As Abdallah Laroui explains, "Just when the state was materially gaining strength, it was unable to win the loyalty of its citizens/subjects due to an ideological legacy that was difficult to eliminate ... The Islamic utopia has remained alive and well, with the inevitable consequences of devaluing the very idea of the state."[42]

Islamist Contestation

Islamism, and subsequently jihadism, developed in a context characterized by profound upheavals: the demographic revolution, the lack of legitimacy of political institutions, and bankrupt development models. The gradual successive disappearance of the leading figures of nationalism and progressivism pointed up the vulnerability of these regimes when they faced social riots and protest movements in the name of Islam. Throughout the 1980s, associations and various interest groups constructed a political alternative. In 1979, Rached Ghannouchi, leader of the Ennahda Party, affirmed with great foresight: "during this century, Islam will go from defence to attack. It will reach new heights. It will be the century of the Islamic state."[43] He was arrested in 1981 and then sent into exile. On 30 August 1990, he announced from

Khartoum: "We've tried everything, both capitalism and socialism, but that did not bring bread to the Tunisians, so we must go back to our values and to Islam."[44] The ideological and moral attrition of the developmental state, whose actions focused mainly on control over its territory and the security of its population, had reached its limits. The widening of inequalities and the lack of future prospects provided fertile ground for an ideology that made Islam *the* solution to all problems. Although already present in the 1920s,[45] Islamist ideology found increasing resonance from the 1980s.

The ideology of a just state embodied by Islamist movements superseded the ideology of a strong state. Socialist-leaning economic policies in Algeria, Tunisia and Libya did not produce the anticipated effect of reducing inequalities. The context was ripe for the emergence of Islamist movements seeking purity, authenticity and restoration of Muslim identity. The social body was no longer a construct made up of peasants, bourgeois and revolutionaries described by revolutionary socialists, but of Muslims who were distinguished by the degree of intensity of their practices.[46]

Thus, at the end of the 1980s in Tunisia, the most "secular" and "modern" of the three states, the government began facing protest in the name of Islam. Algeria, Libya and Morocco were soon confronted with the same calls for a just and uncorrupt state. Islamists early on had denounced the socialist "excesses" of the Algerian and Libyan regimes in the 1960s and 1970s. In the 1980s, they began to decry the "despotic" dimension of the state and in the 1990s condemned its unjust aspect.[47] Islamist demands for a just state gradually wore down the political and moral foundations of the "strong state" embodied by nationalist and progressive movements. These now stood as obstacles, even enemies, of the transition to a political regime based on Islamic values.

In Algeria, the victory of the Islamic Salvation Front (FIS) in the December 1991 general elections raised serious concerns within the army, which terminated the election process and undertook, to use its own term, to "eradicate" the Islamists. All of the state's resources were funnelled toward combating armed Islamist groups that threatened to overturn the "FLN state" and establish an Islamic state.[48] Twenty years later, Syria, Iraq and Libya were faced with the same challenges as Algeria: how to survive jihadi violence. In Morocco under Hassan II

(1961–1999), stringent control of the Islamists reduced domestic threats, and the king's role as Amir al-Mu'minim (Commander of the Faithful) seemed to protect the monarchy.[49] However, the accession of Mohammed VI to the throne and his ambition to establish a just and democratic rule coincided with the increasing popularity of the Justice and Development Party (JDP) and raised concerns about the real or imagined strength of Islamists in the kingdom.[50] Between 1990 and 2000, the states of the region implemented national and international security policies in an effort to contain the Islamist threat. On the eve of the 2011 Arab revolts, the authorities mistakenly believed that Islamist movements had been defeated. The social forces that were shaking up the regimes were thus considered marginal and inoffensive actors coming from civil society.[51]

The nationalist project aimed to build a "strong" state founded on developmentalist ideology and capable of implementing progressive policies. Driven by the "unifying energy" of the state,[52] North African leaders devoted such a large portion of their resources to development that they claimed to manage even the social and economic dimensions of people's existence. The Arab revolts were a call to transform the state in the direction of limiting the "state's action".[53] Between 1970 and 2010, people's standard of living clearly improved even though population growth was higher than economic growth. Neither the building of housing units, roads, schools and universities nor food subsidies and the distribution of natural gas and electricity were enough to satisfy a young population. With the exception of Morocco, North Africa's leaders remained locked into a security logic that to a considerable extent masked the social transformations under way. Between 1990 and 2000, demands emerged from civil society for better governance, more social justice and greater freedom. Obsessed by the Islamist threat, the authorities were blind to them and seemed incapable of providing adequate answers to rampant social injustice and territorial fragmentation.

2

INJUSTICE, A CHALLENGE TO SOCIAL COHESION

The startling outbreak of the 2011 uprisings was interpreted as yet another social upheaval; the authorities realized too late that these revolts were a prelude to revolutions that aimed to bring about regime change and transform social systems that had become fossilized under autocratic regimes. But once the hope or the illusion of a democratic wave[1] or an exit from authoritarianism had passed, real questions arose as to the ability of these states to survive such events.[2] The successive collapse of Iraq and Syria, Yemen, Libya and Sudan pointed up the extreme fragility of the state structures and foundations formed in these Arab countries during the twentieth century. The dismantling of the nation-state and the implosion of the national community were stark reminders of just how tenuous are the ties that hold a state together. Revolts and revolutions challenge the national cohesion that ensures the state's stability and people's security in the region, testing its very resilience. Through that lens, it is possible to analyse whether a state's nation-building process is sufficiently advanced to guarantee national unity.

Like the fall of the Berlin Wall or the collapse of the USSR, the scope of the Arab revolts and the speed with which protest spread throughout each country took the world by surprise. In the space of a few months, the conventional wisdom about the countries of the Maghreb and the Middle East was seriously called into question. Studies of their authoritarianism and solidity routinely overlooked what Sarah Nafissa calls "the blind spots of political science research on the region".[3] The focus of attention on the solidity of these regimes, their ability to dominate, and their techniques for neutralizing opposition led observers to disregard the strength of their societies. "Weak states and strong societies" is one of the findings gleaned from the analysis of transformations in the region.[4] The "strong regime" narrative was so powerful that even civil society actors were unable to imagine any other horizon than authoritarianism. In 2009 in Tunisia, a human rights activist stated with conviction and resignation: "The regimes in place could last for a long time due to the lack of any serious counterpower. These regimes are very strong, they have many years ahead. I don't see why they would change …"[5] Throughout the 1970s and 1980s, authoritarian systems demonstrated their ability to control and contain all forms of protest.[6] However, Algeria's civil war (1991–1999) illustrated the limits of these "systems" in the face of demands for political change expressed by wide swathes of society. Only through ruthless repression was the government able to restore order in politics. Indeed, starting in the 1990s, the countries in the region were faced with profound transformations in their societies: soaring population growth, urbanization, and mass youth unemployment, in particular among graduates. Social tensions and political conflicts emerged in which strong demands were expressed, such as those for better social justice, more transparent public spending, and better political representation. The political regimes were confronted with the demands for both political and economic reform inherent in the awakening of civil society.

The Awakening of Civil Society

In the 1970s, demands for democracy had become muffled in the region, and actors supporting such demands were quickly weakened by the dynamics of populist mobilization encouraged by the political regimes. Charismatic leaders appealed to their historical, religious or revolutionary legitimacy to establish their authority. The people, so often referred to in the fight for independence, once sovereign, became a source of worry. The main goal of the political regimes was to pull the people out of poverty. As Boumediene said in his speech before the

Islamic Summit Conference in Lahore in 1974, "people who are hungry need bread, people who are ignorant need knowledge, and people who are sick need hospitals." It was time for an economic jihad, as Bourguiba claimed, which meant directing efforts to the fight against underdevelopment:

> When he was walking to Mecca with his companions, they were surprised by Ramadan. Some of them held to the fast, others did not respect it. The Prophet broke the fast to encourage the first group to do so. He said to his companions—"Eat! You will be stronger to tackle the enemy"—this applies perfectly to our case. We have an enemy to conquer—poverty. Through the Prophet's voice, God invites us to be stronger, to work and not occupy the lowest rank among peoples.[7]

From 1960 to 1980, the states of the Maghreb were driven by a developmentalist ideology[8] which was not matched by an improvement in living standards for young people. Throughout the entire 1980s, revolts, such as the one in June 1981 in Casablanca, in January 1984 in Tunisia,[9] and in October 1988 in Algiers, were perceived as the product of social and economic frustrations that plagued a segment of the youth. Yet, these riots also expressed social and political demands. Protesters found fault with the state's authoritarianism and the failure of its economic development model. The January 1984 riots in Tunisia "symbolized the end of an era ... The Tunisian government had abruptly decided to revisit its distributive function that had been essential since independence."[10] In Algeria, the October 1988 demonstrators targeted symbols of the "FLN state", which was incapable of providing its youth with the jobs and housing they demanded.[11] After a brutal crackdown, to quell the anger President Chadli Bendjedid (1980–1992) announced the creation of a multiparty system and economic liberalization.

Confronted by social transformations and political change, the security ideology took precedence over economic performance. The political regimes had run out of solutions to "raise people out of poverty", but they had the law enforcement and judicial means to produce short-term security and stability. In the 1990s, the social pact hinged on controlled pluralism in the framework of a hybrid regime that Daniel Brumberg has described as "liberalized autocracy".[12] In the face of the Islamist threat, the state redirected its resources toward ensuring its citizens' security rather than their well-being. The exclusion of Islamists from the political system in the early 1990s triggered a wave of political violence in the name of religious and political freedom. In reaction to governments' conceit, voices of dissent began to be heard. From Algeria in 1989, to Tunisia and Libya in 2011, protesters called for new rules of the game. In view of economic failure and social injustice, the absence of political freedom was no longer justified. Contrary to what the regimes feared, protest was not driven by Islamist revolutionaries, as it was in the 1990s, but rather by civil society actors.[13]

Egyptian political activist Saad Eddin Ibrahim prophetically remarked in an article written in 1998 that the development of civil society was under way in the Arab world and that it was set to experience "a mini-wave of democratization". Pointing to a network of over 70,000 civil associations in 1990 compared to only 20,000 in 1960, Saad Eddin Ibrahim emphasized the "revitalization" of civil society in the Arab political space.[14] One year prior to the Arab revolts, the then-exiled Tunisian politician Moncef Marzouki, in an interview given in the French daily newspaper *Le Monde* (29 October 2009), stated, "Our Arab dictators have Western governments as their allies; we have civil societies on our side." During the first decade of the twenty-first century, amid general indifference, civil society actors would work to maintain social bonds in countries suffering from embargoes or extreme violence and encourage the development of social policies.

During this same decade, one of the issues in state–civil society relations was the development of a public space in the Maghreb. In its 2008 Human Development report on Egypt, the UNDP (United Nations Development Programme) emphasized that the state "must maintain and improve on its role as the key provider of public goods and services, but it should retreat from its monopoly in particular segments in the social services chain so as to make space and crowd in CSOs [civil society organizations]. Examples are in hospital management and university education where the private sector caters for the rich and the CSO sector could play an important role for the non-rich."[15] This demand for greater space for civil society is consistent with a conception of civil society not as a protest actor but rather as an actor that accompanies the state in economic and social development, a role that is fully illustrated in the case of Morocco.[16]

Specialists in Eastern and Central European studies have underscored the essential role played by civil society in the fall of the Berlin

Wall in 1989. Renewed interest in civil society, whether academic, journalistic or even political, is in fact closely tied in with the 1980s. Twenty years later, observers of the Arab revolts continued to highlight the role of civil society in the strategic surprise of the toppling of Arab authoritarian regimes in 2011. Most unexpectedly, actors emerged and revealed an unknown or little-studied aspect of Arab countries: dynamic civil societies clashed with states that were organized and structured in such a way as to facilitate political domination of non-democratic regimes. In 2000, Francesco Cavatorta pointed out, "Laith Kubba has already proclaimed that the 'awakening of society' would lead Arabs to the 'promised land' of democratization, just as it had done for the countries of Eastern Europe in the 1980s."[17] The correlation between civil society and democratization is obvious. The political sociologist Larry Diamond, a specialist in political transitions, wrote in 1994, "It is now clear that to comprehend democratic change around the world, one must study civil society."[18] However, far from being uncontroversial, this liberal conception of civil society raises criticism of its supposed virtues.[19]

In the contemporary Arab world, the expression "civil society" has been used by critical intellectuals from the trade union or advocacy sphere at odds both with regimes and with Islamist movements.[20] In the 1990s, "civil society" as a term was assimilated with non-governmental actors. It was directly associated with the promotion of good governance and encouragement to develop "non-governmental civil societies".[21] In answer to the disengagement of the state, civil society was often promoted as a palliative in sectors deemed vital to development such as healthcare, education, the emancipation of women, and organizational support for youth. The notion of civil society is no longer associated with resistance or viewed as an alternative to political regimes and Islamist movements. However, given the formal or real grip the state has on the development of civil society actors, many observers question civil society's potential.

Civil society mobilization differs according to country. Thus, in the Maghreb in the first decade of the 2000s, Morocco was in the lead as regards social reform. By comparison, Tunisia under Ben Ali and Algeria under Bouteflika appeared as ossified political regimes living in an illusion of security. In 2008, an activist with the Socialist Union of Popular Forces (USFP) stated, "We are a country in transition toward democracy compared to Algeria and Tunisia. Morocco has covered considerable ground in this domain: the Advisory Council on Human Rights (CCDH), the Fairness and Reconciliation Commission (IER), the Moudawana [personal status code] reform, the Royal Institute for Amazigh Culture (Ircam), and so on. Of course there are still many shortcomings, especially regarding social democracy and disparities between the different social classes, but I believe the democratization process in Morocco is irreversible."[22] A similar analysis was made by a National Rally of Independents (RNI) activist who claimed, 'Those who talk about the absence of democracy in Morocco don't want to see our pioneering experience in this area ... Of course we can't compare to Western democracies, but with respect to what's going on in Algeria and in Tunisia, we say, praise God. For us the king is the guarantor of the country's integrity and its identity. Attacking the monarchy as an institution amounts to killing our identity. We must consolidate our progress toward democracy without altering our fundamental principles.[23]

This may be one of the factors explaining the failure of the 20 February Movement in Morocco in 2011. The social reforms initiated by the monarchy defused the risk of revolution in the kingdom, as will be seen in Chapter Five.[24]

Social Transformation and Political Change

During the first decade of the 2000s, many Tunisian civil society actors showed an attitude of resignation. Others wanted change to come about peacefully, the civil war in Algeria (1991–1999) being fresh in mind. For one United Socialist Party (PSU) activist, "as a grassroots activist, I'm in favour of peaceful change, which should affect institutions, political parties, and the monarchy ... for a real rotation of power and to manage it in a democratic fashion."[25] After 2011, the conflicts in post-Qadhafi Libya and the Syrian tragedy confirmed the refusal to adopt a strategy of confrontation with the authorities. Initially triggered by the effect of price increases in raw materials on the price of basic consumer goods, these revolts could have turned into hunger riots and ended with mass arrests in the context of a policy of repression.[26] But, unlike in the past, they turned into uprisings, peaceful ones in most of the countries affected, and an insurgency in Libya. The revolts were inevitable. Social and economic transformations compelled states to undertake reforms and political regimes to alter the rules of the game: Rémy Leveau made this observation many years ago.[27] According to the demographer Youssef Courbage, transformations within the family, for instance, already heralded a "convergence of civilizations". Demographic revolutions entail changes in the relationship to political authority.[28]

And indeed, in a half-century, the population of the Maghreb more than tripled, rising from 25.7 million inhabitants in 1950 to 90 million in 2010. Life expectancy increased by 25 years (from 42 to 67 years), with the exception of Mauritania, where it does not exceed 50 years.[29]

As a result of the demographic revolution, the population of the 20–40 age group rose from 23 million in 2000 to 28 million in 2010. This age bracket now makes up 36% of the total population. It will not begin to diminish until 2030, when it will drop back down to 33%. In the long term, demographic pressure, in particular the proportion of young people in the age pyramid, will decline due to the fall in the birth rate. The pension system, described as "generous", will be exposed to population ageing, "a new issue for the Maghreb, likely to seriously challenge the financial equilibrium of pension schemes in the coming decades".[30]

The fertility rate declined from 7 to 8 children per woman in 1970 to less than 3 in 2000 and then to 2 in 2016.[31] For the time being, the 20–40 age bracket faces low job creation, which has not kept up with population growth.

In the short term, governments were forced to cope with mass unemployment, which often has adverse effects on society.[32] Protests in Libya showed that even in that country, population stress was a breeding ground for mobilization against the regime: in 1973, the Libyan population was an estimated 2 million inhabitants; it reached 5.6 million in 1995 and 6.2 million in 2015. The rejuvenation of the population is clear and inherent in an annual population growth rate of 4.21%, one of the highest in the Arab world. Added to this population increase is ever more rapid urbanization. In 1950, the urban population made up 20% of the total population, 26% in 1960, 45% in 1970, 62% in 1980, and 80% in 2010.

Figure 1: Population growth in North Africa, 1950–2050[33]

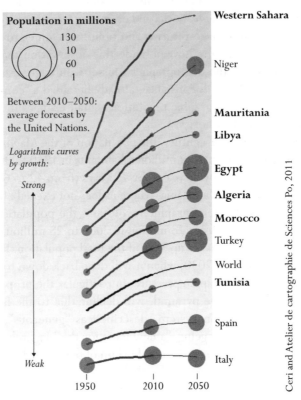

Source: United Nations, Population Division, *World Population Prospects: The 2008 Revision*, http://esa.un.org

Such accelerated urbanization is aggravated by an ailing agricultural sector.[34] In Morocco, 41% of the population lives in rural areas, in Algeria 40% and in Tunisia 36%, making a total of 30 million people. The active farming population is 8 million individuals. It makes up 34% of the total active population in Morocco, 23.5% in Tunisia and 23.6% in Algeria. The agricultural sector remains large in the Maghreb, and it has been the target of several reforms aimed at ensuring food security.[35] Rural dwellers have all the more incentive to move to the city as they have little access to infrastructure (water, healthcare): 56% of the rural population has access to drinking water in Morocco (compared

Figure 2: Young people in North Africa, 1950–2010[36]

Share of the population under 25 (in %)

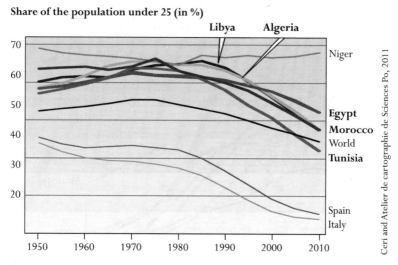

Source: United Nations, Population Division, *World Population Prospects: The 2008 Revision*, http://esa.un.org

to 99% of the urban population); 31% has access to healthcare (83% of urban dwellers). In Tunisia, 60% of the rural population has access to drinking water (94% of urban dwellers) and 62% to health services. The rural population has seen its living conditions improve, but it remains plagued by poverty and underemployment. Internal cityward migration and a prosperous informal economy are better understood in view of this situation. In an area such as the Rif, one of the poorest in Morocco, the primary economic activity is cannabis cultivation, which involves 75% of the villages and 96,000 farms, or about 800,000 people.[37] Cannabis production does keep the population in place and provides additional income for families, but it destroys the ecosystem.[38] The long-term impact on the environment is disastrous: deforestation, soil erosion, massive use of mineral instead of organic fertilizers, and so on. According to the GEFRIF project (participatory management of the Rif forest ecosystems), cannabis is accountable for the disappearance of 1,000 hectares of forestland per year in Morocco: between 1967 and 1987, 40% of the forest cover vanished. In view of this, income from the drug economy for the moment keeps the popula-

Figure 3: Average number of children per woman in North Africa, 1950–2010[39]

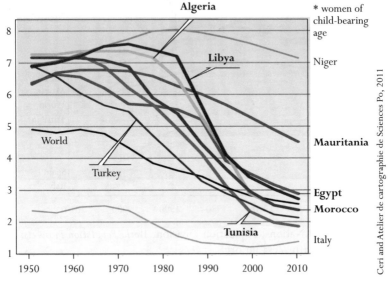

Fertility rate (average number of children per woman*)

Source: United Nations, Population Division, *World Population Prospects: The 2008 Revision*, http://esa.un.org

tion on the land, but destruction of the ecosystem and the failure of projects to develop alternative crops risk driving inhabitants of the Rif to migrate or to revolt.[40]

Lastly, the informal economy plays a considerable role in North Africa. In Morocco, according to various reports, it accounts for 17% of the production of national wealth and in some sectors, such as construction and public works, it makes up 52% of the workforce, 40% of production, and 55% of added value. Women are well represented in the informal sector, especially in the capacity of family caregiver and household help. In rural areas, they are a source of virtually free labour. In Algeria, informal employment was estimated to compose 25% of total employment excluding agriculture in 1985; it rose to more than 40% in 2007. In Algeria, the informal economy corresponds to an "unobserved economy" that can be divided into four segments: underground production; illegal production; informal production by small-

Figure 4: Urbanization in North Africa, 1950–2010[41]

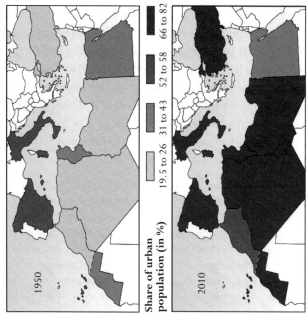

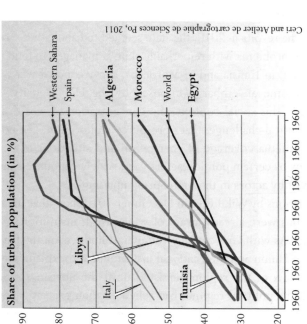

Ceri and Atelier de cartographie de Sciences Po, 2011

Source: United Nations, Population Division, *World Population Prospects:The 2008 Revision*, http://esa.un.org

scale enterprises; and own-use household production. In 2005, this unobserved economy made up 16–17% of GDP and employed 50% of the active population. Even though the informal economy existed during the colonial period, it expanded from the 1970s due to the rigidity of supply. Items sold at administered prices are for instance resold on the parallel market. Likewise, the monopoly on foreign trade increases opportunities to circumvent it. The Algerian authorities gave priority to the industrial sector, which represented the public sector. The private sector was left to informal trade. The informal sector is an answer to

> serious social needs (jobs, housing, income) that have not been met and a response to many rigidities characteristic of the economy in general and in particular in wages, taxation, entrepreneurship, access to foreign markets, currency exchange and financing ... Informal employment, especially common in goods and services in the crafts sector and retailing, is likely to continue in the future as long as liberalization reforms are not completed, or the declared private sector has not reached a level of investment that would enable it to provide strong and lasting stimulation for the job supply, or the unemployment rate has not come down to an acceptable level.[42]

Until the revolts in 2010, the state seemed to handle these social and economic problems with remarkable skill. It managed to fend off riots and revolts (in Tunisia and in Morocco), survive a civil war (Algeria) and overcome an embargo imposed by the UN Security Council (Libya). In this social context, the concentration of wealth raised a major political challenge: that of resource reallocation. The politicization and media coverage of corruption and situations of economic hegemony by certain political actors were widely denounced and called to account by actors in the Arab Spring uprisings.[43]

Revelations by WikiLeaks in December 2010 show that the region's populations were already aware of widespread, institutionalized corruption.[44] As with Greece, only voluntary blindness on the part of the European Union and international institutions can explain why a misleading view of the region persisted until the uprisings. For many decades, the political regimes had relied on their security and intelligence services to neutralize and subjugate "rebel" individuals and groups, but in the face of escalating threats the security apparatuses seemed incapable of accomplishing their aims. In this context of social violence, terrorism, and disenchantment of youth, the countries of North Africa were confronted with the need to implement public policies that could produce the solidarity and loyalty conducive to preserving a sense of community that had been lost in Libya, Syria and Iraq. Until a short time before, these Arab countries had all been considered to have robust regimes. The post-colonial states of North Africa realized how essential it was to find mechanisms capable of generating the national cohesion needed to hold their countries together. The time when nationalists dreamed of strong states seemed far away indeed. The effects of the Arab revolts differed for each country in the region. While the revolts in Tunisia led to a revolution that toppled the Ben Ali regime and paved the way for a democratic transition, in Libya an armed insurgency soon supplanted the initial peaceful demonstrations and dragged the country into armed clashes which brought about the collapse of the state. By contrast, in both Morocco and Algeria, although revolts were crushed, grievances against the state remained intact and obliged the governments in both countries to allocate considerable resources to preserve stability and civil peace.

Chaos in Libya: A Foil for Regional Revolts

In Libya, revolution and a bloody war in which NATO came to the insurgents' aid brought down the Qadhafi regime. On 15 February 2011, the human rights activist Fethi Tarbel was arrested in Benghazi. This run-of-the-mill event in Qadhafi's Libya nevertheless sparked off rioting throughout the city, which soon turned into violent clashes and then an armed resistance movement. Against all expectations, a full-blown jihadi-backed insurgency quickly spread to cities such as Bayda, Misrata and Zawiya.[45] To put an end to the revolutionary situation, regime hardliners brought back the man they had refused to listen to before: Saif al-Islam, one of Qadhafi's sons. In 2007, the government had authorized the creation of private media, most of them belonging to the Ghad Foundation, headed by Saif al-Islam himself. In May 2009 came a new crackdown: the government nationalized private media outlets (Al-Libi satellite channel, Eman al-Libye radio station, and *Quryna* and *Oea* newspapers), putting an end to the fleeting experiment with a free press. Acknowledging his defeat, Saif al-Islam announced his withdrawal from politics, thereby abandoning the reforms he had deemed necessary to ensure the Libyan regime's survival. On 10 December 2010, only months before the insurgency, his Ghad Foundation published a report on human rights in Libya, pointing to "a dangerous regression" in the situation of civil society organizations and criticizing the General People's Congress. Prior to the uprisings, Amnesty International published a report on Wednesday, 23 June 2010, describing the human rights situation as "desperate". The short experiment with media liberalization in Libya was far from without consequence, however. It was what Sarah Nefissa labelled a "pluralist enclave"[46] in an autocratic political system. A number of young journalists employed and then arrested during this period were to place their talents in the service of the rebels by providing media coverage of the February 2011 revolution.

On 20 February 2011, Saif al-Islam, in a televised statement, warned Libyans: "Libya is at a crossroads. If we do not agree on reforms today, we will not be mourning 84 people, but thousands of deaths, and rivers of blood will run through Libya." On 17 March, the fear of harsh military reprisals against the city of Benghazi prompted the UN Security Council to authorize military action to protect civilians. It took the NATO-backed insurgency eight months to reach Tripoli and overthrow the regime. According to Miftah Duwadi, deputy minister of martyrs and missing persons, the number of casualties in the revolution, contrary to estimates of 50,000 dead at the time, was in fact 4,700 dead and 2,100 missing.[47]

An oil-rich country, Libya under Qadhafi, despite its system of redistribution, had fallen victim to the distress of regions such as Cyrenaica and Jebel Nefusa, which always felt the Jamahiriyya (Qadhafi's Libya) had abandoned them. Thus, when Saif al-Islam announced in 2007 that "Libya [would be] a modern country with modern infrastructure and a high GDP ... [that] its citizens [would] enjoy the best standard of living in the region ... Libya [would have] closer relations with the rest of the world and with Africa, as well as a partnership with the European Union ... [and would] join the WTO ...,"[48] only its European and Asian trade partners took him seriously. In April 2006, a World Bank report noted that Libya needed foreign investment in every economic sector: "with more than 50 percent of the population under the age of 20 … Libya is coming under intense demographic pressures. In 2003, 86 percent of the population was urban, compared to 45 percent in 1970."[49] The real economic and social challenge for the Qadhafi regime was to create jobs outside the hydrocarbon sector so as to integrate unemployed youth drawn to Islamist ideology. Despite the sound advice proffered by international consultants, however, the regime remained impervious to reform right until its downfall. Ravaged by corruption and waste, Qadhafi's Libya had been swept by the wind of revolt well before 2011.[50]

Whereas Tripoli had been at the centre of the revolution of 1969, it was merely the scene of a confrontation that totally escaped the grip of revolution in 2011. On 20 October of that same year, Colonel Qadhafi was brutally executed in a symbolic *mise-en-scène* and then transported to Misrata by that city's Revolutionary Brigade. His death brought an end to the regime he had established following a coup d'état in 1969. After having survived many an ordeal throughout its long reign, the regime collapsed, paradoxically, at a time when Libya radiated strength. On the eve of the "Arab Spring", the Jamahiriyya's financial clout, estimated at over $160 billion, was intimidating. The presence of several eminent guests at the September 2009 festivities held in celebration of the fortieth anniversary of the revolution illustrated the regime's return to favour. After Silvio Berlusconi tendered apologies for Italy's colonial rule of Libya (1911–1942), the president of the Swiss Federal Council apologized for the treatment Qadhafi's youngest son, Hannibal, had received at the hands of the police in a five-star hotel in Geneva. In September 2009, the Scottish courts released Abdelbasset Ali al-Megrahi "on compassionate grounds", even though he had been convicted of the Lockerbie bombing. Lastly, in May 2010, Libya occupied the presidency of the UN Security Council for one year. On the eve of his unpredictable overthrow, Qadhafi's Libya was viewed as an Eldorado coveted by lobbies for the oil, arms and civil engineering industries. No one imagined the regime would fall, and all were prepared, if necessary, to suffer the colonel's rebuffs to gain access to this market which had a per annum growth rate of 8% in the first decade of the twenty-first century.

In Morocco and in Algeria, the authorities followed the revolts in Tunisia and the armed insurgency in Libya with concern. However, as will be explained in Chapters Five and Six, both these countries managed to contain the development of protest dynamics that were likely to bring about a revolution. The entire region, however, was experiencing social and political transformations that threatened national cohesion. Youth unemployment, affecting both graduates and the unskilled, and territorial fractures in southern Algeria, the Rif in Morocco and southern Tunisia all made the authorities nervous, given the extent to which the political regimes seemed unequal to the difficulties facing them. The implosion of Libya came as a clear warning of the threats hovering over each of them. The awakening of civil society fuelled public debate on a host of subjects, including those that had seemed the most taboo, such as corruption.

3

TUNISIA

FROM THE SPECTRE OF CIVIL WAR
TO DEMOCRATIC COMPROMISE

President Ben Ali's unanticipated downfall in the wake of a surprise protest movement calls for a reappraisal of the supposed political robustness of regimes in North Africa, starting with a fresh look at the end of the Tunisian paradox. How could an educated society employed in a diversified economy with a strong middle class cohabit for so long with a police regime as brutal and corrupt as Ben Ali's?[1] The answer can be found in the various techniques devised by the Tunisian regime to bring the country's political, economic and social resources under its control, techniques detailed by Béatrice Hibou in her book, *The Force of Obedience.*[2]

The riots that came in the aftermath of Mohamed Bouazizi's immolation in December 2010[3] served to highlight—in a most dramatic fashion—the despair of the youth, whether day labourers or unemployed graduates and non-graduates. But how did they manage to gather such a nationwide following, eventually toppling Ben Ali? Tunisia specialists have pointed out the density of virtual social and informal networks that made it possible to politicize the initial social demands expressed in small towns in the interior; the work of intellectuals in translating their complaints and grievances into the language of poli-

45

tics; their deployment in a symbolic geographical space such as the capital; and the manufacture of an expiatory victim in the Trabelsi clan. The Tunisian opposition pulled off the incredible feat of bringing about the convergence of social and economic demands with political demands in record time—less than a month—enabling the revolt to result in a political outcome rather than ending up in yet another social hunger riot such as those taking place concurrently in Algeria, triggered by skyrocketing wheat prices on the international commodity market. In short, while the dynamics of the uprising seemed linked to the successful politicization of social riots and their confinement to the capital, its success had to do with the army's refusal to fire on the demonstrators, a condition that was not met in Libya.

In 2011, to the world's surprise, the political regimes considered the most robust were challenged by unforeseen forces. Against all expectations, it was not the Islamists, major actors since the 1980s, who were in the vanguard of protest, but instead a league of lawyers, union leaders and human rights activists whose mobilization inspired entire segments of the population to follow.[4] What happened? How can the phenomenon be explained? Did protest movements that grew out of the financial crisis in Europe and the United States influence movements in the region? In other words, "did external crises make certain Arab regimes more vulnerable to internal revolts?"[5] Until the uprisings, discussion of the regimes' vulnerability and fragility was virtually absent from research on the region. Instead, attention was turned to the regimes' robustness, their coercive capacity, and their mechanisms of domination.[6] Their relative success against Islamist organizations between 1980 and 2000 had reinforced the impression of these regimes' strength and masked their fragility. The Euro-Mediterranean (Euromed) policy, together with the Barcelona Process, offered them a façade of legitimacy and respectability that reinforced the feeling inside the country that their political leaders were all-powerful. Some studies did, however, point out the danger of such an approach, and while they did not go so far as to predict the unthinkable—in other words, revolution—they showed how, to use the Chinese saying taken up by Timur Kuran, "a single spark can start a prairie fire".[7] Research on civil society and social movements has described the underpinnings of contestation processes. But it has made only minimal headway in the political sphere.

In fact, in "the prairie", virtually no actor believed fire was possible in a country like Tunisia, as this interview conducted in 2009 in Tunis illustrates: "The regimes in place could last for a long time due to the lack of any serious counterpower. These regimes are very robust, they have many years ahead. I don't see why they would change."[8] Just before the uprisings broke out, the conviction that the political regimes were unshakeable was a firm belief among many civil society actors. Systematic repression in a country like Tunisia left no room for perspective and reflection on the region's future. "We're fighting for survival. We are forced to focus our action on preserving our organization, not even on defending human rights. We're subject to such harassment that we're incapable of it. What can I say about issues concerning the Maghreb, partnerships, Euromed ... These are luxuries."[9] This belief in the power of the political rulers explains why the issue of democratization never managed to leave the realm of utopia. "Dreaming of democracy in the near future borders on utopia. It would be enough to hope for rationality in government policies. The regimes in place today would rather maintain control over the population and the territory."[10] And yet an unexpected and unforeseen popular uprising toppled a regime considered one of the most robust in the region.

Among the factors explaining the success of the Tunisian Revolution, the role played by the army in January 2011 was crucial and too often neglected in analyses of Tunisia's transition.[11] Indeed, on 13 January 2011, General Rashid Ammar, the Tunisian army chief of staff, refused to give the order to open fire on the demonstrators.[12] A hero to the demonstrators, a traitor to former officials of Ben Ali's regime, he by his refusal to join the police in their crackdown on the demonstrators shook the regime to its foundations. This act of disobedience to the political authorities weakened President Ben Ali, who fled the country to Saudi Arabia two days later. On 24 January 2011, as demonstrators were calling for the resignation of the transitional government made up of regime bosses under Ben Ali, General Rashid Ammar assured demonstrators in an impromptu speech on the Kasbah esplanade, "The nation's army are guarantors of the revolution. The army has and will protect the people and the country ... We are faithful to the Constitution. We will protect the Constitution. We will not get out of this framework."[13]

What explains the army's refusal to crush this popular uprising? One answer may lie in the fact that, historically, the army had constantly been "kept in check"[14] or "eclipsed",[15] under both the Habib Bourguiba (1956–1986) and the Ben Ali regime (1986–2011). Unlike in Algeria or Egypt, the army was neither the backbone of the regime nor a pillar of the state. Therefore, "Tunisian troops were constantly declining in number over the last decade, with only 35,000 underequipped soldiers in 2010 … Ben Ali, on the other hand, based his power on a solid police apparatus 120,000 strong."[16] The all-powerful police force under Ben Ali turned the country into a police state feared by all its opponents.

This apparently daunting and unshakeable power nevertheless had its weaknesses, as Sadri Khiari has shown in his work on "community disintegration" in Tunisia.[17] Ben Ali's powerful regime chipped away at the social underpinnings that were nevertheless necessary to enable it to endure. An invisible process of "community disintegration" was at work under his rule. The end of Habib Bourguiba's rule fuelled hopes that the regime would move toward greater openness. Ben Ali's overthrow of the "Supreme Combatant" was justified by the conclusion that "the Tunisian people were ripe for democracy". But very soon, measures taken by the new president suggested continuity with the methods of the past. The fight against Islamists provided a pretext for restricting civil liberties. Institutions, political parties and trade union activities were held in check. By exploiting the Islamist threat, a powerful repressive apparatus was set up and the range of its victims constantly expanded, from Islamists to democrats. The emergence of the Islamic Salvation Front (FIS) in Algeria and the Iraqi invasion of Kuwait prompted a segment of Tunisians to back the security policy designed by the president, for whom cohesion took precedence over democracy.[18] The revelation of a "Nahdaoui conspiracy" by members of the Ennahda party was the prelude to the preventive eradication of the Islamist threat. As Sadri Khiari points out, "Ben Ali put an end to the uncertainties of the later years of Bourguibism, without sowing chaos and disorder. Many were those in the middle classes who identified with Ben Ali's new syncretism: rehabilitation of a non-aggressive Arab-Islamic identity associated with a discourse of modernity—in fact far more technological than social and political—and of progress, essentially concerned with consumerism";[19] a technique borrowed by

Algerian president Bouteflika in the early 2000s, with definite success at the start. The fact remains that, as under Ben Ali in Tunisia, concerns were expressed about the disintegration of Algerian society and its consequences.[20]

Tunisia projected a positive image on the outside, at variance with the violence and despair within. Thus, the context in which Ben Ali came to power in 1987 was characterized by "decline at the topmost echelon of the state, the erosion of trade union and democratic opposition groups, and the Islamist threat". Ben Ali's autocratic behaviour brought an end to state decline, and the establishment of a police regime sounded the death knell for any form of political opposition. From an economic standpoint, modernization primarily profited businesses, as Béatrice Hibou points out in her analysis of the tax structure. Economic liberalization produced inequalities that had obvious social and political consequences. But the establishment of a powerful, effective police state cushioned the regime against upheavals caused by economic policies conducted over the decade. To the attentive observer, the oft-touted Tunisian economic miracle exhibited flaws and weaknesses that have otherwise received little scrutiny, repression being so pervasive as to drown out other voices.

Thus, despite critical studies of the country, especially Béatrice Hibou's analysis, Ben Ali's Tunisia was long held to be the best performer in the Maghreb. Among the factors helping to promote the regime, Tunisia's economic success was constantly highlighted to better distinguish it from its wealthier but less developed neighbours. Thus, according to some, "President Ben Ali took things in hand, improved the country's economy, restored hope in people's hearts, and breathed passion and the desire to excel into business leaders and economic actors."[21] As the French Embassy's Trade Commission in Tunis pointed out in June 2007, "between 1995 and 2006, Tunisia's GDP rose by an average of 4.8 points per year. The growth rate reached 5.4% in 2006 and the government forecasts it will attain 6%." This growth rate partly explains Tunisia's positive image, even if it was driven by credit growth. But for the regime's opponents, these figures concealed the brake which a single clan, the Trabelsi, had on the wheels of all economic sectors.[22]

In this context, Sadri Khiari asked the following question: "What explains that the population's growing discontent has not taken an active and organized form or has delayed in doing so?"[23] Analysis of the failure of the Algerian popular uprising at the end of Bourguiba's rule shows that the various opposition forces were unable to forge a credible and effective alternative. Likewise, investigation into the Islamist movement under Ben Ali's presidency reveals contradictions within it. The Ennahda Party's missteps arose out of its lack of direction, an inevitable consequence of the policy of repression. The radicalism of the democratic movement prevented it from being perceived as a constructive opposition force, because "Ben Ali's obstinate authoritarianism led the movement to call into question the entire political system".[24] Lastly, "union resistance" had to deal with "an accelerating economic transition" that weakened the economic sectors in which trade union influence was strong (education, the metallurgical industry, healthcare, and so on). The "community disintegration" observed by Sadri Khiari portended a radical change. As this author affirmed, "the regime [had] not lost its entire foundation; it still rested on remnants of the social, economic and political system characteristic of the Bourguiba era."[25] Ben Ali's liberal police regime was undergoing a crisis, according to the author, whose duration and outcome were uncertain. But the alarming signs of a state on the verge of breaking up were obvious to him. The "street", silent until then, was likely to witness what Sadri Khiari called "a sudden outbreak of impromptu events" that would have unanticipated consequences. In 2011, the uprisings that produced the Tunisian Revolution confirmed the accuracy and relevance of Sadri Khiari's analysis of "community disintegration".

The Spectre of Civil War

In the months immediately following the fall of the Ben Ali regime, concerns were growing: would transition lead to democracy or civil war? Aside from the surprise victory of Ennahda, the Islamist party, in the October 2011 elections to the Constituent Assembly,[26] revolutionary actors noted with dismay that the end of Ben Ali's regime had been accompanied by a resurgence of Salafi violence. On 19 February 2011, the transitional government granted amnesty to all political prisoners, including many Islamists who had been arrested and sentenced under the 2003 anti-terrorism law.[27] The release of Abu Ayadh, founder of the

Tunisian Combatant Group and leader of Ansar al-Sharia,[28] presented the authorities with the challenge of coping with the jihadi threat within a pluralist and democratic framework.[29] More than 400 police stations were attacked in 2012, as well as cultural centres, cinemas and even Sufi shrines such as Saida Manoubia in Tunis and Sidi Bou Said. The political transition in fact gave Salafis and jihadis the opportunity to attempt to impose their social and religious domination. Some observers maintain that the Salafis benefited from the complicity of the Ennahda Islamists in government. As in Algeria during the FIS period (1989–1991), secular artists and intellectuals were vilified by the Salafis. This noxious climate brought an end to the image of Tunisia as a "haven of peace", fabricated at great expense by the Ben Ali regime.[30] Already in 2012, a large number of organizations "warned of civil war".[31] Disorganized and subject to contradictions within the government, the internal security forces were incapable of restoring security. Being associated with the image of Ben Ali's police regime, they did not have the support or the legitimacy they needed in the aftermath of the revolution. They allowed rallies and demonstrations to degenerate not only for fear of criminal charges but also to remind the victors of the revolution that a political transition without a security force enjoying the people's support left the door open to anarchy, chaos and violence. As for the army, unlike in Algeria in 1991, it remained at a distance from these social and religious clashes which tarnished the image of the Jasmine Revolution.

In fact, between 2012 and 2014, the government headed by the Ennahda Islamists attempted to channel and control radical Salafis, though without combating them. It refused to consider them ideological enemies or a threat to the democratic transition. To avoid conducting the same security policy as Ben Ali, all ideas and beliefs could be freely expressed; only crimes and acts of violence were punished. This approach raised a number of criticisms and concerns.[32] As a moderate Islamist party convinced that Islam could coexist with democracy, Ennahda was faced with Salafi organizations that spurned democracy and were fighting to establish sharia as the basis for law.

In the process of drafting the Constitution in 2013, society was polarized between Islamists and secularists, Bourguiba's heirs, over the question of Islam's place within the state. Tensions also crystallized around the nature of the new regime: parliamentary or presidential? The Constitution adopted in February 2014 provided a constitutional solution to a polarized political situation. The Ennahda party became the first Islamist party to take part in achieving a historic compromise with democracy at the cost of toning down their positions to some extent. Article 1 stipulated that Islam was the religion of Tunisia but did not establish sharia as the source of law. As the Ennahda leader, Ghannouchi, said, "Power lies with the people and no one can incarnate God on earth. We are clearly in favour of a civil state and against a religious state."[33] Tunisia thus became a civil state. In the October 2014 elections, the Nidaa Tounes party won 39% of the seats in the Assembly and took over from the Troika (2011–2014) which had been in charge of the transition. The election of Beji Caid Essebsi as president at first contributed to a coalition frightened by Salafi violence and jihadi threats. However, its lack of an economic programme or an agenda for reform very quickly caused it to fall out of favour with the general population, exasperated as they were by deteriorating living conditions.

For indeed, while from a constitutional standpoint the country concluded the transition and revolutionary period with a new constitution and a transfer of political power, from a social and economic standpoint the decline in the standard of living clearly threatened the stability and especially social cohesion of post-Ben Ali Tunisia. Seeing no improvement in their everyday lives, the poorest regions of the interior have regularly taken to holding demonstrations.[34] The tourist sector, which accounts for about 7.5% of GDP, was hit hard by Islamist terrorism. After the Salafi violence of the 2012–2013 period, the attacks on the Bardo National Museum in Tunis on 18 March 2015 and in Sousse on 26 June 2015 were devastating for the tourism industry. An estimated "280 hotels closed, in other words 50% of the hotel capacity".[35] Out of fear, Europeans, who made up 70% of the tourists in 2010 and only 45% in 2015, put off their trips. Tourists from Eastern Europe and the Maghreb, however, gradually took the place of Western Europeans. The deterioration of the social and economic climate resulted in a drop in foreign direct investment and a sharp rise in unemployment to an overall 15%, but to 35% for the 15–24 age group and a colossal 67% for young graduates.

In January 2016, riots broke out in Kasserine and spread to Jendouba, Kebili and Gafsa, indicating a growing insurgency. Clashes between demonstrators answering the call of the Unemployed Graduates Union and the General Union of Tunisian Students left hundreds wounded. In view of this, self-defence groups formed in a number of cities. Exasperation also reached new heights within the police force, which petitioned for wage increases before the presidential palace in Carthage. In response to the rioting, demonstrations and wage demands, Prime Minister Habib Essid announced measures, especially a new phase of hiring for public jobs, intended to combat unemployment. One of the outcomes of the revolution had indeed been a steep increase in public sector hiring. Between 2010 and 2014, 180,000 employees were hired (40% for security and defence personnel), representing a 30% increase in public enterprise workers, who total about 800,000 employees. With this recruitment drive, public employment accounts for 24% of the employed workforce, "a level that is three times higher than in Morocco". These public sector jobs have increased the wage bill (13.5% of GDP in 2015), which absorbs 56% of tax revenues and amounts to nearly 50% of total expenditures.[36]

On 7 March 2016, against a backdrop of political vulnerability and social unrest, some one hundred jihadis stormed state institutions in the city of Ben Gardane on the Libyan border and sought to foment an uprising among its inhabitants against the authorities. Convinced that the population was disillusioned and disenchanted by successive governments' inability to address their concerns, they hoped that, as in the city of Sirte in Libya, they would be welcomed and supported by the villagers. A fierce battle ensued, stunning the Tunisian population by the scale of the attack and the number of victims: more than 46 among the jihadis.[37] A small town of 60,000 inhabitants in the extreme southeast of Tunisia, Ben Gardane (and especially Ras Jdir, 25 kilometres away) is known to be the hub of cross-border smuggling with Libya. Border trade flourished while Libya was under embargo, and was organized by the Touazine tribe in Tunisia and the Nouayel tribe in Libya.[38] It made the town attractive, causing a population explosion: 6,500 inhabitants in 1975; 9,400 in 1984; 12,000 in 1994; and 60,000 in 2004.[39] "Ben Gardane, a sleepy town in the mid-1980s … has awakened and is now a city that never sleeps. It has become an assembly point for traders from all over Tunisia and a transit point for Maghreban trade."[40] The collapse of the Qadhafi regime heightened activity at the crossing between Tunisia and Libya, which became the centre for all kinds of smuggling (including cigarettes and weapons) and a source of concern for the Tunisian authorities: 15% of Tunisian jihadis who went to Syria and Iraq transited through Ben Gardane.[41] One report published findings that bore out what everyone suspected: thousands of Tunisian nationals, 5,500 of them, had joined the Islamic State organization and 1,500 were allegedly in neighbouring Libya. Tunisia contributes the highest number of jihadis to foreign campaigns.[42] On 19 and 20 January 2016, IS videos issued calls to overthrow the "apostate" Tunisian and Moroccan governments.

As in Morocco and Algeria, the Tunisian authorities unveiled a "strategy to combat extremism and terrorism" in November 2016. It was built on four pillars: *prevention*, "measures aiming to eradicate underlying causes of terrorism and prevent young people from turning to this evil"; *protection*, "establishment of a more effective system of coordination and information sharing among the various intelligence services"; *tracking*, "to thwart the financing of terrorists"; and *response*, "a mechanism to deal with the consequences of terrorist acts". In fact, the terrorist incidents of 2015 radically altered the Tunisian authorities' approach, as the interior minister explained: "the important element that changed for us is that to ensure security and defence, we had to shift from a position of retaliation to one of anticipation and prevention."[43]

International support has proved indispensable in order to combat jihadi organizations that have powerful internal and external networks. In addition to ties with Algeria, Tunisia has the active support of the EU and the United States. From a symbolic standpoint, a 200 kilometre-long barrier along the border with Libya was completed. Built with German funding, it is meant to keep jihadis from entering the country from Libya. In view of the fear of seeing the only democracy in the Arab world destroyed by jihadis, the EU and the United States became somewhat more involved in bolstering the Tunisian regime. In May 2015, Tunisia became a "major non-NATO ally" and the United States committed to training special counterterrorism forces such as the Special Unit of Tunisian Guards (USGT) and the Tunisian Antiterrorism Brigade (BAT). The US bill HR 157, "Combating Terrorism in Tunisia", states: "It is the policy of the United States to further assist the democratically elected Government of Tunisia in eliminating terrorist organizations that operate in Tunisia and neighboring Libya and preventing fighters in Syria from returning to Tunisia."

Accused of letting radical youth leave for lands of jihad, the authorities have prohibited Tunisians under 35 from visiting countries such as Libya, Iraq and Syria. In 2016, the authorities claimed to have prevented as many as 18,000 young people from leaving. Like Algeria in the 1990s or post-Qadhafi Libya, a fraction of Tunisian youth has become radicalized. For the authorities, this process poses a threat to national unity and social cohesion. With a dearth of economic resources, they are at a loss to deal with the dynamics of violence, which prevent a return to stability. In 2017, however, dozens of terrorist cells were dismantled owing to improved coordination among the security services. The fact remains that with thousands of Tunisian nationals joining IS ranks, Tunisia has been confronted with the return of Tunisian jihadis to the country since the collapse of this organization. Over 800 of them have reportedly returned to their homeland, obliging the Tunisian government to devise de-radicalization programmes for these ex-combatants. Some combatants who "return to Tunisia without being tried in court are for instance placed under house arrest and are under surveillance".[44] The handling of returning Tunisian jihadis, and the counterterrorism policy more generally speaking, raise fears among civil society in Tunisia of the resurgence of a police state.

Reform of the Security Sector

The 2003 law defining the legal framework of the fight against terrorism under the Ben Ali regime raised numerous criticisms due to the very broad definition of terrorism. Between 2003 and 2011, more than 5,000 people were sentenced by virtue of this law and 2,000 of them "on grounds of and/or for crimes of opinion".[45] After the revolution, security sector reform was on the agenda. "In transition phases, several states have opted for security sector reform (SSR), based on clear principles, that is, accountability, transparency, equality, civilian protection, democratic norms and respect for human rights."[46] The restructuring of the interior ministry, in particular with the dissolution of the Directorate of State Security (DSE) and the dismissal of the main cadres of the Directorate of Preventive Antiterrorism, has "crippled the fight against terrorism".[47] In fact, security institutions (internal security forces, the army) had to "adapt in three fundamental ways: to the new democratic framework, to the jihadi threat, and to demands for social justice that were unleashed by the fall of the dictatorship and radicalized by the authorities' poor mediation capacity".[48] Under the Ben Ali regime, people's fear of the police was a major factor in maintaining regime stability. Tens of thousands of informers throughout society kept security forces apprised of various situations. The deployment of informers in all sectors (universities, factories, the media, transportation and so on) provoked a self-censorship reflex among the population.

After the revolution, the police bore the brunt of people's rejection and anger. In an explosive security and social context, they had not only to regain the population's trust but also to overcome suspicion among the new political representatives, who were eager to curtail the police force's prerogatives. This situation generated a sense of insecurity among the police.[49] As they were unable to achieve the level of security to which the population aspired, expectations turned toward the army. Revered for its attitude during the revolution, the army was mobilized for several purposes: securing natural resource extraction sites, protecting borders and combating jihadi groups. To fulfil these roles, the army's budget was doubled, from 400 million euros in 2010 to 800 million euros in 2017. Although engaged in a fight against terrorism, the army was underequipped to deal with the regular skirmishes it faced in the mountainous areas of the north-west and attacks on the Tunisian–Libyan border (March 2016 in Gardane). The loss of 68 soldiers in addition to more than 135 wounded in its ranks pointed to the need to modernize its matériel and strategy.[50] Restoring security in Tunisia proved fundamental not only to reviving the tourism industry but also, and above all, to guaranteeing the democratic transition. The collapse of several economic sectors and the government's difficulty in restoring security heightened concerns about the country's transition to democracy.

Like other countries in the region, the Tunisian government is faced with jihadi violence.[51] Security measures today encompass not only the identification and neutralization of terrorists but also the task of mobilizing civil society and Islamist parties so as to deconstruct the jihadist discourse. Salafi violence and jihadi terrorism require moderate

Islamist parties, such as Ennahda, to dissociate themselves from violent acts and promote public discussion of tolerance and respect for the plurality of not only opinions but also interpretations of Islam. Several initiatives in Tunisia aim at devising strategies to prevent radicalization and violent extremism, as other states in North Africa and in the Sahel have done.[52] These strategies mobilize religious actors to promote and spread traditional values of Islam (tolerance, respect, sense of justice) which they use to counter the literalistic and radical interpretations of the Quran that the Salafis convey. The official discourse on the dangers of jihadi Salafis contributes to strengthening national unity and social cohesion. Moderate Islamists, republicans, democrats and nationalists converge in their refusal to accept jihadi ideology and practices. Furthermore, the equation made between jihad and criminality at the borders, and delinquency and martyrdom in suicide bombings, has helped to deconstruct the jihadi narrative, which portrays the combatants as pious Muslims defending Islam. As in Algeria in the 1990s, jihadis in Tunisia are involved in a criminal economy that provides a livelihood for entire regions. De-radicalization strategies can therefore only be successful if the populations in the most destitute and neglected regions are targeted by territorial and social policies that can reintegrate them into legal activities and restore ties of loyalty to the state and a sense of belonging to the national community. Tunisia's decentralization policy is a response to the feeling of abandonment in interior, "useless" regions of Tunisia.

As Béatrice Hibou has pointed out, the state in Tunisia is characterized by its "asymmetric formation", with public investment concentrated solely on developing the coastal regions.[53] Between 1990 and 2000, whereas Tunisia's growth rate was 3.4%, the unemployment rate in the city of Kasserine went from 30% to 49.3% and in Sidi Bouzid from 39% to 49%.[54] Article 12 of the 2014 Constitution stipulates, "The state shall seek to achieve social justice, sustainable development and balance between regions based on development indicators and the principle of positive discrimination." According to the provisions of Article 14, "The state commits to strengthen decentralization and to apply it throughout the country, within the framework of the unity of the state." As Jean-Philippe Bras explains, "The 2014 text bears the mark of events that led to the previous regime's downfall."[55] The revolution aimed to rectify a historical imbalance by transferring new prerogatives and resources to local authorities.[56] In May 2018, Tunisia's first free municipal elections were held. Some 57,000 candidates ran for office in the 350 municipal councils, the first stage in the participatory democracy laid out in the new Constitution. While the two main political parties came out victorious in these elections—Ennahda won 25% of the seats and Nidaa Tounes 22%—voter turnout was only 33.7%. The electorate's very low mobilization supports the thesis of profound post-revolutionary disenchantment.[57] The election outcome underscores the need to stimulate economic growth and restore security so as to renew citizens' confidence in political parties and democracy.

4

LIBYA, A MULTINATIONAL STATE?[1]

Eight years after Qadhafi's ouster, the international community gauged the scope of the problem and stated that its goal was to "build a state in Libya"[2] so as to impose a political order on local dynamics that escaped institutional control.[3] Along with the overthrow of Colonel Qadhafi's regime came the disintegration of the Jamahiriyya (the "state of the masses"), the political system that attempted to organize Libyans' social relationships.[4] Without a state, the Libyan nation withdrew into the various tribal and community networks that offered the only guarantee of protection in a violent environment. Far from being solely destructive, this violence can be viewed as a resource in the service of new actors—the militias—that are seeking to reconfigure the emerging state to their advantage.[5] Borders, oil fields, migrants, and arms trafficking are all new and lucrative sectors that the protagonists of post-Qadhafi Libya are trying to control. Territorial fragmentation mirrors the struggle for monopoly over local resources: in the south, Toubou and Tuareg are vying for border control;[6] along the coast, those paying allegiance to Tripoli or to Tobruk are at war for control of the oil fields and oil terminals. In the middle of these two major economic areas, clashes break out over control of roads and stopover cities. Jihadi organizations have gained strongholds in this violent reconfiguration for the control of resources,[7] and offer the people an alternative to the chaos surrounding them by promoting the formation of an Islamic emirate or an Islamic state.[8] In the space of a few years, Libya has moved from a socialist, revolutionary and pan-African regime to a territory controlled by a host of local and regional authorities.

The Arab revolts raised hopes of seeing the region slip peacefully into a democratization process, leaving authoritarianism behind to join other political regimes undergoing a democratic transition.[9] This vision proved to be an illusion. With the exception of Tunisia, the so-called democratic wave paradoxically paved the way for jihadi groups with a non-democratic political project conveyed through violence. In Libya, opposition to the Qadhafi regime quickly took an insurrectional turn. As Saif al-Islam stated regarding Tunisia and Egypt, these countries experienced "true revolutions, with millions of people in the streets" demonstrating "peacefully and unarmed for days on end … In Libya, the streets are now full of armed militias." These armed militias, which overthrew the Qadhafi regime with NATO support,[10] had a very different agenda from the National Transitional Council (NTC), which was acting as the representative of the Libyan government. Once Qadhafi's forces were destroyed, Libya was left to tribe-based militias that have laid down the law.[11] This abandonment by the countries most involved in NATO proved to be a dramatic strategic error.[12] Libya became a country at the mercy of jihadi groups and armed militias that pillaged the huge store of weapons stockpiled during the Qadhafi regime. Libyans discovered with horror that NATO members had no post-Qadhafi strategy other than to let them face on their own the countless challenges awaiting them, including the most perilous of all: how to avoid sliding into civil war.[13] This occurred in 2014, three years after the regime was toppled. Contrary to expectations, the July 2012 elections did not pave the way for a democratic transition but proved rather that the new political regime in Libya was ruled by the militias.[14] Between July 2012 and July 2014, they managed to impose their authority, and from July 2014 they unleashed a series of attacks to gain control of the symbols of state (cities, oil production, airport, central bank and so on). Libya splintered into a multitude of local powers and then gelled into two regional blocs: east (Benghazi) and west (Tripoli), redrawing the historical fault lines of the Libyan state that have existed since its foundation.

LIBYA, A MULTINATIONAL STATE?

An Insurrectional Process

From the very start, an insurrectional process defined the relationship with the former regime. It was framed as a confrontation that left the Guide no other alternative than exile or death. As Fathi Fadhli wrote, "Qadhafi, his sons and his supporters are not part of Libya anymore, they are no longer Libyans." Unlike the Tunisian and Egyptian revolutions, the Libyan revolution rapidly took a confrontational turn, leaving little room for negotiation or compromise. For many, Qadhafi made his fatal error on 15 August 2011 by calling the rebels "rats" on live television, after over six months of conflict. "The end of the colonizer is near and the end of the rats is near. They flee from house to house while the masses hunt them down." For Hakim, a veterinarian in Tripoli and former member of the Suq al-Jum'a militia, this insult was a pivotal moment in the insurgency then taking place in the Libyan capital. It galvanized the rebels, who were determined to take revenge for the offence. "Many people cried with rage when they saw and heard Qadhafi call them rats; some of them took this as a worse insult than being called dogs. After all the strife we had just lived through, he called us rats. I think that's what spurred the revolutionaries on after these insults [November 2012]." During the civil war, words could be as deadly as weapons. The people of Tawergha (35,000 inhabitants) were called slaves, negroes and animals by the revolutionaries in Misrata, who accused them of taking part in the destruction of their town on the side of the loyalist forces. They were driven to take refuge in camps on the outskirts of Tripoli, and more than 1,300 of them are still in custody, missing or dead. Similarly, Zintani brigades called the inhabitants of Mashshiya "Qadhafi's dogs" for having backed the loyalists.[15] In 2018, the Misrata militias continued to prevent residents of Tawergha from returning to their homes, and hundreds of people are still in prison or have been "disappeared".[16]

In Jebel Nafusa, in villages near the town of Nalut, Berber revolutionary brigades also called inhabitants suspected of sympathizing with the regime "Arab dogs".[17] An estimated 550,000 were displaced in the course of the civil war in their effort to escape the dangers and violence. In the new narrative of post-Qadhafi Libya, there is little room for truth in this regard and even less for justice, which seriously compromises any chance of reconciliation. In post-Qadhafi Libya, the Tuareg and the Africans are considered repugnant. Racism against Africans, already apparent in the 1990s, was fully expressed during the insurgency, when attacks on African migrants exemplified a determination to terrorize them and force them to flee. Under the former regime, African migration was a sign of Libya's opening up to the continent, part of Qadhafi's Africa policy. During the revolution, the Tawergha were accused of massacres in Misrata, sparking a wind of hatred toward all Africans living in Libya. Ishak Ag Husseini, representative of the Tuareg Coordination of Libya, accused the revolutionaries of "collective liquidation" during the civil war. "The situation is dire: Libya's Tuareg are suffering horribly due to the manhunt against them by the revolutionaries, who consider them to be Qadhafi supporters."[18] In the 1970s and 1980s, thousands of young Tuareg had left Mali and Niger for Algeria and Libya, where some joined the Islamic Legion, a military instrument in the service of Qadhafi, where they learned soldiering. In the 1990s, the Libyan regime backed Tuareg demands for autonomy, which again descended into armed uprisings in Mali and in Niger.[19] In 2005, an unlimited residence permit was offered to all Tuareg from Mali and Niger. Since the Tuareg had been integrated into Qadhafi's security apparatus, they were all lumped together when the 17 February revolution broke out. Considered as supporters of the regime, they were driven out of Libya.

Convinced that they alone brought about the fall of Qadhafi, the revolutionaries have no doubts about the success of their insurgency. While the history of the civil war remains to be written, the dominant version for the moment is that of the victors. In this formulation, the others—those who did not take part in or did not back the insurgency—no doubt enhance the combatants' role. Yet, seen from Benghazi, Tripoli's change of course was a long time coming. For the Tripolitans, the reason for their belated engagement was the massive presence of regime security forces in their city. In contrast to Benghazi, Tripoli was the Qadhafi family's place of residence, as Dr Ahmed al-Atrash, of the University of Tripoli, points out:

> Qadhafi resided in the centre of Tripoli, his men were there, the security forces as well. People here did not believe the revolutionaries would get this far and take the compounds. Most people stayed here

and waited. Life in Tripoli went on as usual. We were very afraid, but we kept going. The bombings were surgical. Only the military compounds and intelligence and security facilities were destroyed. Here we could not revolt like they did in Benghazi and Adjdabiya: Qadhafi's forces were here because he and his family were here.[20]

The Predictable Failure of the Political Transition, 2012–2014

In the first free elections in post-Qadhafi Libya, held on 7 July 2012, 2,639 candidates took part, representing 374 political parties, lists or independents. The contenders included many women: although invisible during the uprising against the former regime, women are playing an active role in the new "civil and political society".[21] Mahmoud Jibril's National Forces Alliance won 39 seats out of the 80 reserved for political parties; the Justice and Construction Party, an offshoot of the Muslim Brotherhood, came in second with 17 seats; and the National Front, an offshoot of the historic opposition party, the National Front for the Salvation of Libya founded in 1981 by Mohamed Youssef Magarief, came in third with only 3 seats. The Union for the Homeland and the Wadi al-Hayat party each took two seats, and the remainder of the seats were divided up among several political parties. The other 120 seats were reserved for independents, who hold a de facto majority. Some of them are voluntary organization leaders, such as human rights activist Juma Atiga; others are notables representing ethnic groups such as El-Tahir Makni, elected by the Toubou in Qatrun, in Murzuq district, who is also an activist in the Wasat party.

On 9 July 2012, the General National Congress (GNC) elected its president for an interim term of eighteen months: Mohamed Yousef el-Magarief, a long-standing opposition figure, was chosen. And on 8 August, during a historic ceremony for the Libyans, the president of the National Transitional Council,[22] Moustapha Abdeljalil, transferred authority to the GNC, and each of its members swore to uphold the aims of the 17 February revolution. The elections offered a snapshot of the new Libya. The United Nations secretary-general did not fail to "warmly congratulate the Libyan people for the country's first free election in a half-century" on 8 July. On 12 September 2012, following intense negotiations and against all expectations, Mustapha Abu Shagur was appointed prime minister, beating Mahmoud Jibril by two votes, although Jibril had won the ballot. Among the government's objectives, aside from restoring security, the new authorities then outlined a precise political agenda: the drafting of a new Constitution to be approved by referendum. But hardly had he been designated when Mustapha Abu Shagur was replaced on 14 October by Ali Zeidan, a former diplomat who had left Libya in the 1980s and had been active in the National Front for the Salvation of Libya, an opposition movement against Qadhafi's regime.

Although at first the outcome of the 7 July poll suggested that, unlike the situation in Tunisia and Egypt, the Libyan Islamists had lost the elections, the constitutional drafting process attested to the strong influence of the Muslim Brotherhood's Justice and Construction Party. The revival of the political scene in Libya, moreover, witnessed the emergence of media and civil society actors who spontaneously became involved in debates on the Libyan transition. For instance, regarding plans for the new Constitution: should the commission in charge of drafting it be elected or appointed? While a consensus was reached as to the number of its members—60 in all,[23] 20 for each of the three regions in Libya (Tripolitania, Cyrenaica and Fezzan)—the controversy raged on until 6 February 2013, on which date the members of the General National Congress came out in favour of electing a constituent assembly to draft the Constitution by a vote of 87 out of 97 members present. This decision satisfied the Justice and Construction Party and confirmed that the GNC was under the control of the Muslim Brotherhood.[24] Actually, the choice illustrated more than anything the desire of members of the GNC to avoid a clash with proponents of federalism, for whom one of the goals of the 17 February revolution was to restore the autonomy that provinces and regions had lost under Qadhafi's regime, especially in Barqa—Cyrenaica in Arabic.

The aim of the July 2012 elections was to give the country a parliament that would establish the institutions needed to form the Libyan state. Despite the legitimacy the elections accorded them, successive governments could only acknowledge the weakness, not to say insignificance, of their authority compared to the main victors of the post-Qadhafi era: the militias.[25] Following the fall of the regime, tens of thousands of combatants, grouped into brigades associated with towns or districts, occupied public places abandoned by the old regime security forces, to protect the revolution. For the political representatives of Libya in transition, disarming them and integrating them into the national security forces was a top priority. Following the elections, the Libyan authorities issued an ultimatum that remained unheeded: "The National Mobile Force, which comes under the central command, requests all individuals, armed groups and units currently occupying military compounds, public buildings and property belonging to members of the former regime or children of Qadhafi in Tripoli or the surrounding towns, to evacuate these sites within forty-eight hours." Some 1,700 groups, organized into 300 militias, are believed to have taken part in the uprising, and in 2012 over 150,000 Libyans were considered to be armed. In 2014, they numbered from 200,000 to 250,000. For the government, while the militias made it possible to keep order to a certain extent after the regime collapsed, they eventually had to be either disarmed or absorbed by the new Libyan army or security forces under the interior ministry. Convinced that the state could never become an autonomous agent concerned with protecting its territory and inhabitants, Libyan militias have taken over control of their own territories and the security of the people residing there. The overthrow of the Qadhafi regime left a distressing security vacuum: no more police, army or security services. The "state of militias" replaced the "state of the masses".[26] The Islamist militias did all they could to prevent the emergence of a political authority that was not under their thumb. On 11 March 2014, Prime Minister Ali Zeidan was removed from office.

Non-existent Political Institutions

Was the descent into chaos of post-Qadhafi Libya predictable? "By the end of about 20 months, the Libyan people will have elected the leaders they want to lead their country," the National Transitional Council representative in London announced in October 2011. Yet, following the overthrow of the Qadhafi regime, Canadian legal expert Philippe Kirsch, the United Nations envoy to Libya, said: "In other countries, institutions start functioning again after a conflict. In Libya, such institutions simply do not exist," and he added, "During the course of my visits, I realized to what extent Qadhafi's legacy was devastating to

Libyan society."[27] The question of the nature of the Libyan state in fact immediately emerged after Qadhafi's political mantle was removed. The February 2011 revolution not only toppled the former regime (1969–2011), but also paved the way for the reconfiguration of social relationships in Libya through violence. Regional secularism has been compounded by tribal antagonisms that were exacerbated by the old regime as well as by ideological rifts between Islamists and nationalists. Added to these problems is the fight for control over hydrocarbons. The new authorities are not equipped to face these challenges. Unable to exercise control over the territory, Libya has disintegrated into a multitude of local power centres.[28] After the regime was overthrown, the international community failed to provide support for Libya's transition. Instead, there is a pervasive feeling of incomprehensible abandonment, as this Libyan French teacher in Tripoli explains:

> France helped to free us and then left. There's a lot of disappointment about France here. Why aren't the French more present? We don't understand. We don't know what they are afraid of here. Al-Qaeda? The Libyans are against al-Qaeda, too. After the attack on the consulate in Benghazi, people were really angry with the terrorists; for forty years, Qadhafi humiliated us; he gave Libya a ridiculous image. All Arabs made fun of us. We're not going to let al-Qaeda give us a terrible image. We're against what they did in Benghazi, but you can't flee Libya because there are terrorists. You should help us build up a police force and an army to fight them.[29]

The Qadhafi regime was taken by surprise by NATO's military intervention alongside the Islamist insurgents. Saif al-Islam, one of Qadhafi's sons, expressed great bitterness toward powers such as France and the United Kingdom, which he had considered Libya's friends or at least partners: "When your regime is strong, everybody kowtows to you. But when things collapse, everybody says 'bye bye: see you'."[30] After decades of conflictual relations with France and the United Kingdom, Qadhafi's Libya believed that after the 1991–2003 embargo was lifted, the regime would be viewed as an ally. Qadhafi was convinced that by participating actively in the "global war on terrorism" and opening up the oil industry to foreign investment, his regime would be absolved of its past sins. As for the NATO powers, they did not realize to what extent the Libyan state was essentially buttressed by the regime's strength. Like the Bush administration in Iraq after it had invaded the country, the NATO powers had no post-Qadhafi plan. Unlike its neighbours in the Maghreb and Egypt, the state in Libya had remained embryonic, in gestation, devoid of a unifying force. Libyan nationalism did not promote any sense of communal belonging like that observed among its neighbours in the 1970s.

Western powers naively believed that the National Transitional Council would be able to implement its hidden political agenda. Instead, NATO's war against Qadhafi produced rifts and fractures that drew the country into a civil war. As Diane Ethier writes, "History teaches us that civil war does not produce democracy, unless the belligerents voluntarily subscribe to rules and procedures that enable them to resolve their disputes by working out a compromise, or if such compromise is imposed on them by foreign occupation forces ... with uneven success. Neither of these scenarios currently exists in Libya."[31] Regime change in this case is clearly the result of war, and "disputes" between Libyans are settled through violence. Unlike the case of Tunisia's transition, the victors of Libya's revolution seem incapable of reaching the necessary compromises. Why is that? Is the political violence in post-Qadhafi Libya the consequence of the insurrectional path chosen by revolutionaries? Why did Libya go down the path of revolution and insurgency to overthrow the Qadhafi regime? Does the "sultanic" nature of the Qadhafi regime explain the violence it took to topple it? These hypotheses disregard an essential factor: the political imaginary of the actors and their practices. In fact, in Libya's case, those who fought in the revolution—the militias—did not aim so much to install democracy as to replace the paramilitary groups that ruled during the Qadhafi regime.[32] A Tocquevillian analysis shows the transition in Libya to be proceeding more on a continuum with political practices handed down from the old regime than making a clean break with them. Thus, the militia rule characteristic of the Qadhafi regime shows resilience, despite the regime's collapse and the disintegration of state institutions. Libya's transition also bears out certain hypotheses regarding democracy: Linz and Stepan hold that there can be no democracy without a homogeneous nation-state.[33] From this standpoint, the Libyan experiment is doomed to fail.

Sliding into War, 2014

General elections were held in June 2014. Two hundred members of the House of Representatives were supposed to replace the elected members of the GNC. Voter turnout was low, in stark contrast to the July 2012 elections: most Libyans no longer believed in their political representatives.[34] Sectarian and partisan, they are incapable of reaching the compromises needed to address the multiple grievances of Libyan society. Instead, Libya has become the theatre of inter-militia clashes: in July 2014, the "Dawn of Libya" alliance comprising militias from Misrata attacked the Zenten militias, which controlled the airport in Tripoli, ousting them after five weeks of fierce fighting. The Dawn of Libya Islamists took control of Tripoli and forced the provisional government formed after the June 2014 elections to flee to Tobruk. "Ministerial headquarters and state agencies in Tripoli are occupied by armed militias that are preventing civil servants from gaining access to their offices and threatening their superiors," the government claimed. In September 2014, the Libyans were living with two parliaments and two governments: the legitimate government formed after the June 2014 elections and recognized by the international community, in exile so to speak in Tobruk; and another government in Tripoli, formed by the GNC, and backed by Islamist militias and the Muslim Brotherhood. In Tripoli, a National Salvation Government was formed by Khalifa al-Ghawil. This body, made up of Muslim Brotherhood members, was under the protection of the powerful Islamist militias of Misrata and was backed internationally by Turkey and Qatar.[35]

The Islamist militias are well regarded by the population of the capital. Hakim, a veterinarian residing in the Suq al-Jum'a neighbourhood of Tripoli, joined the revolutionaries like many others with the deep conviction that Libyans did not deserve to continue living under Qadhafi's regime. Once it was toppled, he returned to work and thanked the "good militias"—the Islamists—for protecting Libya and its revolution, as Hakim claims:

> There are bad militias, they are criminals. The good militias fight them, the good militias are the bearded men [he says jokingly], they're the best. They protect people if they are attacked. But people don't want violence or war, they want to live in peace. For instance, if a

group of armed men live in a neighbourhood and in the evening they drink, smoke hashish and shoot off their guns, the army or the police aren't going to come, it's the good militia in the neighbourhood that will come. In the evening, they'll surround the house and fire warning shots at it. But they'll come because the committee of wise men has asked them to intervene. The committee of wise men represents the neighborhood.[36]

Not without humour, Hakim explains that the "bearded ones" are the good guys, the true revolutionaries, those who want Libya to become a stable and developed country and are against the "criminals", those who are taking advantage of the revolution and simply want to replace the "criminals of the former regime". The Islamist militias ensure security, which the state at present is unable to do:

I'm sure that in a few years, things will work out. The militias are a good thing; without them it would be chaos. They replace the police and the army until the army and the police are able to function. Today the militias are the ones capable of the job. But they are highly organized: each militia has a commander, they are gathered together in a camp and a militia is not allowed to leave its territory. The Nawasi militia covers Suq al-Jum'a. It's not going to go into another neighbourhood. Each militiaman is registered with the interior ministry. They are paid by the ministry of the interior or defence. They are well paid, and that's why they want to stay in the militia. They get paid between 1,000 and 1,500 dinars, the salary of a university professor![37]

The revolution has provided many unemployed young Libyans with "occupations" that were reserved for members of the revolutionary committees under the Jamahiriyya: thief, gangster, criminal. The lucrative criminal economy, which under Qadhafi's regime was structured and organized around the custodians of the Jamahiriyya, is now coveted in the new Libya. Drugs, alcohol and weapons are the currency around which networks and organizations are rebuilt, fostering the integration of thousands of young people into activities previously reserved for a privileged class. In their ultimate form, these organizations are set up as "criminal militias", in other words as social organizations that use violence to secure and guarantee transactions.

The desire to join a militia is extremely widespread in Libya: over 250,000 people claim to have taken part in the revolution and are demanding the attendant benefits, such as integration in the army or the police. In truth, a number of them never actually took up arms against the former regime, but the material advantages associated with militia status are so great that they attract thousands of youths. These latecomers to the militias arouse mockery, sometimes anger, from those who define themselves as "true revolutionaries"—meaning those who took the risk of defying the old regime right from the start of the uprising. They view the new Libya as the product of their courage, and they are prepared to use their weapons to make the "criminal militias" and "last-minute militiamen" pay for their misdeeds. As it happens, the Islamist militias are the ones who define themselves as the "true revolutionaries". In this transition period, the militias are seeking to form the backbone of post-Qadhafi Libya. Many of those who support them, either because they fought alongside them or because they recognize the merit of their having worked for the "good" of Libya, still hope that eventually the state's security forces will take over from them. The narrative of patriotic Islamic militiamen struggling to keep Libya going while waiting for the return of the state in fact nourishes the hopes of many Libyans.

Yet, many are aware that such a narrative does not reflect reality. For if Tripoli is hoping for the return of the state in order to impose its authority over the entire territory from Cyrenaica to Fezzan, this Tripolitan view is hardly shared by all. In Benghazi, jihadi groups have taken over the city and are extending their influence throughout the region. According to Hakim, if life in Tripoli goes back to normal, the rest of Libya will follow suit. He believes the return of the state in Tripoli will convince the provinces tempted by autonomy that it is in their best interest to remain under the authority of the capital. Thus, surprisingly:

> The state is functioning well in Tripoli; its administration is very effi-
> cient. Employees are paid every 20th of the month. Before, under
> Qadhafi, the state was two or three months behind on paying salaries,
> sometimes more. Qadhafi's regime collapsed, but not the state or the
> administration. Luckily for us, this isn't Iraq. That's why economic and
> social life has returned: schools, banks, etc. The only thing that isn't
> working yet is the police and the army. There's a problem: some people
> don't want those who worked in the police and the army under Qadhafi
> to hold state jobs now. Others say they were forced but that they
> backed the revolution and they should be integrated. It's a thorny issue.
> Gradually an army and a police force will come together.[38]

Many people no longer viewed Tripoli as Libya's capital. To the east, the government faces military opposition from General Khalifa Haftar, Colonel Wanis Boukhamada, head of special forces, and Colonel Fernana, commander of the military police. Military support from Egypt and the United Arab Emirates for this anti-Islamist military coalition plunged Libya even further into civil war. The anti-Islamist coalition led by General Haftar was fuelled by nationalism and its corollary, a strong central state. While his actions against jihadi militias in Benghazi, such as the fight against Ansar al-Sharia, found resonance, it prompts rejection when it targets militias associated with the Muslim Brotherhood-affiliated Justice and Construction Party, which controls the GNC in Tripoli.

In Misrata, the brigades (40,000 strong), equipped with tanks and rocket launchers, ensure this port city's autonomy. Similarly, the region of Cyrenaica proclaimed its own government on 25 October 2013 and set up a regional council as well as a security force. Abd-Rabbo al-Barassi, head of its executive bureau, claimed, "We are not defying the government ... We are insisting on our rights" and added, "Power lies where the natural resources are": 80% of the oil reserves as well as most of the oil terminals are in the east (Sedra, Ras Lanuf, Hariga, etc.). The 2012 and 2014 elections hastened the process of division: when they proved unable to reconstruct a political space, the elections tipped the militias into confrontation for control over a historically fragmented territory.

The Disintegration of the State: A Process Predating the Revolution

Unlike Tunisia for instance, the Libyan state never managed to promote cultural or administrative unity. Under Qadhafi, the centralizing dimension of the Libyan state was reinforced, but it never succeeded in establishing the legitimacy of state sovereignty over the territory. Qadhafi's Libya instead strengthened traditional community groups such as the tribes.[39] Thus, unlike other states in North Africa, Libya's monarchic and then revolutionary political regime fortified tribal ties within the state. Likewise, and in contrast with its neighbours, the nation-state remained embryonic owing to its inability to permeate society. It never identified ideologically, culturally or emotionally with

71

the Libyan nation. Rather than devoting himself to Libya, Qadhafi turned his zeal to the causes of Arab nationalist ideology in the 1970s, and then to pan-African unity from the 1990s. National identities and the original territorial fragmentation persisted. Only through his despotic use of force and autocratic distribution of oil revenue did he manage to maintain a territorial unity that was otherwise lacking.

The process of territorial unification is recent. The state was formed from the amalgamation of three provinces (Fezzan, Cyrenaica and Tripolitania) during the Italian colonial regime (1911–1942). The violence of the Italian conquest, including the incarceration of over half of the Libyan population in concentration camps, sparked strong resistance, which became the breeding ground for Libyan nationalism. But regionalism remained characteristic of Libya right from the start of the Idris monarchy, in 1951. The capital was moved temporarily to Bayda, in the Cyrenaican region of Jebel Akhdar. Qadhafi's coup d'état in 1969 was at once a reaction to this regionalism and to the monarchy's supposedly "decadent" ways: "a process", as his Green Book explained, "of radical change in the political, economic and social structure of human society. Its duty [was] to destroy a corrupt society to rebuild a new and just society."[40] To achieve this, the state, political parties and democracy were destined to be replaced by the tribe, the "natural social umbrella" according to Qadhafi, as "by virtue of social tribal traditions, the tribe provides for its members collective protection". In Qadhafi's revolutionary Libya, "the state is an artificial political, economic, occasionally military system, bearing no relation to humanity." He believed that society should thus be founded on the tribe rather than the state. For Qadhafi, "the tribe is a family that has grown as a result of births. It follows that a tribe is a big family. Even the nation is a tribe which has grown demographically."[41] In fact, the tribal imaginary is the product of contemporary political transformations: Qadhafi's Libya was part of a continuous process in which the Libyan state, ever since its independence in 1951, evinced the characteristics of its tribal nature. The roots of King Idris's monarchy in the Islamic brotherhoods were also deeply influenced by the tribal confederations of Cyrenaica, as the historian Ali Abdullatif Ahmida has shown.[42] From that perspective, the army and the state were perceived as two obstacles to the revolution's success. These perceptions of state and army persist among today's militias. With the overthrow of the regime, the state very naturally disinte-grated, plunging the country into violence.

Furthermore, in contrast to Egypt and Algeria, the army was not a central power figure. Power instead resided in a balance of paramilitary forces skilfully chosen from among tribes that had sworn allegiance to the regime, thus enabling them to be represented and take part in governing. The army was perceived as a threat to be neutralized, even if that meant weakening it and making it ineffectual from a military standpoint. The army was thus unable to promote its own values and interests as a body or institution—unlike other military institutions in the region—or develop an economy within Libyan society that might have enabled it to retrain its staff or establish influential ties.[43] The political determination to sabotage the Libyan army's development can be explained by the complex, subtle and contradictory relationship between the Libyan Jamahiriyya and the state. In the philosophy of the Jamahiriyya, the state was destined to disappear, to make room for local political structures in which tribes would play a fundamental role.

Power Is Where the Oil Is

As previously under Qadhafi, the National Oil Corporation (NOC) today serves as a war chest for the authorities in Tripoli: in 2012, hydrocarbon exports brought $55 billion into the country. Added to that are some $100 billion in funds and assets held by the Central Bank of Libya and the Libyan Foreign Bank, unfrozen by the UN Security Council on 22 December 2011. The Libyan authorities also control the assets held by the Libyan Investment Authority (LIA), a sovereign wealth fund established in 2006, which according to its chairman, Mohsen Derregia, has $50 billion in financial assets and $20 billion in real estate and infrastructure assets. Owing to the startling resumption of oil production, Libya's growth rate in 2013 was 17% according to the IMF, after having shrunk by 60% in 2011, and a record 120% in 2012. Under the Jamahiriyya, the hydrocarbon sector accounted for 95% of exports, 90% of government revenue, and 70% of its GDP. Libya holds the largest or second-largest reserves in Africa: 47.1 mil-lion barrels.[44] Seen from Benghazi, Tripoli is a thief that must be made to return the spoils it stole and that monopolizes all the country's resources, an accusation echoed by Tahani Mohammad ben Ali, leader of the Benghazi Workers Union, a powerful trade union in the Arabian Gulf Oil Company. "The objection is that it is like before—everything is controlled by Tripoli; this is not what we had a revolution for." That means control over exploitation of the hydrocarbons sector in Cyrenaica. Out of the 1.6 million barrels produced daily, 1 million come from NOC branches operating in Cyrenaica. In 2013, after much discussion, the NOC, despite demonstrations staged by its employees in Tripoli, took the initiative of starting a subsidiary in Benghazi, a gesture toward those advocating the decentralization of hydrocarbon management and exploitation. Even if the NOC stays in Tripoli, the new company (National Company for Oil Refining and Petrochemicals) will have its own budget ($30 million) and will enjoy partial autonomy in hiring practices and oil infrastructure in the east. This concession from Tripoli to the demands of the Benghazi elites reassures those who feared the oil infrastructure in Cyrenaica would be held hostage for lack of a compromise: Libya's largest oil refinery, Ras Lanuf (220,000 bpd), lies in the east of the country along with two oil terminals, Es-Sider and Marsa al-Brega.

The modern history of Cyrenaica is punctuated by conflicts. In the early years of the twentieth century, under the leadership of Omar al-Mukhtar, the region of Jebel Akhdar was the centre of Libyan resistance to Italian colonization.[45] During the Second World War, Cyrenaica became a vast battlefield where the Allied forces fought the Germans and Italians. The fighting that took place there resulted in the total destruction of some cities, such as Tobruk. In 1951, following Libya's independence and under the Idris monarchy, the area, ravaged by military offensives and counter-offensives, underwent a serious subsistence crisis, any movement being hampered by vast minefields.[46] The Libyan Arab Force had taken part in the battle of Derna-Tobruk in 1942 alongside the British. The Sanussi Legion, which fought on the Allied side during the war, became one of the pillars of the Idris monarchy. Libya's Nasserists in fact obsessively dreaded that the British would revive the Sanussi emirate in Cyrenaica on the model of Jordan. In 1969, after Colonel Qadhafi's coup, certain army units put up violent resistance against tribes that remained loyal to King Idris, while the Revolutionary Command Council promoted schemes to build farms on land belonging to religious foundations in Jebel Akhdar.[47] Colonel Qadhafi's regime never ceased hunting down the Sanussi leaders. Once the Jamahiriyya was set up, the revolutionary committees shut down the last small shops in Benghazi, thus depriving several Sanussi families of their livelihood. From the 1990s, such tales fuelled Islamist opposition to the regime, to which was added an anti-Islamic interpretation of the Jamahiriyya, in this regard falling in line with the Muslim Brother-hood.[48] The question of a return to federalism today, which also raises the question of what is meant by autonomy, separation and independence, thus crystallizes the identity claims of a region that views itself as the cradle of Libya, its independence in 1951 and the revolution of 17 February 2011.

Forty years after federalism was abolished in Libya, a segment of the Libyan population wants to see it restored as a way of fostering a better and more equitable distribution of wealth. Federalism, for Cyrenaica, means the right to control the exploitation of its hydrocarbon resources—hence the end of the NOC monopoly. In addition to threatening to cut off oil supplies, representatives of Cyrenaica have several other ways to make their voice heard: much of the country's water supply, transported by the Great Manmade River, is found in Cyrenaica, and most water wells are located on land belonging to the Zawiya, one of the largest tribes in the region.[49] One of the main priorities of the Libyan revolution is thus to "renegotiate" the country's material and political resources.[50] There is fierce debate in Libya about how the oil wealth should be distributed: its outcome will determine the country's future and its political stability. For Tripoli, decentralizing the management and redistribution of the hydrocarbons sector means taking the risk of weakening the only corporation—the NOC—that provides the authorities with the financial means to secure the militias' allegiance.

Restoring Civil Peace

Left to its own devices after the overthrow of the Qadhafi regime, Libya descended into a civil war that paved the way for IS to establish itself in the city of Sirte. The fear of seeing Daesh on Europe's doorstep and in a country that has the second-largest oil reserves jolted the international community into action, prompting it to place restoration of the state in Libya at the top of its priorities.[51] For Libya's neighbours, in particular Tunisia, Algeria and Italy,[52] this was an essential element in the fight against terrorism and the control of migration flows from sub-Saharan Africa. After intense negotiations between the main protagonists (representatives from the GNC and the House of Representatives), an agreement was signed in December 2015 in Skhirat, Morocco, under the aegis of the United Nations. It envisioned the formation of a national unity government, a presidential council and legislative elections.[53] According to the former special representative of the UN secretary-general and head of the United Nations Support Mission in Libya (UNSMIL), Martin Kobler, this "roadmap" was guided by the following principles for Libyan unity: "to ensure dialogue prevails over confrontation, unity prevails over division, and security prevails over chaos."[54]

In March 2016, Fayez al-Sarraj, prime minister of the Government of National Accord (GNA), unanimously endorsed by the Western powers, arrived in Tripoli to face opposition from radical Islamist militias who defined themselves as "guardians of the revolution". They were opportunistically supported by a situational alliance, Khalifa al-Ghawil's National Salvation Government, which refused to recognize the government formed after the 2014 general elections and forced Sarraj to take refuge in Tobruk, in the eastern part of the country near the Egyptian border. These militias, close to the Muslim Brotherhood and with various interests, are associated with local authorities in fragile and shifting alliances. They control the territory and are responsible for the city's security and protection. Although paid by the interior or defence ministry, they do not answer to the political authorities. Thus, with no army or police force, the prime minister of the GNA, Fayez al-Sarraj, is under the protection of militias such as the Rada special deterrent force, the Tripoli revolutionary brigades and the Ghewa brigades. The government aims to form a national guard that can ensure security when it resumes control of official government buildings. In February–March 2017, fighting raged between the militias of the two governments in Tripoli and ended with the eviction of the National Salvation Government militias from Tripoli. In April, a new security plan for Tripoli was deployed, aimed at amalgamating the various security and defence units.

Sarraj believes this victory is deceptive as long as his government remains isolated and lacks local political support. Accused of being a foreign import and abandoning Libya "to foreign powers", Sarraj suffers from a legitimacy deficit that considerably hampers his ability to implement his economic policy, all the more as his government can hardly be said to have the financial means to meet the country's economic and social problems. Even so, despite the prevailing lawlessness in Libya, the central bank has continued to pay the salaries of state employees, in other words the overwhelming majority of the active population. Thanks to its dollar reserves, the central bank was able to offset the collapse of production and of the price of oil between 2014 and 2016. The fact remains that oil reserves have been diminishing and the per barrel price of oil has not risen again; only oil production increased in 2017 to 1.25 million bpd, matching the 2013 production level. It should be noted that with the exception of IS, which carried out attacks against oil installations in January 2016, the UN experts pointed out: "The warring parties in the oil crescent have largely refrained from damaging oil installations, and they have consistently given authority over the terminals to the National Oil Corporation management, even though control over the region has changed hands repeatedly."[55]

In the course of 2017, General Haftar, favouring a "military solution" to restore the sovereignty of the Libyan state, reinforced his positions in the east. His attritional war against jihadi militias of Ansar al-Sharia Benghazi and the Benghazi Revolutionaries Shura Council (affiliated with al-Qaeda) paid off in July 2017: after three years of conflict, the city of Benghazi was declared to have been liberated. Haftar's "national army", backed by Egypt, the United Arab Emirates and Sudanese mercenaries from Darfur, finally achieved tangible results. His strategy of eradicating jihadi militias seems so disproportionate to the size and means of his "national army" that it continues to raise several questions. The victory in Benghazi, however, paved the way for retaking cities such as Derna and Bin Jawad, which have been jihadi strongholds for decades. Libyan National Army (LNA) chief of staff Abdulrazek al-Nadoori was appointed military governor. The southern military region of Sebha has also come under LNA command. General Haftar's territorial gains have opened opportunities for him that the powerful Misrata Third Force hopes to diminish. In May 2019,

General Haftar set out to conquer Tripoli. He encountered unexpected resistance from Misrata militias defending the capital.[56]

Between the establishment of the Government of National Accord in Tripoli and the tightening of General Haftar's grip on Benghazi, the powerful Misrata Third Force militias that support the Presidential Council launched Operation Al-Bunyan al-Marsous on Sirte, which had been under Islamic State control since 2014. After six months of fighting and heavy losses,[57] the city was liberated in December 2016. Even though they were expelled from Sirte, the Daesh jihadis, many of them foreign, continue to sow terror by perpetrating attacks throughout the oil crescent. The victory of the GNA and the Misrata militias nevertheless offered the international community proof of the new authorities' commitment to the fight against terrorism.

The victories in Sirte and Benghazi reinforced the protagonists' international standing. They gave the impression that the disintegration of Libya into a multitude of local powers had been stemmed, giving way to a concentration of forces within regional blocs. In this context, several regional and international initiatives have been striving to bring General Haftar and Serraj, chairman of the Presidential Council, to the negotiation table to work out a means of implementing the Libyan political accords. On 2 and 3 May 2017, the two leaders met in Abu Dhabi and then again on 25 July in Paris. Despite a disastrous security situation, they pledged to hold general elections in 2018.[58] The fear was that they would decide to go to war with each other rather than to seek a compromise. For the Libyans, time is of the essence. In his August 2017 report, the UN secretary-general said he was "concerned about the prevailing lawlessness in the country. Abduction and hostage-taking, including of children; torture and other ill-treatment; summary executions and unlawful killings; enforced disappearances; and arbitrary, incommunicado and prolonged detention should end. Criminal syndicates, including those involved in the smuggling of petrol to neighbouring countries, pose a direct threat to the rule of law and undermine efforts to restore stability."[59] Lawlessness has, moreover, fostered the presence of criminal militias that exploit a lucrative market of human beings, weapons, drugs and petrol from the coast to the edge of the Sahara. In addition to this violence there are the humanitarian needs of 940,000 people.[60]

5

MOROCCO

BENEFICIAL REFORMS

A Constant State of Revolution

Paradoxically, during the Arab revolts Morocco, a country in which the wealth gap is one of the highest in the world,[1] did not experience the dynamics of social protest likely to produce a revolution. The thorny issue of the kingdom's stability was raised once again with the Arab revolts: would it withstand the uprisings that were shaking the Arab world? Unlike in Tunisia and Libya, institutional actors (the army, trade unions, political parties) remained loyal to the monarchy, which quickly gauged the weakness of the protest movement. The 20 February Movement in 2011, which at first mustered a diverse group of political and social actors,[2] gradually came under Salafi influence, thus repelling democratic and socialist opponents of the regime who were concerned by this drift. In reaction to the unease generated by a social protest movement in which Salafis—who have the stated ambition of over-throwing the monarchy—participated, the 20 February Movement imploded and shrank to its most radical fringe. The young jet set and, more generally, the discontented middle class distanced themselves once and for all, thereby depriving the movement of important connections in influential social spheres. Far from seeking to bring down the

79

monarchy, a segment of the movement was demanding political and social reforms to improve governance and state capabilities.

In fact, since the 1970s, Morocco specialists have pointed out its paradoxical nature: it has had a huge "revolutionary potential" ever since independence, although this has always been neutralized by reforms.[3] In the 1950s, for instance, Istiqlal, the powerful nationalist movement, posed a threat to the monarchy, urging it to adopt its project for a Greater Morocco (which would include Mauritania, Western Sahara and part of Algeria);[4] in the 1960s, it was the revolutionary left behind Ben Barka that wanted to overthrow the monarchy; in the 1970s, the army made two coup attempts; in the 1980s, it was the Salafis, buoyed by the virulent sermons of Sheikh Yassine, who hoped to see the hated monarchy collapse.[5] All in vain. Under King Hassan II's rule, the monarchy adopted Istiqlal's nationalism and co-opted its elites: the annexation of Western Sahara in 1975 and the war against the Polisario Front enabled the monarchy to present itself as the embodiment of Moroccan nationalism in the face of its Algerian enemy, which backed the Sahrawi Arab Democratic Republic (SADR). The Western Sahara conflict has been used adroitly by the monarchy to manufacture nationalist sentiment. As for the army, its failed confrontation with the monarchy resulted in its weakening. The army was deployed in Western Sahara, far away from the king's palaces. The revolutionary left was violently crushed, culminating in the kidnapping of its leader Ben Barka on 29 October 1965 in Paris. His body was never found. His third-worldist political movement never recovered from this trauma. Like Istiqlal, the leaders of the revolutionary left were gradually co-opted and ended up accepting the monarchy's legitimacy. In 1996, in the framework of a controlled transfer of power, Driss Jettou, head of the Socialist Party, was appointed prime minister. Ultimately, only the Salafis persisted in claiming the monarchy was illegitimate. The Arab Spring gave the monarchy an opportunity to bolster the Muslim Brotherhood-affiliated Justice and Development Party (JDP), in the hope that it would absorb and weaken the Salafi movement.

The 20 February Movement

The monarchy's experience in handling and integrating rebel and protest movements, gained over the long term, has given it a degree of skill that was again exemplified in its handling of the 20 February Movement in 2011. While the movement sought to demonstrate that Morocco shared the same symptoms as the other countries in turmoil—and hence ran the same risks—the monarchy managed to exploit their demands by implementing a programme of institutional and political reform.

When the revolts in Tunisia and then in Egypt toppled their rulers in January and February 2011, Moroccans took to the streets. Thousands of young people, organized via social media, began mobilizing in February in over fifty cities in the kingdom. Several demonstrations were held by the 20 February Movement, which brought together Islamist activists in the Justice and Charity movement (Al-Adl wa-al-Ihsan), secular NGOs and cyber-activists. They were not demanding the removal of King Mohammed VI, but ambitious constitutional reform instead. The person of the monarch did not attract the same rejection observed among demonstrators in neighbouring countries. The 20 February Movement was not seeking confrontation with the monarchy, but instead was calling attention to certain grievances and fighting for a parliamentary regime in which the king would rule without governing.

To curb the protest, on 9 March 2011, Mohammed VI announced the establishment of a Consultative Commission for the Revision of the Constitution. On 17 June 2011, during a televised speech, the king announced a plan for constitutional reform. The project, officially adopted in a referendum on 1 July 2011 by an overwhelming majority (98% of the vote), aimed to transfer some of the king's powers to the prime minister. The head of government would henceforth be selected from within the party that had won the legislative elections instead of being appointed by the king. He also became the only person with the power to dissolve the houses of parliament. However, the king retained considerable executive powers: he would preside over the Council of Ministers and remain Commander of the Royal Armed Forces and Commander of the Faithful.

Even though the 20 February Movement insisted that Moroccans were suffering from the same ills as their neighbours—huge social inequality, high youth unemployment, the absolute power of a single leader, widespread corruption and a muzzled opposition—Mohammed

VI managed to make Morocco an exception in the region. Even if the referendum did not put an end to political protest in Morocco, it did enable the monarchy to demonstrate that resorting to political means can be an effective weapon to neutralize adversaries. In the wake of the Arab Spring, early legislative elections were held on 25 November 2011. They were won by the JDP, which came in way ahead of Istiqlal. The king appointed the winning party's leader, Abdelilah Benkirane, to the post of prime minister, as stipulated in the new Constitution. According to some newspapers, this was the start of a "cold war" between the royal cabinet and the Islamist government. While for some, the JDP embodied hope for greater social justice, it raised concerns among others, particularly because of its vain ambition to moralize customs (condemning homosexuality, certain music festivals, certain rights won by women, and so on). In this period of crisis, the Islamists proved to be the monarchy's best allies, as it were, in that they transferred the problems from the political arena to that of morals, thus subverting the demands of the 20 February Movement.

Yet, those contesting the monarchy point out that the kingdom is far from being a haven of social justice. According to UNDP indicators, Morocco is ranked 123rd on the human development scale, with a poverty rate of 18.1%; 5 million inhabitants live on 10 dinars per day (one euro); the minimum wage is 55 dinars per day (5 euros).[6] It became imperative to implement economic and social reforms. Morocco has experienced steady economic growth (around 5%–6% per year) since 2003, allowing it to reduce unemployment from 22% in 2003 to 10.7% in 2017.[7] But joblessness remains particularly widespread among young people, who make up 37% of the unemployed. This over-representation is probably one of the government's biggest challenges, and one which fuels the EU's worst fears: Islamic radicalism, migration, social unrest. Social issues are all the more pressing as radical Islamist movements preach violence to resolve them. Like Algeria twenty years before, Morocco has become the breeding ground for radical Islamist organizations prepared to engage in strategies of violence. Moroccan jihadis indicated their hatred of the monarchy in a document published on 4 September 2008 on an Islamist website (elshouraa.ws—since taken down), entitled "The day will come when we play football with his head in the streets of Islamic Morocco". The document criticized the monarchy as follows:

It is the worst monarchy the world has ever seen, in which the King owns the people and the land and does what he wants with them. He rules supreme, protecting all sorts of traffickers. He plunders the country and protects the other plunderers in his entourage who were also close to his father, Hassan II, and are just as corrupt as he is. He is the king of prostitution, of deviance, drugs, and corruption, who has no qualms about selling the bodies of Moroccan women to the princes and other businessmen in the Gulf.

It urged Mohammed VI, dubbed "King of the Poor", to repent and invited him "to mend his ways, starting with returning the billions extorted by his father, by his entourage and by himself to the detriment of an impoverished people deprived of their rights. People kept in obscurantism and ignorance ... while their king lives in palaces out of the One Thousand and One Nights."[8]

These criticisms are based on the fact that Moroccan society is structured by very stark inequalities. *Forbes* magazine estimated the wealth of the monarchy at $2.5 billion in 2011; in 2000, it was put at $500 million.[9] The National Investment Corporation (SNI), which absorbed the Omnium Nord-Africain (ONA) group, whose majority shareholder (60%) is Copropar (a subsidiary owned 100% by the Siger/Ergis Group), is a holding company owned by the royal family and presided over by Mohamed Mounir el-Majidi. The SNI[10] has holdings in diverse sectors: mining, steel, cement, supermarkets, insurance, renewable energy (Nareva), packaging (Sevam), furniture (Primarios), textiles (Compagnie Chérifienne des Textiles), sugar and edible oil (Cosumar), and the Centrale Laitière dairy firm. SNI holdings in the Attijariwafa Bank are estimated at 48.3%. The family holding company has local alliances with Lafarge, Danone, Renault and others. Added to these assets are agricultural properties, twelve royal palaces, an automobile fleet estimated at $7 million dollars, 1,100 items on the national budget, an allowance of $70 million per year, and a monthly stipend of 160,000 euros paid to the royal family (the monarch, his brother and sisters). An inventory of the monarchy's wealth made big waves throughout Moroccan society, fuelling social and political protest. In the wake of the WikiLeaks revelations, while the monarchy turned out not to be the largest landowner in the kingdom, it still appears as a hegemonic actor that does little to combat corruption. "While corruption practices existed under Hassan II, they have been much more institutionalized under King Mohammed VI," wrote the US consul in Casablanca.[11] The 20 February Movement cited two persons responsible for these corruption practices: Fouad Ali el-Himma, president of the Party of Authenticity and Modernity (PAM), and Mohamed Mounir el-Majidi, chairman of the royal holding company. The phosphate mining group OCP, presided over by Mostapha Terrab, partly escaped popular wrath. It was decided to repeal the decree that had authorized the OCP to pay part of the profits from phosphate exploitation to the monarchy since the time of the French protectorate. While under Hassan II, the OCP, which had been nationalized in 1973, was viewed by the opposition as a slush fund, the OCP group has been a limited liability company since 2008.[12]

Criticism of the concentration of wealth in the hands of the monarchy prompted divestment of certain royal interests. Still, the new Constitution preserves the monarch's prerogatives that ensure his hegemony in Morocco's business affairs. That said, the king has so far enjoyed the population's loyalty, a factor lacking for all other heads of state in the region. In popular discourse, it is the monarch's entourage and not his person that arouses indignation.

High Expectations

On 30 July 1999, Mohammed VI ascended to the throne of the Kingdom of Morocco, succeeding his father Hassan II's long reign (1961–1999). His accession kindled hopes of seeing the kingdom open up its political space and devote more attention to social justice. Hassan II's Morocco, under the stewardship of interior minister Driss Basri, overcame threats jeopardizing the regime, such as the riots in Casablanca and the Rif in 1965, the coup attempts of 1971 and 1972, and the social uprisings of the 1980s, but at the cost of countless violations of human rights and basic freedoms. Three months after Mohammed VI came to power, Driss Basri, a symbol of the "years of lead", was dismissed.[13] This symbolic gesture indicated the king's readiness to regenerate a monarchy that had been lambasted by the international press. During the first decade of the 2000s, when Morocco was experiencing social, religious and economic transformations, Mohammed VI set in motion several reforms, in particular of the

Labour Code in 2003 and the personal status code in 2004. He also established a new body, the Fairness and Reconciliation Commission (IER), in charge of investigating human rights abuses committed during Hassan II's reign. He launched the National Human Development Initiative in 2005 with a view to reducing poverty and unemployment. Lastly, he organized reform of the Constitution in 2011, in the context of the Arab Spring.[14] Yet, at the same time, the king preserved a system that generates deep social and regional inequality.

Popular protest is latent. Even though there are various social and religious tensions in the country, the population seems more marked by "the feeling of being abandoned by the central government than by revolutionary aspirations". During the Arab Spring, the king thus announced constitutional reforms as early as 9 March 2011, intending to transfer new powers to parliament and the prime minister. This enabled him to defuse a very tense political situation. The early months of Mohammed VI's reign generated high expectations within Moroccan society. On the domestic front, regime opponents who were condemned to exile under Hassan II hoped to see an end to the years of state-sponsored violence and win a reprieve. Abraham Serfaty, for instance, a communist and later extreme left activist who threw his support behind the Polisario Front, made a triumphant return on 30 September 1999 after nine years in exile and seventeen years in prison. As for the press, it hoped to be able to treat sensitive topics without fear of legal action.

Institutional changes were not prominent, although in September 2002 the first legislative elections were held, followed by the appointment of Driss Jettou as prime minister and the formation of a new government. Mohammed VI's readiness to break with the past and establish a relationship with the population nevertheless considerably improved Morocco's image on the international stage. Only relations with Spain remained strained. They even deteriorated in July 2002 during a sovereignty conflict over the tiny island of Perejil (west of Ceuta). Madrid retook the island seized by Moroccan soldiers, but the incident awakened Spanish concerns regarding Morocco's ambitions regarding the cities of Ceuta and Melilla.

Within the police apparatus, many were concerned about changes taking place. With the international media spotlight trained on

Morocco, the police were compelled to respect human rights in their fight against the kingdom's opponents and enemies, in particular radical Islamists. After the terrorist attacks in Casablanca on 16 May 2003, security again became a state priority. As the country is highly dependent on tourism, foreign investors and its image as a peaceful haven, these attacks caused Morocco to fear that it had become a target for terrorist groups. Mass arrests were made throughout the country and counterterrorism measures multiplied to reassure people of the Moroccan government's ability to keep control.

Social Reform and Security Policy

Morocco established the Fairness and Reconciliation Commission (IER) at the behest of Mohammed VI in November 2003. Based on the principle of transitional justice, this commission was set up to investigate human rights violations so as to help bring Moroccans to terms with their terrible past. Mohammed VI agreed to consider recommendations made by the Moroccan Human Rights Association (to uncover the truth about forced disappearances, return bodies to families, establish death certificates, rehabilitate victims and pay compensation). On 30 November 2005, the IER submitted its final report to the king.[15] While the creation of the commission reassured human rights advocates, its outcome produced mixed reactions, particularly due to the state's refusal to identify perpetrators of violations and bring them to trial. Furthermore, in contradiction to the very principles of the IER, the government's fight against terrorism involved more mass violations of the rights of those accused, including the use of torture.

Security concerns notwithstanding, the government implemented a series of reforms aimed at meeting long-standing social demands. Under Driss Jettou's government (2002–2007), a reform of the Labour Code was passed in July 2003. It was considered a social revolution. Following negotiations between the government, the major trade unions and the Moroccan business federation (CGEM), the new labour code respected the right to organize in the workplace, readjusted legal severance pay rates, reorganized working hours and provided social protection for workers. In January 2004, a new family code was also passed. It redefined relations within the family, in particular relations between married couples. Children became the responsibility of both parents. Women no longer required a mentor to marry and the minimum age of marriage was raised from 15 to 18. Child custody was granted primarily to the mother. While polygamy remained allowed, it was made more difficult: a court authorization was required, the request to marry a second or third woman had to be sufficiently justified, and the applicant was obliged to prove his financial ability to support his wives. The new family code was a victory for women's rights organizations in Morocco which had been campaigning since the 1990s to win legal equality for men and women in the family.[16]

The Fight against Poverty and Social Exclusion

Since 2003, Morocco has enjoyed a sustained annual economic growth of between 5% and 6%, enabling it to reduce unemployment. Mass youth unemployment in Morocco remains without a doubt the government's biggest challenge. From 2001 to 2014, the Moroccan Planning Commission (HCP) indicated that "the number of poor had gone from 4.5 million to 1.6 million".[17] Despite considerable progress since the beginning of the twenty-first century, the rural population remains faced with problems of poverty and underemployment that encourage migration to the cities.

"Concrete jungles" began to crop up in the urban sprawl created by this rural exodus. Unknown until recently, these slums, particularly those in Casablanca, became security and public policy issues in the wake of the 2003 attacks. In July 2003, the Moroccan housing ministry launched an ambitious "Cities without Slums" programme targeting 95 Moroccan cities. Ten years later, some 240,000 families are believed to have benefited from the programme and 43 cities were declared slumless. In this framework, on 18 May 2005, Mohammed VI established the National Human Development Initiative, a project aimed at combating poverty and social exclusion. Ten billion dirhams were earmarked for the project over a five-year period, which aimed to provide the most destitute with access to water supply, electricity and healthcare facilities. From the outset, 360 rural municipalities and 250 urban neighbourhoods were targeted as priority areas.[18]

Serious regional inequalities remain nevertheless. Major investments and development have taken place throughout the entire northern region, for instance, which had been neglected under Hassan II's reign: construction of the port of Tanger-Med (2004–2007), a Renault factory in Tangier in 2012, renovation of the Tangier city centre, construction of a high-speed railway between Tangier and Casablanca begun in 2011 as well as several marinas. Even if political and social unrest continues to rumble in average-size cities in the north and east, the public authorities have turned new attention to them. That is because cities such as Ceuta, Melilla, Tetouan and Fnideq are considered "breeding grounds for Islamists"[19] and, as mentioned previously, the main economic activity in the Rif region, one of the poorest in Morocco, remains cannabis cultivation: 75% of the villages, or 96,000 families, make their living from it.[20]

All this provides the context of violence and insecurity in which legislative elections took place on 7 September 2007. Istiqlal, the long-standing conservative nationalist party, came out on top, to no one's surprise. The fear of Islamists proved disastrous for the Justice and Development Party, which was associated with the Islamist terrorist violence in Casablanca. The election results offered reassurance to all those who doubted the new monarch's ability to control the JDP Islamists. Mohammed VI showed that he retained a firm grip on the political agenda and imposed his will to rule and govern by strengthening the regime of controlled transfer of power established by his father Hassan II.

The Terrorist Threat

Like other countries in the region, the Moroccan authorities have to contend with AQIM and IS violence.[21] The kingdom is under threat and its engagement in the fight against these groups is international in scope.[22] More than 1,200 Moroccan nationals, including 700 reportedly from the north of Morocco, have joined the ranks of IS, comprising the third-largest foreign contingent after Tunisians and Saudis. Unlike their neighbours, Moroccan jihadis still have not managed to gain a foothold in the country owing to the effectiveness of the government's counterterrorism strategy.[23] The fact remains that, according to the interior ministry, between 2011 and 2016 86 terrorist cells were dismantled, 38 of them during the year 2016 alone.[24] However, since the first decade of the 2000s, the monarchy has been regularly threatened and attacked, as illustrated by the election-year Casablanca attacks on 16 May 2003: Morocco's economic capital was shaken by five suicide bombings perpetrated by terrorists from the Sidi Moumen slum, killing 45 people.[25] On 13 August 2007, an attack on tourists in Meknès failed. When on 3 November 2007 Ayman al-Zawahiri, al-Qaeda's then second-in-command, called on Muslims in Maghreb to proclaim jihad, he confirmed the Moroccan authorities' worries.[26] These calls provoked fears that the Islamists might erupt on the political and social scene during the Arab uprisings. Like the other countries of the Maghreb, over 600 Moroccan jihadis had gone to fight in Afghanistan, Bosnia and Chechnya.[27] Following the 13 November 2015 attacks in Paris, the Moroccan Council of Ulamas issued a fatwa on jihad, condemning the terrorist acts by Daesh and distinguishing legitimate jihad from terror.[28]

Mohammed VI's Morocco has implemented several beneficial reforms, which, according to many observers, have "defused" revolt.[29] In addition to the extensive regionalization project, the kingdom has engaged in promoting and exporting its model for preventing radicalization, emphasizing a "moderate" interpretation of Islam and support for the various brotherhoods, which have a considerable role and influence in the country.[30] In the wake of the May 2003 attacks in Casablanca, Morocco defined its "comprehensive strategy" in this way:

> Morocco is pursuing a comprehensive, integrated and proactive strategy aimed at eliminating festering fanaticism and uprooting terrorism. In sum, the ultimate goal of Morocco's counterterrorism strategy is to strengthen the national social fabric and protect it from all forms of radicalism and fanaticism impervious to otherness and modernity. The Kingdom of Morocco has therefore adopted a multidimensional proactive and reactive approach ... through political, institutional, economic, social, cultural, educational, religious and media reforms to combat extremism, poverty, social exclusion, job instability and illiteracy via human development and the strengthening of the rule of law.[31]

The Hirak Movement

Although the monarchy handled the political and social effects of the Arab Spring with remarkable dexterity,[32] it was unable to demonstrate the same control when a vast protest movement, Hirak, emerged in the Rif in October 2016.[33] The ensuing repression and intimidation revived the wounds of a region that felt itself ignored by the monarchy, and raised concerns about Morocco's national cohesion. As Pierre Vermeren writes, "Berber identity has long been neglected and regional—Rifian, Soussi and Saharan—particularisms disregarded."[34]

For on-the-spot observers, Hirak was a continuation of the 20 February Movement; for others, it expressed feelings of profound injustice at the *hogra* (contempt) of the authorities.[35] In October 2016, the tragic death of Mohsen Fikri in Al Hoceima, capital of the Rif, close to Ajdir, reawakened the traumas of an area whose inhabitants had long been described as riffraff (*awbash*) both by colonial France and Spain and by King Hassan II. Since 28 October 2016, tensions in the Rif have run high. The authorities feared that Mohsen Fikri's death would become the focus of all forms of discontent in the kingdom. The scale of the demonstration in Rabat on 11 June 2017 in support of the Hirak Movement took everyone by surprise, as did the attempts by the Salafi movement Al-Adl wa-al-Ihsan to turn it to its advantage.

On 26 June 2017, bloody clashes occurred in the city of Al Hoceima. A month before, on 26 May, Nasser Zefzafi, who led the protests, entered the main mosque in Al Hoceima during the imam's sermon, titled "Security Is a Blessing", in which he accused the demonstrators of stirring trouble. Nasser Zefzafi interrupted the imam and asked worshippers in the mosque: "What does *fitna* [strife] mean when our young people have little to eat?" "Who do the mosques belong to? God or the government?" He was arrested for "interfering with freedom of worship". Dozens of other activists were also hauled in and jailed. A support committee for the Hirak Movement claimed that 400 were arrested. Most of them were detained on charges of "threatening national security, undermining loyalty to the state and actions against national unity", according to the communiqué issued by the prosecutor in Casablanca in June 2017.[36] Some forty detainees were pardoned by King Mohammed VI in July and September 2017, and some fifty other activists in the movement, including its leader, Nasser Zefzafi, were tried before an appeals court in Casablanca. The Hirak Movement was on trial. The proceedings gave activists the opportunity to denounce the neglect of their region and especially the failure to implement development programmes there. In October 2015, the regionalization process had in fact earmarked for the city of Al Hoceima 650 million euros over a five-year period. In answer to accusations of misappropriation and fraud, Mohammed VI ordered his government to perform an audit to uncover the reasons for the delay in implementing the programmes planned for the region. The audit concluded that the delay was due to bureaucratic inertia and not corruption or fraud.[37]

Protest in the Rif and oppression of the Hirak Movement undermined "the notion that Mohammed VI had made historic reconciliation with the Rif, a region left by the wayside by his father for forty years".[38] The Rif's political identity was shaped in the early twentieth century through armed resistance against Spanish and French occupation. After the battle of Annual (July 1921) in which Abdelkrim el-Khattabi's troops defeated Spanish King Alfonso XIII's royal army, the former proclaimed the Rif Republic, making Ajdir its capital, in July 1923. Its territory ranged from Tangier to Melilla. In 1925, France and Spain joined forces and managed to obtain Abdelkrim's surrender in May 1926.[39] The Rif Republic was vanquished. Exiled first to Réunion Island and later to Cairo, Abdelkrim continued his fight; he founded the Army of Liberation and dreamed of driving Spain and France out of Morocco. Shortly after independence, in 1958, the Moroccan monarchy declared the Rif region a military zone by royal decree and sent in the army to eradicate the threat of an embryonic armed resistance movement.[40] When Hassan II succeeded his father Mohammed V to the throne in 1961, he decided to punish the Rif by depriving it of economic investment and structurally impoverishing it: social and economic marginalization characterize the eastern Rif compared to the rest of Morocco. The local people managed to make ends meet by cultivating hashish and emigrating en masse to Europe.[41] Between 1982 and 2004, the population of the Rif dropped by 34%.[42] With Mohammed VI's accession to the throne in July 1999 came a policy of recognition of Amazigh identity in general and reconciliation with the Rif region in particular, which became the target of an intense economic investment policy. While this economic boost is beneficial for the Rif, it is insufficient: the economic reasoning during the Spanish protectorate (1912–1956) was "primarily control of the territory and exploitation of its resources for Spain's benefit",[43] and after independence the conflict with the Hassan II monarchy marginalized the region.

The twenty-first century began with the opening up of the region. Several major infrastructure projects were undertaken in northern Morocco (Tanger-Med port, the two-lane coast road RN16 between Saïdia and Tangier, the construction of an international airport in Nador). Redevelopment of the Rif to integrate it into the national economy raised expectations and generated frustrations among the population. With the exception of cannabis traffickers whose economic success is a source of envy,[44] the population accused the authorities of misappropriating public funds and practising corruption. People were exasperated and believed that opening up the territory did not produce the expected economic and social benefits. The Hirak Movement's demands provide a concrete illustration of the region's expectations.

The movement published a list of 21 demands that amounted to a social and economic agenda for the region. In addition to a full investigation and the trial of those responsible for Mohsen Fikri's death, the movement demanded the repeal of the royal decree of 1958 declaring the Al Hoceima region a militarized zone. But above all, the movement demanded that the state invest heavily in education, by building a university and establishing training institutes in all skill areas. It called for a university hospital to be set up as well as dispensaries and healthcare facilities. From a cultural standpoint, it wanted to see the completion of the Museum of the Rif, as well as the construction of a regional library and a cultural centre. Regarding the environment, the deterioration of the ecosystem prompted the Hirak Movement to demand protection for the forest sector.[45] Economically, the movement called for an end to the economic siege and marginalization of the area and the region's integration into the country's railroad and highway network. But for Hirak Movement activists, the Moroccan state's answer to these demands seemed like a continuation of the crackdown. Unlike the handling of the 20 February Movement, that of the Hirak Movement was left to the police and the courts. Many NGOs reported arbitrary arrests, disproportionate use of force, and torture.[46] The crackdown on the movement raised fears of the kingdom being destabilized by unrest in a region whose ties and loyalties to the state and monarchy are historically tenuous.

6

ALGERIA

A SOCIETY ON THE BRINK

Against all expectations, Algeria was spared the Arab Spring uprisings, even though analysts for many years have said the country is "at war with itself" or on the brink of revolt.[1] Since Abdelaziz Bouteflika came to power in 1999, the Algerian economy has benefited from rising oil prices, which have enabled 40 million Algerians to see an improvement in their standard of living. Rather than try to overthrow a president who is not perceived as a symbol of power, workers took advantage of the revolutionary mood to bargain for pay hikes. Unlike Tunisia's General Workers' Union, UGTT, which joined in the opposition against the Ben Ali regime, Algerian trade unions defended their various occupational categories, thereby depriving the unemployed of a formidable instrument of mobilization. Algeria thus did not experience revolts.[2] Despite the hundreds of demonstrations staged, none of them evolved into a mass movement. They were for the most part sector-based and did not demand that Bouteflika step down; instead they demanded pay increases.[3]

The trauma of the civil war continues to haunt Algerian families, who have no desire to engage in political contention that could lead to an increase in politically motivated violence.[4] The Algerian authorities skilfully exploited the fear many families felt of seeing Algeria sink once again into civil war, like Libya and Syria. In March 2014, they believed they had overcome the threat of the Arab revolts. Prime Minister Abdelmalek Sellal even said something to the effect that "the Arab Spring is a mosquito that we'll eliminate with Fly-Tox."

In fact, between 2003 and 2013, a time when oil prices were high, the government earmarked half of the oil revenue for social transfers (770 billion dinars) or about 13% of GDP, in attempt to offset the devastating effects of the oil counter-shock (1986–2001). The era of financial abundance (2003–2013) made it possible to restructure networks essential to ensuring the regime's stability. The political apparatus built by Bouteflika, which draws its support from interest groups, is considerable: political parties such as the National Liberation Front (FLN) and the National Rally for Democracy (RND), the Algerian General Workers' Union (UGTA), all received support; and the veterans' lobby, through the Association of Mujahideen, saw its transfers virtually triple from $900 million in 2000 to $2.3 billion in 2013. The academic sphere was not left behind: during the first decade of the 2000s, 92 new institutes of higher education were established and thousands of teaching fellowships were offered to PhD students. The Forum of Algerian Business Leaders[5] is a staunch supporter of the president, for a simple reason: 97% of Algeria's businesses have fewer than nine employees. These are essentially family-run, and 76.6% of them have been founded under the Bouteflika presidency, with financial assistance from the state, either through the National Investment Agency (ANDI) or through the National Agency for Youth Employment Support (ANSEJ). For managers of public companies with more than 250 employees, dependence on the regime is even greater, owing to the lack of transparency in public procurement procedures.

In addition to the regime's involvement in the political and administrative spheres as well as in trade unions and society at large there is the pivotal role of the army, the police and the security apparatuses. Military spending increased from $2.7 billion in 2000 to $11 billion in 2012: between 2006 and 2010, Algeria became the world's eighth-biggest arms importer for that period. Under the leadership of General Ahmed Gaïd Salah, deputy minister of defence and chief of general staff, the military has been a pampered institution. This explains why the General Staff, with the exception of once powerful but now retired generals (Hocine Benhadid, Mohamed Mediène, Khaled Nezzar), prefers to pursue its lucrative partnership with political institutions in the president's orbit rather than entering into conflict with the regime.

While Bouteflika's redistribution policy helped considerably to improve the regime's stability and restore public authority over territories that had totally escaped it, it must be recognized that at the same time an "Algeria on the margins of the state"[6] has also developed, and poses a threat to social cohesion, being a real cause for concern. Nine million Algerians were still living in poverty in 2015, according to the World Bank. Approximately four million people have no social protection and continue to work in the informal sector. In support of the idea that the unemployment rate seems to rise with educational level (17% of the unemployed have a university education), 500,000 youths leave school prematurely each year with no qualifications. Moreover, Algeria has made no progress in battling corruption, as its ranking by the NGO Transparency International indicates: rated 115, it is one of the most corrupt countries in the world. The Algerian Association Against Corruption is not surprised at this ranking, arguing that no progress has been made owing to the lack of political will.[7] From the Sahara to Kabylie, protest movements erupt, calling attention to social injustices and inequalities and accusing the public authorities of indifference. Added to these regional demands is a sense that society has become highly fragmented, and the bonds of solidarity are expressed solely within the family. While the sense of belonging to the nation persists, loyalty to the state has been "seriously weakened".[8] In such a context, it is impossible for the authorities to undertake a transformation of society, given the extent to which the social order produced by the political institutions is disputed by many people.

The constitutional revision of March 2016 aimed to restore trust in the state and its representatives. Article 2 provides that "a National Commission for Corruption Prevention and Control shall be set up", corruption being considered a scourge and a destabilizing factor for social cohesion. According to the preamble of the new Constitution, "youth shall be at the heart of national commitment" and "the Algerian people faced a real national tragedy which put the survival of the nation in jeopardy". The document also emphasizes that the state is determined to "keep Algeria away from sedition, violence and all sorts of extremism". Also, in a context of territorial fragmentation and separatist claims, the new Constitution (art. 4) designates Tamazigh as "a national and official language" and states that the state shall work toward "its promotion and development". Such recognition of the Kabyle language was part of an effort to preserve national unity.

In the Algerian authorities' approach, the preservation of national unity and social cohesion is virtually an obsession. The civil war continues to haunt not only families but the political leadership as well, all the more as the situation in Libya and in Syria has revived the memory of this tragedy. The Algerian authorities deftly exploit the population's fear of seeing Algeria once again slide into violence. However, the idea, conveyed by AQIM propaganda, of combating the regime finds little resonance among the population, even among Islamists themselves, who have undergone a considerable transformation.[9] The surge of violence in Libya, Syria, Yemen and Iraq has reinforced the conviction of the Algerian authorities as well as a segment of the population that revolts and revolutions are dangerous. Many also believe that the Arab "conservative powers" in the Gulf are willing the destruction of socialist, progressive, republican states. In addition to this view is the belief that the region is not prepared for a democratic transition, as long as none of the countries appear to have the required safeguards at hand. Freedom without security is a godsend for the Islamists, who can impose their new moral order. Algeria moreover claims in all seriousness that it wishes to "protect Tunisia's democracy" from the dangers threatening it, as terrorist violence in Tunisia reminds Algeria of its recent past.

In the early 1990s the regime was in danger of being overthrown by armed Islamist groups.[10] Algerian security forces were not equipped to fight a guerrilla war. It was not until 1993 that an elite counter-guerrilla corps was formed, commanded by General Lamari. Upon its creation, this army corps was made up of 20,000 men from the various security forces; it numbered 60,000 in 1996. However, owing to its inability to procure adequate military equipment on the international market (helicopters, night vision devices, etc.), it was unable to "eradicate" jihadi groups. According to General Touati,[11] there were approximately 27,000 Islamist combatants in 1993,[12] spread over remote regions that were hard to access. However, the "total war" on which the regime embarked destroyed the Islamists: in 2002, their numbers had dwindled to an estimated 700: 20,000 were killed and 6,000 laid down their arms in the context of the "Civil Concord" amnesty law. To counter the violence, the regime managed to mobilize militias that wiped out sanctuaries used by Islamist groups. According to the newspaper *Jeune Indépendant*, 500,000 people were armed to form self-defence groups and communal guards.

Initially isolated in their fight against Islamist groups, after the attacks of 11 September 2001 Algeria's rulers felt vindicated in their understanding of Islamist violence: they felt Algeria was the victim of a conspiracy. At an international conference on terrorism held in Algiers in October 2002, Redha Malek, a former head of government and member of the High Council of State, insisted that

> fundamentalist terrorism, which draws its sources from the war in Afghanistan, has spread with the help of the Gulf oil monarchies and the CIA. It was implemented by the former FIS [Islamic Salvation Front], and it was encouraged by the laxity of the authorities at the time. The rise of the FIS in 1991 and 1992 coincided with the return of the Afghan Algerians (2,000 to 3,000 people) who formed the spearhead of terrorist violence.[13]

Accused of having put an end to the "democratic experiment", General Belkheir[14] answered: "I regret nothing; I decided to spare Algeria the fate of Afghanistan. The price was high, but the worst was avoided: a true civil war with millions of victims and refugees." General Atailia,[15] on the other hand, believed it had been a mistake to interrupt the democratic process:

> Those who worked to stop the electoral process must assume responsibility for it. If they had listened to me at the time, we would have prevented a catastrophe; I told them that we had to let the FIS govern as long as the president had all the constitutional prerogatives to redress the situation in the event of deviation, for it is difficult to pass judgment on a party that has not governed. If we had given the party the opportunity, the people would have quickly abandoned it because it potentially favoured many misguided practices.

Yesterday's fiery debates in Algeria are topical today in Morsi's Egypt, in Syria and in post-Qadhafi Libya.

Algeria managed to emerge from civil war owing to a national reconciliation policy. In April 1999, the election of Abdelaziz Bouteflika to the presidency put an end to a decade of conflict between former FIS Islamists and the military rulers. The Civil Concord referendum held on 16 September 1999 confirmed Algerians' deep wish to return to civil peace. Officially, 96% of them answered "for" to the question "Are you for or against the general policy of the President of the Republic, whose goal is peace and civil concord?" On the strength of the outcome of this referendum, Algeria's president claimed in July 1999 that his action was justified by a desire to prevent the civil war from dragging on any longer: "I am trying to act with a modicum of good sense to get to the bottom of a tragedy which will soon have lasted for eight years. My personal feeling is that it is time for all this to stop. Life is not going to improve if we have 200,000 or 300,000 dead and three million victims of terrorism. The accounts have to be settled some time or other."[16] In January 2000, the president issued a decree "granting amnesty to members of the so-called 'AIS' [Islamic Salvation Army] … in return for their unilateral decision to call a ceasefire in 1997, in order to help unmask the enemies of Algeria and Islam."[17] According to other government sources, some 5,500 members of armed groups surrendered in the period between July 1999 and January 2000; and 5,000 prisoners convicted of terrorist or subversive acts were released through a presidential decree issued on 5 July 2000.[18] In August 2005, a referendum on national reconciliation finalized the amnesty process for former FIS Islamists that had begun in 1999 with the Civil Concord law. The authorities now saw the challenge as one of having to combat radical jihadis who refused to recognize the state and the legitimacy of its institutions.

A De-radicalization Strategy

Well over a decade later, the authorities are aware that national unity and social cohesion are fragile and that a transition to democracy in this context would bring the Islamists back to centre stage of the political scene. The army may have won the fight against jihadi groups, but it lost the ideological battle: Salafism has spread considerably in Algeria. The Ghardaïa riots[19] were a stark reminder of how tenuous national cohesion is. The Algerian authorities view Islamist "radicalization" as the primary threat to national unity and social cohesion. Like other countries, Algeria has implemented a comprehensive de-radicalization strategy[20] that differs from similar strategies specifically targeting jihadi groups.[21]

In September 2015, the foreign affairs ministry issued a document summarizing Algeria's de-radicalization strategy.[22] Like Morocco's, Algeria's strategy is all-encompassing: "Algeria firmly believes that the battle to be waged against this dreadful scourge has to be on a daily basis and in all areas of activity, whether political, institutional, economic, cultural, religious, educational or social."[23] As regards economic development, the ministry points out that in an effort to reduce social injustice, the state spends almost 12% of GDP annually on behalf of the disadvantaged. In addition to this social expenditure is an effort focused on "identification of radicalization centres; isolation of radical groups and advocates of violent extremism; and the limitation of the settings that allow individuals to develop extremist ideas."[24] Thus, measures are applied in the prison environment, aimed at separating "those involved in terrorist acts from the other categories of prisoners, through their isolation in strictly separated cells or cell blocks", and to "have incarcerated terrorists approached by theologically learned imams ... primarily to evoke ideological repentance among the most radical prisoners."[25] To regain control over the discourse on Islam, the authorities created more than twelve institutions specialized in training imams. In 2015, the ministry of religious affairs and waqf endowments created the institution of the Mufti of the Republic. Similarly, to re-establish control over the mosques, a national charter for mosques was developed and the theme of preventing violent extremism was introduced into the sermons of imams. There is a plan to establish a new Academy of Fiqh Sciences that will "bring together all the dogmas of Islam", and the Algerian Islamic University emphasizes the "propagation of a moderate and tolerant Islam" in the higher education of imams. The authorities have also mobilized the zaouias (Islamic religious schools) and Quranic schools, as they are "important platforms for the dissemination of positive and constructive ideas and beliefs about Islam, and form a bulwark against violent extremism and radicalization". The zaouia is a space that "expresses spirituality in the setting of the conviviality and ancestral wisdom of Muslim humanism". Moreover, attention has been given to "the creation of the Algerian radio station and TV channel on the Quran, whose solid programmes will contribute toward the presentation of an Islam of peace, tolerance, humanism, and solidarity, as it has always been lived in Algeria."[26]

Educational programmes were revised so as to foster the transmission of "Republican and democratic values …; standard national identity values …; and universal values". In Islamic education, the topics taught focus on "the human and moral values preached by Islam, namely, tolerance, generosity, a sense of justice, work, and honesty". The authorities insist that "the Algerian school system plays an important role in deradicalization and in the fight against violent extremism".[27]

To reduce the space "radicals" have for expression, the authorities have implemented measures in a number of areas, including a policy of media awareness targeting families and financial assistance for the voluntary sector. To raise awareness among youth, 25 private television stations received government approval in the context of the liberalization of the audiovisual sector. "Some of the most positive results have been the shift of the Algerian youth from the extremist rhetoric purveyed by some TV channels." A radio station is aimed specifically at a young audience (Jil FM) and strong media coverage is devoted to "moderate opinions expressed by famous Muslim thinkers". In the area of culture, one of the targets of jihadi groups during the civil war, Algeria renewed its cultural policy: 176 international, national and local festivals received public funding in 2015 compared to only 28 in 1998. Over 300 libraries were established between 2010 and 2014. There is a will, at least in the discourse, to protect the country's cultural heritage. The ministry of culture provided financial support for several films to contribute "to greater awareness of fundamentalism and obscurantism. These feature films include *El Manara*, by Belkacem Hadjadj, *Rachida et Yamina*, by Yamina Bachir Chouikh, *Douar de femmes*, by Mohamed Chouikh, *Les Suspects*, by Kamel Dehane, *Autopsie d'une tragédie*, by Ait Aoudia, *Parfum d'Alger*, by Rachid Belhadj, *Morituri*, by Okacha Touita, etc." Also, to encourage "dialogue among cultures and to protect Algeria's intangible heritage as a bulwark against fundamentalist messages", the government also instituted a symposium entitled 'Culture, Music, and Sufism'. The symposium allows researchers to "debate various cultural aspects of the worship rituals and spiritual heritage of Islam and other religions".[28]

The fight against radicalization is a top priority for the Algerian authorities. The development of Salafism and jihadism in the region is posing a threat to national unity once again. The discourse of the authorities is based on stability and security. Regional instability is a fact, and while Algeria now has the military means to secure its territory, protecting its citizens against the "jihadi contamination" forces it to mobilize means other than military. The Islamist counter-discourse and mobilization of all sectors of society are the levers of the state's strategy, as is the government's rhetoric portraying Algeria as the victim of potential conspiracies and calling on the population to unite with the government against them. The authorities interpreted the Arab Spring as a plot hatched by Qatar and its Arab and Western allies to destabilize the region.

Kabylie, a Source of Wild Imaginings

Alongside the jihadi threat, the authorities have been trying for two decades to quell tensions in Kabylie. The death of high school student Massinissa Guermah on 18 April 2001 in the Beni-Douala gendarmerie headquarters triggered riots that were harshly put down by the authorities. The scale of the repression—resulting in over one hundred deaths among the rioters—sparked a protest movement that spread beyond Kabylie, reaching towns in the Babor mountains. The gendarmerie, the government and the state were heckled by groups of demonstrators made up of young unemployed, managers and so on.[29] Like young FIS sympathizers in the early 1990s, they shouted their anger at the scorn (hogra) shown toward them by the security forces. Although the protesters were confined to Kabylie, the resentment they expressed resonated throughout the country. For the regime, the events in Kabylie marked the opening of a "second front" after its war against the former FIS Islamists.[30] The call for regional autonomy issued by certain Kabyle figures and rumours circulating about the formation of Berber armed groups stoked fears of lasting instability in Kabylie. To appease the rioters, the government announced the gendarmerie's withdrawal from the region.

But the calm was short-lived, swept away by reports of evangelization taking place in Kabylie. Since 2004, the local press had been reporting on such a phenomenon. The account given in *El Watan* newspaper (26 July 2004) of a symposium held at the Emir Abdelkader University of Islamic Sciences in Constantine seems to have triggered the "scandal". The author of the article summed up remarks made about the phenomenon by various participants, redolent of a conspiracy theory: Algeria was allegedly the target of a campaign focused on Kabylie but actually directed at "the entire country". According to the author, "The truth is that officially there are many churches in Kabylie. They are being created at lightning speed throughout the entire region," and he added, "Although evangelization in Kabylie is not new, its growing scope, its obvious ideology, its unavowed aims and its instrumentalization by national and international forces will produce additional crises in a Kabylie and an Algeria already saturated with all sorts of crises."

After colonialism and Wahhabism, some believe Algeria is now a victim of Christian evangelists. "Evangelization in Kabylie is not spontaneous today any more than it was in the past. It is the result of proselytism organized and funded by a global strategy to evangelize Muslim peoples," the author claimed. The investigation concluded with an appeal to the government authorities: "It is dismaying to note that the government hardly utters a critical word in response to the new American colonial policy." Although there is no reliable data on the number of non-Muslims in Algeria, they are estimated at about 5,000. According to figures supplied by Christian community leaders, there are 3,000 members of evangelical churches—most of them living in Kabylie—and 300 Catholics.[31]

On 20 March 2006, Parliament passed Ordinance 06–03 that laid down "the conditions and rules for worship of other religions than Islam" and reiterated that the state guaranteed tolerance and respect between the various religions, but then listed the new conditions governing non-Muslim religious worship:

Art. 5. The use of a building for religious worship is subject to prior approval by the national commission; any activity in designated places of worship other than their intended use is forbidden.

Art. 7. Group worship will take place solely in structures set aside for this purpose, open to the public and clearly identified on the outside.

Art. 8. Religious services must take place in designated structures; they are open to the public and subject to prior approval.

The conditions in which religious worship may take place are subject to criminal provisions. This fact did not fail to provoke outrage. According to Article 10, "one to three years' imprisonment and a fine of 250,000 to 500,000 DA may be levied on anyone whose speech or writing posted or distributed in places of worship, or conveyed by any other audiovisual means, contains an appeal to resist the enforcement of laws or decisions by the public authorities." Article 11 provides for two to five years' imprisonment for anyone who

> incites, constrains or utilizes means of seduction tending to convert a Muslim to another religion, or by using to this end institutions of learning, education, health, or of a social or cultural nature, or training institutes or any other establishment or any other means; [or who] makes, stores or distributes printed documents, audiovisual materials or another medium with the intent of shaking the faith of a Muslim.

The anxiety generated by this marginal phenomenon is amplified by the fact that it is located in Kabylie. The author of the investigative report notes: "Many missionaries dream of turning Kabylie into a new multiconfessional Lebanon. Currently without legitimate elected officials but with 'illegitimate' officials, Kabylie gives the impression of being colonized by a foreign power. The idea of autonomy gaining ground, the ingredients for Kabyle secession multiply day after day amid general political indifference."[32] Having thus posed the issue, the author then appealed to the authorities, urging them to act because danger was afoot. And yet, a Christian presence in Kabylie is nothing new and the Christian myth of an artificially Islamized land is tenuous.[33] Already in the nineteenth century, under colonial rule, Kabylie became a political and religious issue in which colonization was associated with Christianization. The work of Catholic missionaries, based on the notion that Islamization was less frequent among Kabyles, was intended to facilitate their reintegration into the "religion of their ancestors". Once viewed as a colonial policy, today as an American strategy of evangelization, conversion of the Kabyles to Christianity still remains a huge source of anxiety and wild imaginings in Algeria. The affair of the Kabyles' "conversion to Christianity" fits in with the post-traumatic context enveloping the regime and society at large. It comes all the more as a surprise since Algeria's religious landscape has grown increasingly uniform in recent history: Islam is now professed by 99% of the population. Algeria is undergoing a serious cultural and religious crisis. Algerian Muslims were deeply affected by the years of violence perpetrated in the name of Islam. Redefining one's relationship with the divine has become a matter of personal quest.

The Algerian state managed to survive the civil war and not founder. Its civil administrations continued to function as best they could and the security apparatuses maintained the necessary cohesion for a counterinsurgency. It nevertheless remains clear that the civil war caused tragedies resulting in deep changes to individual behaviours. It lastingly traumatized Algerian society, which paid a high price for the collapse of its national community. The end of the FLN state monopoly on what defined the Algerian national community paved the way for a radical questioning of Algeria's history and identity. Owing to the civil war, the state has sought to redefine its foundations: Abdelaziz Bouteflika's approach opened new perspectives for Algeria on a symbolic level. In his many speeches, the president readily points out that the regime's revolutionary legitimacy has passed away and that the state must now be built on other foundations than the war of independence. His calls for reconciliation are addressed as much to Islamists as they are to former Algerian-born colonists and Jews.[34] For the first time since independence, a head of state has sought to redefine the components of the state's identity which until then had rested on the triad of Islam, Arab and nation.

The Algerian state has been influenced by the maxim of reformist Sheikh Abdelhamid ibn Badis (1889–1940): "The Algerian people are Muslim and are part of the Arab world."[35] This principle has prompted the state to restrict other forms of religious expression in the name of official Islam. It has sometimes pitted them against one another so as to neutralize them. As Sossie Andezian has pointed out, "The independent Algerian state, openly hostile to mystic trends, gradually modulates its policy to the tempo of national interests, to ostensibly encourage its expression as historical heritage during certain periods in an effort to counter Islamism."[36] State Islam must not obscure "the diversity of relationships to religion in independent Algeria, despite standardization by the state of belief systems and practices of worship," she insists.

Thus, the will to control the religious practices of non-Muslims fits in with the same perspective as that prompting the state to control Muslim worshippers. Algeria is witnessing the arrival of new Christians from sub-Saharan Africa who either cross the country in search of a passage to Europe or who settle within its boundaries.

According to some NGOs, 100,000 black African migrants are living in Algeria illegally. They come under the law of 2008 regulating entry and exit from the country, and over 56,000 people have been convicted of crimes and violations.[37] Since 2014, the authorities have been brutally expelling these migrants,[38] and the UN in particular estimates that 28,000 migrants from Niger have been repatriated. In response to criticism of Algeria's anti-migration policy—some media outlets mention "roundup and deportations" of black African migrants—the government claims that migrant networks are permeated with "robbery, terrorism, crime and subversion".[39] Like the fear of evangelization, xenophobia against black Africans is a symptom of the Algerians' difficulty in accepting and tolerating a pluralist society. It must be said that after a decade of abundance (2003–2013), the economic and social situation has deteriorated steadily owing to collapsing oil prices since 2014.

After Bouteflika: Is Algeria Ripe for Collapse?

Today, as oil wealth is dwindling ($112 billion in 2014, $49 billion in 2017) and reserve funds have shrunk considerably ($200 billion in 2014; $50 billion in 2017), there is growing concern as to whether the Algerian regime can endure. Following the collapse of the price of oil to below $70 pb, the Algerian government enacted measures to curb spending and reduce its deficit. The two-point increase in VAT (from 7% to 9% and from 17% to 19%, depending on the product) is an example of such measures.[40] Faced with an excessively high import bill ($45 billion in 2017), the government hoped to disburse only $30 billion in 2018 and imposed a rather symbolic ban on the import of some 900 products. Other reforms, more structural in nature, have been announced, such as an increase in the retirement age over 60. But the scale of mobilization and the fear of social unrest make the government hesitant to implement such reforms. Faced with high inflation

(7%) and rising taxes, the population has borne the full brunt of the drop in oil prices.

Ailing and weakened by a stroke in 2013, Abdelaziz Bouteflika has defied all medical prognoses concerning his demise. His survival has compelled Algeria to remain in an absurd political situation in which everyone has been waiting for the president to breathe his last before they can finally design and imagine changes. His election to a fourth five-year term in office, in 2014, was already widely criticized, particularly as the head of state seemed unfit to fulfil his duties. And then, in January 2019, it appeared that he would run for a fifth term. His inner circle claimed that his health had improved. Farouk Ksentini, former chairman of Algeria's National Advisory Commission for the Promotion and Protection of Human Rights, stated:

> I met with President Bouteflika last week. We spoke for an hour. It's the fourth time I've met with him this year. Our acquaintance goes back more than thirty years. It was clear that he has a strong desire to run for a fifth term. He is entitled to do so and we support his wish. The Constitution does not prevent him from running. The verdict of the ballot box must be respected.[41]

This life presidency thwarts the hopes of those who would like to see more competitive elections (Abdelaziz Belaid,[42] Abdallah Saadallah Djaballah,[43] Ahmed Benbitour,[44] Ali Benflis[45]) and puts any likely successors (Ahmed Ouyahia,[46] Abdelmalek Sellal[47]) in a state of intolerable expectation. At the top of the list is his brother, Saïd Bouteflika, considered the strongman, the "viceroy behind the scenes" for his sick brother.[48]

Although in the 2017 legislative elections, the FLN and its ally, the RND, won a majority in parliament, with 35% and 20% of the vote respectively, voter turnout remained very low—scarcely 35%, even less than in the 2012 legislative elections, when an estimated 43% voted. The parties in government have retained their hegemony over the political scene, generating distrust among the majority of the population. And the survival in office of a terribly weakened president has aroused concern about Algeria's future both domestically and abroad: a report put out in February 2017 by the American think tank American Enterprise Institute rightly points out, "Algeria today looks strikingly similar to Libya, Tunisia, and Egypt in 2010. With high youth unemployment, a corrupt banking system, unsustainable welfare programs, and an ossified ruling class presided over by an ailing dictator, Algeria is ripe for collapse."[49] The oil rent which for a long time enabled Bouteflika to distribute funds to maintain social peace is running dry, while serious rivals are emerging in the eastern Mediterranean (Egypt, Cyprus, Israel) for the export of natural gas.[50] The country's needs remain considerable: Algeria still imports over 70% of its food, and military expenditure has decreased only slightly. The regional context is equally alarming: the war in Mali, the collapse of Libya and terrorism in Tunisia all pose serious threats to Algeria. Moreover, the collapse of the Islamic State organization in Iraq and in Syria has prompted the redeployment of over 6,000 Daesh combatants in Africa.[51]

In the face of such challenges, a number of Algeria's partners are hoping for a new president to take the reins, one who would be able to address the domestic economic problems and regional threats. The local press has drawn a profile of the ideal successor. The person should be a consensual figure between the presidency and the military high command, and close to the security apparatus. For the moment, the person who matches this profile is the chief of police and former gendarmerie head, Abdelghani Hamel, who is the subject of a campaign to promote his candidacy.[52] Meanwhile, Algeria has withdrawn into itself over the course of Abdelaziz Bouteflika's fourth term (2014–2019). In fact, the fear of contagion from the Arab revolts reinforced the tendency for the country to isolate itself. A fifth term may have caused its implosion, which everyone fears and dreads.[53] The violent crackdown on a demonstration of more than 15,000 healthcare workers in Oran on 3 January 2018[54] was perceived as a sign of panic in the face of social unrest.

The Awakening of Civil Society

The fragile balance that Bouteflika had established over the years collapsed with the 10 February 2019 announcement of his candidacy for a fifth presidential term. An unexpected, peaceful and unprecedented popular protest movement caused the head of state to give up the idea of running for another term. Starting on 22 February 2019, hundreds of thousands of demonstrators gathered every Friday after the collective prayers to denounce the "Bouteflika system" which had led Algeria into a political and economic impasse. This system was characterized by the establishment of powerful crony networks, which in turn help to explain the longevity of Bouteflika's presidency (1999–2019). The increase in public spending made it possible to develop and consolidate alliances between the presidency, the main trade unions and the Business Leaders' Forum; and an increase in the defence budget helped strengthen the army chief of staff vis-à-vis his peers. In fact, between 2003 and 2013, when oil prices were high, the government spent half of the oil revenue on social transfers, i.e. about 13% of GDP, to correct the destructive effects of the oil counter-shock (1986–2001). Financial abundance made it possible to restructure the networks needed to ensure the regime's stability.

Abdelmadjid Sidi Saïd, chief of the Algerian General Workers Union, declared "on behalf of the workers, those retired, men and women, Bouteflika is our candidate" as early as January 2019. Later the same month, Ali Haddad's Business Leaders' Forum, the parties of the presidential alliance (the National Liberation Front, the Tajamou Amal el-Jazaïr, the Hope of Algeria Rally) as well as the National Democratic Rally, the Algerian Popular Movement, the Association of Mujahideen and the chief of staff of the Gaïd Salah army welcomed the president's proposed candidature. The isolated opposition parties—the Rally for Culture and Democracy and the Front of Socialist Forces—announced a "massive, active and peaceful" boycott of the elections. The leader of the moderate Islamist party, the Movement of the Society for Peace (MSP), Abderrazzak Makri, declared his candidacy for the presidency while specifying, in February, that Bouteflika's candidacy "was not in his interest but in that of those who benefit from this situation ... They will take full responsibility for what happens and the dangers that threaten the country", he added.

Three main factors must be considered. The first is that the concerns that ensued from the civil war of the 1990s have faded. Today's Algerian youth no longer refer to that period and aspire to something else. Secondly, the strong instrumentalization of the regional situation by the authorities during the Arab Spring has diminished. The "fear effect" of the wars in Syria or Libya no longer succeeds in inhibiting society. Finally, the third important factor is that, from 2014 with the collapse of the price of oil, Algeria has embarked on a policy of increasing taxes and limiting imports. Overall, there is less money to redistribute, leading to growing social discontent, which exploded during spring 2019.

Forced to renounce his candidacy, the outgoing president announced major political reforms capable of "renewing the nation-state" and establishing a new republic. An inclusive national conference was announced, which would have "all the prerogatives of a constituent assembly", chaired by the diplomat and politician Lakhdar Brahimi. Its aim was to draft a new constitution that would be submitted to a referendum. To make this transition a success, Noureddine Bedoui, appointed prime minister, and Ramtane Lamamra, deputy prime minister, promised a "broad-based dialogue with youth and opposition political forces".

However, this all came too late. For the demonstrators in the citizens' movement,[55] Bouteflika had to resign along with all his entourage, his "clan", his "gang". Bouteflika's long-time strongman, army chief of staff Gaïd Salah, urged the president to step down, and he became a mouthpiece for the protesters' anger. In a few days, all of the head of state's relatives were ousted: Ali Haddad, the powerful and wealthy chief of the Business Leaders' Forum, was arrested and imprisoned in El-Harrach prison. Saïd, the president's brother, was also arrested. General Tartag, head of the security services, was dismissed and then arrested. More spectacularly, General Tawfiq, the former head of the secret service, considered one of the most influential men in the country, was also arrested and jailed. The president of the powerful oil company Sonatrach was also dismissed. Abdelmadjid Sidi Saïd, the leader of the UGTA, was pressured by his followers to resign or retire. Ministers and prime ministers were arrested with considerable fanfare. However, the dismantling of President Bouteflika's networks was not enough for the demonstrators, who demanded that "the entire system" be done away with.

In a matter of months, Algeria found itself confronted with a political transition for which it was not prepared. The disrepute of political parties put the army in the front line to manage a change of which it was frightened because of the uncertainty surrounding it. The failure of the transition that began in the late 1980s is in everyone's mind. The military no longer has the abhorrent image it had after the bloody repression of the October 1988 riots. Seriously disparaged for their massive human rights violations during the civil war (1991–1999), the military leadership virtually went into hiding, if not mothballed itself, by vanishing from the political radar and media screens. Over the past ten years, relieved of the burden of managing political affairs, the Algerian army has become more professionalized and better equipped. In an uncertain regional context, the institution has been striving to restore its former glory by making a show of its military might. Unlike demonstrators in the 1980s and 1990s, those of 2019 express no hatred toward the army. But by effectively taking political power, the army is now exposed to criticism from demonstrators, who fear that Algeria will follow the route of Sisi's Egypt.

In such a climate, the army relies on the Constitution to counter the resignation of the president. This provides for the appointment of Abdelkader Bensalah, a faithful member of Bouteflika's entourage and the president of the Council of the Nation (Algerian Senate), as interim president for 90 days, the time needed to organize a new presidential election. Far from appeasing the demonstrators, this transition, under the constraint of the rules of the Constitution, is perceived as a subterfuge in order to maintain the status quo. In fact, over the next three months, the army may try to find a new political figure, with a broader social base than Bouteflika, with whom to set up mechanisms for sharing power and wealth. Indeed, at this historic moment for Algeria, two scenarios seem to be emerging. Either the army lays the foundations for a new political pact that will pave the way for a transition to a new political regime and a state open to a cohort of youth that aspires to a future other than emigration; or it takes the risk of becoming the target of demonstrators, if it simply renews "the Bouteflika system". In this second perspective, in the absence of a transition to democracy, Algeria would be moving towards an entrenchment of the regime. However, this transition is taking place in a difficult economic context, as oil revenue dwindles.

Faced with such challenges, many of Algeria's partners hope that the country will find a peaceful political solution. The demonstrators obtained concrete changes from the dismantling of the Bouteflika network. This initial victory is a very significant one. They now expect "to accelerate the start of a peaceful democratic transition through an electoral process that embodies the break with the dictatorial and corrupt system and ensures the establishment of legitimate and credible institutions".

7

THE DECONSTRUCTION OF NATION-STATES

THE JIHADIS' REVENGE

Since the 1970s and 1980s, Islamist movements associated with the Muslim Brotherhood or with Salafi groups have been attempting to expand the space that states devote to "Islamic values".[1] Their entryism in the education and justice ministries, for instance, has resulted in the strengthening of Arabization policies. "Bottom-up Islamization" remains a central objective. Pursuing it avoids direct confrontation with the nationalists, who are more concerned with defending a traditional Islam shaped by brotherhoods and zaouias within the framework of an authoritarian state. Political liberalization in the late 1980s enabled Islamist parties in the orbit of the Muslim Brotherhood, such as Ennahda in Tunisia and the FIS in Algeria, to take part in the election process. However, the fear of seeing these Islamist parties, described as populist, rise to power through legal channels prompted political and military leaders to seek to exclude them from the political arena.

Hounded, crushed and imprisoned, Islamists vanished from the official political scene in the 1990s and 2000s. During that time, jihadi groups such as the Armed Islamic Group (GIA) in Algeria and the Salafist Group for Preaching and Combat (GSPC) in Libya embarked on a war against their regimes, which they called "tyrannical" and "apostate", with the support of veterans of the anti-Soviet jihad in

Afghanistan.[2] Defeated militarily, combatants in these groups went into hiding in border areas in the Sahara and there joined the al-Qaeda organization, subscribing to its plan for a deterritorialized "global jihad". Those in prison renounced violence and were released within the framework of reconciliation policies. The authorities considered jihadi groups beaten and no longer posing a threat. Thus, to compensate for the disappearance of Islamist parties, the authorities encouraged the development of quietist Salafism.[3] This strand, unlike the Muslim Brotherhood, does not participate in politics, and does not seek to penetrate the state or become part of the government. Meanwhile, in this world they strive to remain "pure" in an environment considered "impure". The state, the constitution and political parties are perceived as phenomena foreign to Islam and thus despised. Unlike the jihadis, they submit to the political order and do not seek to overturn it and impose the sharia. Under the regimes of Ben Ali, Bouteflika and Colonel Qadhafi, quietist Salafi movements therefore spread considerably, enabling these regimes to disprove accusations made by jihadi organizations that they behaved like "enemies of Islam".

With the Arab revolts, the jihadis took their revenge. The overthrow of the Ben Ali regime and the collapse of Qadhafi's Libya resulted in the release of thousands of Islamist prisoners, including many jihadis. Organizations such as Ansar al-Sharia and IS exploited the vulnerability of regimes in transition and sought to impose their rule in urban areas deserted by security forces.[4]

Emirate and Islamic State: Post-Qadhafi Surprises

Starting in 2012, the al-Qaeda-affiliated jihadi network Ansar al-Sharia engaged in a campaign of murdering and kidnapping former regime figures in Benghazi. On 11 September 2012, it attacked the United States consulate, prompting the hasty departure of Westerners from the region and considerably undermining international support for the political transition. Ansar al-Sharia arose from the merger of two groups active in Cyrenaica's two main cities: Ansar al-Sharia Brigade in Benghazi and Ansar al-Sharia in Derna.[5] With a strong foothold in the region, the jihadis set out to replace Qadhafi's rule by instituting an Islamic emirate: they staunchly opposed the emergence of democracy and a pluralist political scene. Between 2012 and 2014, alongside its terrorist activities, Ansar al-Sharia implemented social service programmes designed to broaden its social base.[6] Paradoxically, the jihadis settled in a region that is the historical cradle of the Sanussi brotherhood, where several Sufi shrines were located, which they had no qualms about demolishing. On 30 July 2014, Ansar al-Sharia proclaimed the city of Benghazi an "Islamic emirate". The jihadis' activities and the drift toward an Islamic state in Cyrenaica raised fierce resistance within civil society, as illustrated by the reaction to the murder of the US ambassador on 11 September 2012 and placards posted throughout the city stating "Libya is not Afghanistan".[7] Three days after the attack, Cyrenaican tribal chiefs met in Benghazi, and after several hours of discussion, they issued a declaration condemning the violence, the attack against the ambassador, and the destruction of Sufi shrines.[8] In May 2014, General Haftar launched Operation Dignity against Ansar al-Sharia in Benghazi and in Derna. It would take him three years to run the group out of Benghazi, partly destroying it in the process.

Further west, IS managed to gain a foothold in Sirte, a stronghold of the former regime abandoned to its fate after Qadhafi's overthrow. In fact, already in 2013, the leader of ISIL, al-Baghdadi, had sent an emissary to Derna where the Shura Council of Islamic Youth had pledged allegiance to Daesh. Control of Derna by other jihadi groups such as the Shura Council of Mujahideen, adversaries of Islamic State, provoked clashes and caused the departure of Daesh combatants from the city.[9] IS managed to establish itself in Sirte without opposition and reorganized the city with the backing of tribal organizations such as Qadhafa, Furlan and Amamra.[10] For Islamic State, Libya became the three provinces referred to by the names they had under the Ottoman Empire: Wilayat Tripoli; Wilayat Barqa (in the east); and Wilayat Fezzan (in the south). In September 2015, al-Qahtani, head of Islamic State in Libya, invited "Muslims" to perform *hijra*[11] and join him to strengthen Daesh control. He explained that he needed staff to administer the territory.[12] The appeal met with great success; between 3,000 and 6,000 combatants arrived: "70 percent of the Daesh's fighters in Libya were non-Libyans, with the majority coming from Tunisia and the remainder from Algeria, Chad, Egypt, Morocco, Niger, Nigeria, Senegal and Sudan."[13] In November 2015, a 25-year-old Senegalese student of medicine at the Cheikh Anta Diop University gave an interview to the Reuters news agency and on his Facebook account, expressing his pride in having joined the Islamic State group: "I left Senegal a year after embracing the ideology of the Islamic State. Joining ISIS in Libya was relatively easy and accessible. I wanted to contribute to the establishment of a caliphate in Libya … I am a jihadist doctor there."[14] The material and symbolic advantages offered by the ISIS group were an incentive for him to go.

IS's establishment in Libya is strategic. It provides a gateway to North Africa and sub-Saharan Africa, taking the threat closer to Europe.[15] In 2015, ISIS controlled a territory of about 200 kilometres around Sirte and could seriously disrupt oil production: the Ras Lanuf petrochemical complex and the oil field, which handled 80% of Libya's production, are close by.

The ease with which Daesh established itself in Sirte was due to the desertion of the city by the main Libyan protagonists.[16] Divided and abandoned, Libya became a sanctuary for IS jihadis who planned to apply throughout North Africa and sub-Saharan Africa the strategy of violence developed in the Middle East. Between 2012 and 2015, Libya was a safe haven where combatants fleeing northern Mali after the French operation could take refuge. The arrival of Daesh in Libya stirred fears of a wave of brutality such as that seen in Syria and Iraq, northern Cameroon and Nigeria. Certain regional organizations, such as Boko Haram, which pledged allegiance to IS on 7 March 2015, have succumbed to its appeal. The group's strategy of violence has stoked fears of the entire region descending into extreme violence. The strategy was outlined in a volume edited by Abou bak Naji, entitled *The Management of Savagery: The Most Critical Stage through Which the Islamic Nation Will Pass*.[17] It involves unleashing violence in Muslim countries so as to exhaust official government forces. "Jihad cannot be continued with softness," it declares. To restore the Umma (or Islamic community), violent, cruel stages are necessary, including beheadings, crucifixions and enslavement. Terrorist violence is required to overwhelm local regimes. Then the violence unleashed must be brought to the attention of the media through acts of savagery capable of wearing down people's resistance. To counterbalance the terror conveyed by propaganda, protection, social services and financial benefits are offered in exchange for allegiance to ISIS. Reconciliation occurs by restoring justice and applying the sharia. Tested in Iraq and in Syria, in Nigeria, and in north Cameroon, this strategy has met with less success in Libya. With the exception of its Sirte stronghold, IS quickly encountered local and regional resistance. It nevertheless took a month of warfare in 2017 to drive the jihadis out of Sirte: liberation resulted in considerable casualties—dead and wounded—among the Misrata militias. IS's move into Libya, the Sahel and West Africa jolted the international community into action: in 2015, several initiatives emerged in an attempt to find a solution for Libya.

This could be partly because IS in Libya does not hesitate to threaten France and Italy directly, as can be seen in a Daesh video bearing the title "Paris before Rome", posted in August 2015. Libya was presented as the key to entering Europe in order to conquer Rome. The true enemy to be brought down remained France, however. Jihadis close to al-Qaeda[18] and those affiliated to ISIS share the common goal of expelling France from the area.

The Arab Revolts: An Opportunity for the Jihadis

The overthrow of the Qadhafi regime turned Libya into a platform for jihadis. One of the countries where Islamists had been the most harshly repressed has become a safe haven for jihadis from the entire region. Throughout the 1990s, jihadi violence had remained confined to the territories of Algeria and Libya.[19] During the first decade of the 2000s, jihadis, having failed in their goals, scattered into the Sahara and the Sahel. The 2011 revolutions miraculously enabled them to return to the coastal cities and threaten the incumbent authorities. During the 2011 uprisings, they wisely left front stage to human rights advocates, who were better able to humanize the revolts against the "dictators". While Islamist parties (Ennahda in Tunisia, the Justice and Development Party in Morocco, the Muslim Brotherhood in Egypt, and the Party for Justice and Development in Libya) successfully set out to take over parliaments, jihadi groups undertook to conquer territories so as to reconfigure the political order in the region. They were out to destroy the nation-states resulting from colonization and restore the caliphate or an emirate. To do so, they implemented a strategy of capturing oil production facilities and destroying tourist infrastructure in the region as the first stage in permanently weakening enemy governments. At the same time, another declared objective was to expel France and the French from the region. After the nationalists in the 1950s and 1960s, it was the turn of jihadis to attempt to chase out the former colonists, now labelled "infidels". Although jihadi groups attack vital interests in Algeria and Tunisia, their real target is in fact France, their "best" enemy. The French military intervention in northern Mali revived the figure of the "French invader" peddled throughout the colonial period, in addition to which the jihadis, turning history around, made Algeria out to be an ally of France: "Decisions in Algeria are always formulated and approved under pressure from France and Western countries ... without taking the people's dignity into account. Don't think we have forgotten your betrayal after your collaboration with France in the war in northern Mali; what has delayed our response is the fact that we have been busy with the war against the French invaders," the jihadis proclaimed.[20]

As remarkable as it is paradoxical, Western support for the insurgents contributed to the return of jihadis in countries such as Libya that had for decades been chasing them out. Thus, against all expectations, it was a member of the Libyan Islamic Fighting Group (LIFG) who was installed in office with the help of NATO in Tripoli. In March 2013, Abdul Hakim Belhaj, former leader of the Tripoli Military Council, in a letter addressed to the British prime minister David Cameron, thanked the UK for its support of the rebels, but nevertheless asked for an apology and the symbolic amount of six dinars in damages. In 2004, this co-founder of LIFG was kidnapped by British security services in Bangkok and handed over to the CIA in conjunction with the global war on terror waged by the Bush administration. The LIFG leader was extradited to Libya, where he remained incarcerated for four years in Abu Salim prison. In 2009, he renounced violence and, in a document entitled "Corrective Studies", declared that the jihad against Qadhafi was illegitimate, which got him released on 23 March 2010. One year later, he led the protest against the regime and, heading a group of rebels from the east whom he had trained along with former LIFG combatants—including Abdel-Hakim al-Hasidi, leader of the Derna section—reached Tripoli on 22 August 2011. When he founded the LIFG in 1995 with Shaykh Abu Yahya, Anas al-Libya (Nazih Abdul Hamid al-Raghie), Abu Bakr al-Sharif, Salah Fathi bin Suleiman (Abu Abdul Rahman al-Hattab), Belhaj little imagined he would someday be the equivalent of governor of Tripoli in 2012. In March 2011, LIFG combatants announced that their organization would pledge allegiance to the National Transitional Council under the name Libyan Islamic Movement for Change (LIMC). Quite a change indeed!

Between 1995 and 1998, the LIFG conducted guerrilla operations against security forces in the Benghazi region, prompting a strong response from the regime in the form of bombing raids on the mountainous regions of Jebel al-Akhdar where the Islamist militants had their hideouts. The regime associated them with the imperialist threat: "our revolution", Qadhafi claimed in 1993, "is a fundamental revolution, a revolution of authenticity. We are the leaders of an authentic and fundamental revolution; only the revolution and pan-Arabism can combat imperialism and its local allies which are the Islamists." For many socialist and progressive regimes such as Libya, Algeria, Iraq and Syria, the Islamists were perceived in the 1980s and 1990s as allies of the West owing to US and Saudi support for the "Afghan resistance" after the Soviet invasion of Afghanistan. Many North African jihadis had joined organizations founded by Bin Laden. After Soviet troops left Afghanistan, jihadis from the Maghreb commenced jihad in North Africa, hoping to topple regimes they considered "apostate".

On 31 May 1998, Islamist groups based in the region of Benghazi staged an attempt to assassinate Colonel Qadhafi, whose convoy was ambushed in the region of Sidi Khalifa as he returned from a trip to Egypt. Qadhafi was wounded in the elbow, and three of his guards were killed. The LIFG called for a jihad against the Qadhafi regime to put an end to the plight of "Libyan Muslims", who could only be saved by the institution of an Islamic state.[21] Hounded by the Qadhafi regime, the LIFG jihadis swore allegiance to the al-Qaeda organization in November 2007, thereby boosting the presence of Libyan Islamists in Iraq, where they made up the second-largest contingent of foreign fighters after the Saudis. While the GSPC and the LIFG seemed to have been defeated, even totally wiped out prior to the 11 September 2001 attacks, the US invasion of Iraq in 2003 enabled them to rise from their ashes. Under the influence of al-Qaeda, these two organizations revised their strategy and decided to join forces for the purposes of a regional jihad.[22] Their war economy is based not only on the "kidnapping industry",[23] but also on the cross-border smuggling of products such as cigarettes. However, AQIM is not a "major actor" in the Sahel drug trade.[24]

The declaration of jihad in 1995 did not bring about the anticipated insurgency. It was not until the Arab Spring in 2011 that a groundswell of protest enabled former LIFG militants to seek their revenge. Convinced that the Islamist fighters were no longer a threat, Saif al-Islam offered them a general amnesty as a gesture of national reconciliation. Abu Salim prison, a symbol of the regime's repression of the Islamists—in 1996, over 1,200 Islamist prisoners perished in a mutiny there—was demolished; in October 2009, members of the LIFG were released and later, in March 2011, they would join the insurgency. Although some jihadis had been converted to democracy, such as Abdel Hakim Belhaj, who founded his own party, Al-Watan, not all of them renounced jihad. Some preferred to join the Umma al-Wasat party led by Sami al-Saadi, the LIFG ideologue, hardly a proponent of democracy. In fact, former LIFG combatants were outdone by those more radical than they: ISIS and al-Qaeda jihadis, who were planning to bring their war against foreign forces and allied regimes into the Sahara and the Sahel.[25]

Africa in Perspective

While Europe has certainly had to face its share of terrorist attacks, sub-Saharan Africa is subject to the tribulations of terrorist violence virtually on a daily basis.[26] Almost non-existent more than fifteen years ago,[27] jihadi groups are destabilizing states by their strategy of violence and are terrorizing communities that feel deserted. After North Africa and the Middle East, the rest of the African continent is becoming a space for the expansion of jihadi groups that seize the opportunities offered in these regions.[28] Unlike those in Arab countries, the armies of the nations of sub-Saharan Africa are weak and do not have the capacity to resist a war of attrition without international support, due to the vastness of their territories.[29] The legitimacy of the state is seriously put to the test in these countries, where its presence is perceived as aggression. Furthermore, the area's demographics provide an inexhaustible pool of combatants and the presence of the former colonial powers helps to construct the trope of an enemy that plunders the country and props up leaders who are more interested in personal gain than in the general interest. For jihadi groups, sub-Saharan Africa is extremely fertile ground where porous borders enable them to conduct their criminal activities unhindered.[30] In fact, the ease with which jihadis have operated since Qadhafi's overthrow illustrates the extent to which these groups have permeated various communities in the region, such as the Tuareg, the Fulani and so on.[31] Jihadi groups have taken their revenge in the wake of the Arab revolutions: the implosion of Libya, the toppling of the police state in Tunisia, and the fall of Blaise Compaoré in Burkina Faso have all provided them with a previously unimagined realm of possibilities. Local jihadi groups have formed new alliances and have enabled Daesh to gain a foothold in the region. A host of jihadi groups affiliated to al-Qaeda or Daesh have spread out from the Algerian Sahara to West Africa. It is their ambition to destroy the nation-states resulting from colonization and restore the caliphate.

The establishment of jihadi groups is the product of a combination of structural variables (poverty, poor governance, sense of injustice, land disputes) and cyclical variables (pre-existing armed conflicts, the activism of entrepreneurs of violence, dissemination of radical ideology by itinerant preachers). These factors politicize land, ethnic and economic conflicts and aggravate the fragility of states, whose presence is sometimes purely nominal in vast parts of the region's territories. The strategy of jihadi groups in the region is currently to establish themselves in areas that can provide both shelter and food, such as forests, parks, lakes and cross-border regions.[32]

Since 2011, Libya and Mali have been at the centre of the problems affecting the Sahara and the states of the Sahel, partly as a result of AQIM's looting of Libyan arsenals with support from the Islamist brigades in Cyrenaica. The communiqué of the ministerial conference held in Paris on 12 February 2013 highlighted "the urgent priority for Libya to effectively control its borders", thereby illustrating international community expectations concerning Libya's transition. Yet, even before the collapse of Qadhafi's regime, southern Libya and the Sahel were already causing concern. As Modibo Goïta, a Malian expert, pointed out in February 2011, "AQIM is increasingly well integrated into local Sahelian communities and many of its leaders are in collusion with public officials and security chiefs. If energetic measures are not taken to counteract AQIM's new strategy in the Sahel, the situation could lead to the establishment of sanctuaries, amounting to Waziristans in the Sahel."[33] Algeria's south-west, the mountainous areas of Timetrin in Mali, the north of Niger and Mauritania are areas where AQIM katibas (brigades) have been operating for many years.[34]

In the 2000s, the Sahel offered them a secure and lucrative environment. Learning from the experience of Algeria's GSPC, members of the LIFG took refuge in the area of Illizi, in Algeria, where several Sonatrach natural gas production facilities were located and where the local population was exasperated by the lack of economic benefits from the oil wealth. By some accounts, commenting on the attack on the In Amenas gas facility, young men in Tiguentourine said, "We don't give a damn if the complex burns. Anyway, Sonatrach has never done a thing for us." In March 2016, AQIM claimed to have "launched two ground-to-ground missiles and, one hour later, ten rockets" at the Kherichba gas facility, located 200 kilometres from Ain Salah and exploited by British Petroleum and Statoil. "We announce to all Western companies investing in shale gas [in southern Algeria] that we will target you in a direct way, and we will use all our capabilities to deter you from these projects." AQIM warned Algerians to stay away from Western oil and gas facilities, cleverly taking up the defence of local populations opposed to shale gas exploitation in southern Algeria. The disintegration of the Libyan state has enabled jihadi combatants to move about freely and preach in villages in neighbouring countries. Online videos show how the jihadis enter villages and urge the people to revolt and join them in the name of Islam: "We are Muslims, not Fulani, Toucouleur, Bambara, Tuareg, etc.," the jihadi combatants claim. Libya's descent into civil war has fostered the establishment of jihadi groups, which have set about destabilizing the region through repeated terrorist attacks in Tunisia's border regions, the Algerian Sahara and the countries of the Sahel.[35] The area must also contend with constant pressure from Boko Haram and propaganda promoting the caliphate by travelling preachers from neighbouring countries.[36] Permeable borders make it possible to carry out attacks throughout the Sahel and West Africa.[37] Burkina Faso, spared under Blaise Compaoré supposedly because of personal ties between the former president and terrorists,[38] has become the scene of a number of jihadi attacks.

The Appeal of Jihadi Groups

Why do people join jihadi groups? A number of authors have underscored the attraction that the radical ideology of jihadi Salafis holds for potential recruits. This radical current—jihadi Salafism—has long existed, but its appeal is recent in North Africa and in the Sahel. What could have happened to make this long-standing ideological offering attractive today? Several studies have highlighted the economic and social dimensions among the mobilizing factors:[39] jihadi groups are also economic operators who invest in and redistribute resources.

Jihadi groups such as the Islamic State in the Greater Sahara (ISGS), composed of West Africans in eastern Burkina Faso, have successfully established themselves by addressing the demands of the local population. According to various sources, members of ISGS are also former Movement for Oneness and Jihad in West Africa (MOJWA) members expelled from Gao, Mali. ISGS established itself in eastern Burkina Faso, a region considered to be one of the poorest in the country, despite its rich subsoil and soil and its high tourist potential.[40] The success of the jihadi foothold in the region may be explained by very negative representations of the state due to a feeling of abandonment. The question remains whether such a presence is sustainable. The choice of Park W, at the borders of Burkina, Niger and Benin, offers many opportunities: in the Gayeri region, a settlement strategy has been carried out since 2018. The death threats against all those who collaborate with the state underscore the will to impose a new political and religious order (women are forced to wear the veil, children are enrolled in Quranic schools, and so on). In return, jihadi groups allow local populations to defy prohibitions imposed by the authorities on hunting in protected areas, fishing, transhumance and gold panning.[41] Jihadi groups collect a tax (*zakat*) on livestock (1,500 CFA francs per cow): an estimate of Boko Haram's revenue in the region of Lake Chad shows that the various taxes on livestock generate a monthly income of one billion CFA. Such revenues attract all sorts of people who are willing to join the ranks of jihadi fighters if they generate lucrative activities. Former highway robbers and gangs of deserters find in Boko Haram a profitable outlet for their criminal deeds, endowing them with religious meaning.[42]

The experience of Islamic State in Sirte (June 2015–December 2016) is instructive: hundreds of African volunteers joined ISIS in this eponymous city. Chased from the town, jihadi combatants withdrew to the district of al-Jufrah, south of Sirte, in the Wadi al-Load and Wadi al-Bay valleys. After reorganizing, they carried out more than twenty terrorist attacks in 2018 against political institutions (ministry of foreign affairs in Tripoli; the Political Committee) and economic targets (the National Oil Company). Travellers were stopped at bogus road-blocks built on the Sebha–Jufrah road and forced to pay a tax. Like other non-jihadi armed groups, criminal groups in southern Libya take part in smuggling of migrants, particularly from Sudan. The spread of Islamic State fighters in the Sahara is reminiscent of the dispersion of jihadi fighters chased from northern Mali.

It should be noted that seven years after Operation Serval, even if jihadist groups in north Mali have been run out of their sanctuary, they have moved to bordering states and are seeking other refuge areas. With the emergence of Katiba Macina (or Macina Liberation Front) in central Mali in 2015, the entire region has been plunged into a state of insecurity as a result of murder and kidnapping. For some observers, the region has become the "epicentre of jihadism". Jihadi groups have succeeded in settling in territories where the population feels abandoned and where state structures are failing. The disintegration of Libya and the implosion of Mali have given jihadis the opportunity to create new bonds of solidarity and loyalty in sub-Saharan Africa that cut across the borders and identities developed during the colonial period. The jihadi enterprise is reflected in the restoration of religious, cultural and economic ties between populations whose lives had been deeply affected by the divergent foreign policies of states in the region. The reconfiguration of this area seems obvious because movement and circulation are easy in areas structured by traditions of exchange and demographic pressure. Disruption of agro-pastoral modes due to global warming and land pressure has resulted in internal migration, generating conflicts between communities.[43]

THE DECONSTRUCTION OF NATION-STATES

The appeal of jihadism in the region is also fuelled by a rejection of the West in general and of France in particular, as a former colonial power. Jihadism holds sway in a context characterized by weak states, poor governance, poverty and crime. These factors heighten feelings of injustice and humiliation among populations who feel, rightly or wrongly, abandoned by the state. In an environment considered corrupt, impure and dishonest, jihadis offer an alternative based on a Salafi-inspired radical ideology of the social order. The development of Salafism has thus brought about a questioning of religious tradition and practices and a moralization of manners and customs to such an extent that it provokes tensions and clashes. Sectarian Islam encouraged a grounding of Islam in this sect and produced its current structures, but today jihadi Salafis are rejecting it. In 2015, Boko Haram joined this radical tendency of Sunni Islam when its leader, Abubakar Shekau, swore allegiance to the ISIS caliphate installed in Iraq and Syria.

Saudi Wahhabi religious entrepreneurs started promoting this radical (quietist or pious Salafi) interpretation of Islam after the Iranian revolution of 1979, encouraging a rigorous and fundamentalist interpretation of Islam in Africa. Those working to spread this version of Islam are students who go to study in Saudi Arabia; Islamic NGOs which, through social service organizations, foster the "Wahhabization" of Islam; and Saudi-trained imams who preach in mosques funded by wealthy merchants.[44] The jihadi version has been adopted by organizations such as al-Qaeda and ISIS since the 11 September 2001 attacks, and it encourages terrorism. Various American, Russian and French military interventions over the past twenty years in the Middle East, the Caucasus and more recently in Libya and Mali, have fanned an anti-Western jihadi ideology. Al-Qaeda and IS have been very well received by the many local jihadi groups in Algeria, Libya, Mali, Nigeria and north Cameroon (AQIM, MOJWA, Boko Haram and so on), resulting in their joining forces.[45]

The success with which Wahhabi Islam spread throughout Africa fits within a particular political context. As a result of cuts in international development aid and the destructive effects of the structural adjustment plans of the 1980s, the Gulf countries largely contributed to taking on some of the aid and invested heavily in the education and religious training sectors. Wahhabi ideology resonates with the younger generation, as a number of field studies point out, particularly in Burkina Faso, Guinea, Côte d'Ivoire and Benin, given the material and symbolic advantages it carries.[46] In West Africa, from the 1980s, the Islamic banks also encouraged the propagation of Wahhabism.[47] While officially they offered loans and banking facilities on the basis of strictly "Islamic" banking guidelines, they provided a powerful means for Wahhabis in Guinea to obtain loans, donations and funding that enabled them to recruit thousands of Guineans in Conakry living in working-class neighbourhoods in the outer suburbs. The Guinean authorities left to Saudi Arabia the role of training religious personnel. Hundreds of theology scholarships were offered in Saudi universities. On returning to their country, these students became imams in mosques built with funding from Saudi Arabia, Kuwait and Qatar and propagated a Salafi interpretation of Islam that is at odds with the Sufi brotherhoods and masters. In Mali, Sufis in the Group of Muslim Spiritual Leaders accuse the Wahhabis of promoting violence and supporting terrorism.[48] Salafi-leaning Quranic schools purport to replace the "Islam of the forefathers" with an "Islam of God".[49] In northern Cameroon, Muslim students rarely go to public school, owing to the prohibition issued by marabouts on attending public schools, considered bastions of Christianity. As a result, Muslims in northern Cameroon are some of the least schooled communities in the country.[50] This state of tension about the place of Islam in society provides fertile ground for the Salafis, who are welcomed within the Fulani community in particular, a community that has particularly suffered from abandonment by the state.

In Côte d'Ivoire, Wahhabism is the most orthodox strand within the Muslim community.[51] Although the causes of violent extremism in Côte d'Ivoire are many and cannot be boiled down to a single factor,[52] there is an urgent need to restore national cohesion. The ethnic, religious and geographical fault lines dividing the nation provide levers that foster the establishment of jihadi groups. The disputed election of Laurent Gbagbo to the presidency in 2000 reinforced the logic of a claimed division between a "Muslim north and a Christian south", despite the contrary evidence of the demographic data from the 1998 and 2014 censuses.[53] The occupation of the country's north after rebellion broke out in 2002 was accompanied by a process of political radicalization. Alassane Ouattara's victory in 2010 and his power grab after the "battle of Abidjan" in spring 2011 occurred in a context in which Gbagbo's evangelist supporters did not give up hope of his return being enabled by "divine intervention". The risk lies in the fact that Christian Ivoirians suspect the Muslims in the northern border regions of being sympathetic toward jihadi groups, either out of self-interest because of the profits made in cross-border trafficking or out of religious conviction. Furthermore, the uneven and incomplete disarmament policy has encouraged the development of countless criminal-related activities. In the context of a weak state, this phenomenon heightens the sense of insecurity among populations that already feel abandoned.[54] Endemic youth unemployment in these regions only aggravates conditions that are conducive to the establishment of jihadi groups.[55]

The fact remains that serious concerns have been expressed about countries such as Côte d'Ivoire and Cameroon. As an Institute for Security Studies report published in 2015 points out:

> Religious radicalism in Côte d'Ivoire has not, for the moment, reached the scale seen elsewhere in the region. However, the country is not immune to the phenomenon … The crisis in neighbouring Mali, which has highlighted the existence of a jihadist terrorist threat, as well as the Boko Haram insurgency in north-eastern Nigeria illustrate the problem of radicalism that currently affects Islam. This context highlights the relevance of investigating the existence of trends, sources or risks of development of certain types of fundamentalism and violent extremism within the Islam practised in Côte d'Ivoire.[56]

The fear is that the outbreaks of violence that have occurred in various countries of Central and West Africa will plunge the region into chaos similar to the Middle East. The exponential growth of jihadi groups is fuelled by societal conflicts. Moreover, by terrorizing civilians in the areas it controls, Boko Haram manages to levy taxes that supply it with a considerable source of revenue. The fact that Boko Haram leaders belong to the Bornuan ethnic group does not make this people a natural accomplice to their actions. Bornuans are, moreover, not the only Muslims in this border region.[57]

Clearly, jihadi groups manage to establish themselves effectively in territories where the population feels abandoned and government structures are failing. Since the 1970s, the Islamist utopia has been built on a devaluation of the state, described as *Taghut*, a Western import that divides the Muslim community.[58] ISIS in the Middle East, or Daesh, was the first experiment in building a transnational political order on the deconstruction of the borders drawn during the colonial period. The disintegration of Libya and the implosion of Mali have given jihadis the opportunity to produce new ties of solidarity and loyalty in North Africa and sub-Saharan Africa that cut across the borders and identities fashioned during the colonial period. Nationalist ideology, for instance, provided the fuel for political movements a half-century ago in the region; today it is devoid of meaning for the local populations. The spread of jihadi ideology is combined with the construction of a new model of political organization based on a re-reading and "revolution-ary" interpretation of Islam: restoration of the caliphate, establishment of an emirate, and so on. The jihadi enterprise takes shape in the re-establishment of religious, cultural and economic ties among the populations of North Africa and the Sahel, ties that had been considerably loosened as a result of the divergent foreign policies of governments in the region. Reconfiguration of this space seems straightforward in view of the ease of transport and demographic pressure.[59] The authorities have thus attempted to devise a border control policy with EU support in order to restore a sense of security. For it to be lasting, it requires faith in state institutions and especially the effective participation of local communities and actors in the mechanisms of prevention and response. National cohesion remains a goal to be achieved. Public land, development, education and social policies can help to reduce territorial fractures as well as hostile religious and political representations and perceptions. To avoid sinking into a war without end, the fight against "Islamist terrorism" must be conducted within the perspective of restoring or installing state institutions in the region, and devising mechanisms able to produce security and trust, so as to provide justice and combat the region's extreme poverty.

The Arab revolts gave a chance for Islamist movements, parties and groups that had been harassed and banned in the 1990s and 2000s, to seek revenge. Although they were absent in the early stages of the uprisings and revolutions, the Islamists quickly turned to their advantage the political and social opportunities offered by the weakening and eventual toppling of regimes. From Tunisia to Libya, they emerged as formidable political forces. Tunisia's Ennahda Party and Libya's Justice and Construction Party snatched political victories that handed them majorities in parliamentary assemblies. They became part of the state machinery and were complacent about jihadi groups that wanted to exploit the disintegration of the Libyan state and the weakening of Tunisia's security apparatus after Ben Ali's ouster. It was revenge for the Nahdaouis, for when Ben Ali came to power in 1987, the Ennahda movement was beheaded and a police regime installed.

In Morocco, the Islamist Justice and Development Party (JDP) won the legislative elections and governed under a new constitution. Under Hassan II, the interior minister Driss Basri's *adab sultaniya* (art of government) encouraged strict control of the Islamists, which suggested that the king's status as Emir el-Mu'minin (Commander of the Faithful) made Moroccan society immune to the "Islamist virus". But Mohammed VI's accession to the throne and his desire to establish a fair and democratic regime were accompanied by the rise of the JDP, which aroused concerns about the real or imagined strength of Islamists in the kingdom. In Morocco and in Algeria, moderate Islamist parties serve to channel this social and religious discontent. The JDP acts as a safeguard against the radicalization of Islamist tendencies. But for how long? Like Algeria, Morocco, with its glaring inequalities and mass youth unemployment, provides fertile ground for radical Islamist organizations ready to embark on a strategy of violence. Many are those who joined the ranks of AQIM or ISIS after the revolts of 2011 and were involved in attacks in Europe. Added to the collapse of certain Arab states, there is now the risk of seeing the countries of the Sahara and the Sahel also descend into violence, given the growing success of jihadi groups established in the region. Jihadis are like the pirates of precolonial Maghreb who sowed terror in the Mediterranean. This threat was ultimately answered precisely by colonization of the region in order to destroy the "Barbary states" protecting them.[60] Foreign military interventions revive fears of the former colonial powers re-establishing a presence in the region on the pretext of bringing security to friendly or partner countries in the framework of a policy of combating "Islamist terrorism".

129

8

SECURITY BREAKDOWN
AND REGIONAL DISINTEGRATION

The security disaster resulting from the civil war in Libya and the conquest of northern Mali by AQIM and its allies shattered hopes of a
peaceful political transition. North Africa's southern frontiers drew
attention because the Sahel–Sahara borders became the epicentre of
the restructuring of jihadi groups in the region.[1] The wonderment and
enthusiasm with which the world beheld the Arab revolts at first were
swept away by concern and then the threat of an entire region descending into lawlessness and violence. No sooner had it come into being
than Tunisia's democracy had to face economic and security challenges
that threatened to be its undoing. The collapse of tourism aggravated
social tensions that were already running high. Thus, after the revolutions in Tunisia and Libya, the failures of the 20 February Movement in
Morocco and the Coordination for Change and Democracy in Algeria
came as a relief to the European Union (EU). Indeed, these two countries appeared to be the last pillars of stability in the region. A transition to democracy is no longer on the agenda: in January 2013, the
French military intervention in northern Mali (Operation Serval)
reactivated the security paradigm throughout the region.[2] The fight
against Islamist terrorism in the form of al-Qaeda and ISIS became an
imperative for the French defence minister.[3] The Tunisian authorities
managed to prevent Ansar al-Sharia from sabotaging the political tran-

sition and making Tunisia a "land of jihad", as was the ambition of its leader, Abu Ayadh, but the exact opposite came about in post-Qadhafi Libya, as the preceding chapters have shown.

Whereas the Algerian civil war (1991–1999) took place behind closed doors, so to speak,[4] the Libyan civil war was fought by regional and international powers.[5] After NATO's controversial intervention,[6] support for the various protagonists given by countries such as Turkey, Qatar, the United Arab Emirates, Egypt and Russia turned the failure of Libya's political transition into a regional war pitting states with divergent visions and interests against one another. In this tragedy, the United States and the EU, although they were responsible through NATO for the overthrow of the Qadhafi regime, were marginalized in a conflict and in a region that is strategic for security reasons, in particular for Europe.[7] As has already been pointed out in the preceding chapters, this security disaster in North Africa and the Sahel presents a threat not only to the countries in the region, but also to economic sectors such as the hydrocarbon, mining and tourism industries. Thousands of foreign companies established in the region face security issues unparalleled since the wave of independence.

Regional Disintegration

Long past are the times when there was a shared dream of regional integration. In 1989, the countries of North Africa had plans to unite within the Arab Maghreb Union (AMU). After 2011, each of them barricaded itself behind its borders. In this security-anxious chaos, Morocco looked to Africa to broaden its horizons.[8] Given the absence of perspective from the EU, the states of North Africa were prompted to reconsider their neighbourhood relations and focus on Africa. Prior to that, only Qadhafi's Libya had devoted to the continent the attention it deserved.[9] In May 1997, Libya was promoting the Community of Sahel and Saharan States (COMESSA), which first included six and then ten African states. At the Organization of African Unity (OAU) summit, Qadhafi put forward the idea of a constitution for the "United States of Africa" and laid out an ambitious plan for the development of the continent:

> An entity that will be known as the United States of Africa … will be the historic solution for the continent … As I see it, Africa is abso-

lutely not a poor continent. Perhaps cash is lacking, but it has resources and raw materials. I regard Africa as a rich continent. However, the capitalist countries have put a veto on Africa. They don't want our continent to develop. They want to keep Africa as it is, in order to steal its raw materials.[10]

In 2002, Libya had brought over 130 projects to fruition in 26 sub-Saharan countries, having invested as much as $4 billion.[11]

The United States of Africa represented an opportunity to set up the infrastructure needed to attract foreign investment, the creation of a fund for Africa, an African development bank, and, especially, a single currency for Africa. Such a plan could have offered a solution for all the border security and demarcation problems. Instead of seeking to alter borders through conflict, with the risk of seeing foreign powers inter-fere, Colonel Qadhafi claimed that they should simply be abolished: "If the decision were made to allow Africans to travel freely and live in any country on the continent, we would sidestep the problem of frontiers. Africa is not like Europe. Europe is made up of nations. Africa is made up of tribes. The tribes were torn apart by the colonizing powers. The state in Africa cannot survive, as it is artificial." From this perspective, Africa would be better equipped than Europe to become a "United States" than would Europe. "In Africa," he said, "there is one race—the black race—united and composed of various tribes." The disintegration of Libya put an end to this project and consequently opened up migra-tion routes toward Europe for African emigrants. Libya became a high-way for migrants to Europe and a safe haven for jihadis.

In Europe, concerns of seeing the continent submerged by "waves of migration" and terrorist attacks have never been higher. With the attacks in Paris in November 2015, in Brussels in March 2016, and then in Barcelona in August 2017, to mention only these three, the terrorist threat has become tangible. In 2016, terrorist attacks claimed the lives of 270 persons,[12] and more than 5,000 European Muslims went off to join ISIS ranks between 2014 and 2016.[13] Jihadi groups have revived ancient fears that have punctuated the long history of the Mediterranean on both shores. In his book *L'an mil*, the historian Georges Duby recalls the main external threats facing the continent: they came from the Vikings, Magyars and Saracens. One thousand years later, Scandinavian countries are peaceful democracies envied by all.[14]

The Magyars have become Hungarians who, although still unruly under Viktor Orban's rule, have become part of the EU.[15] While Europe no longer appears to be plagued by any particular threat to the north and to the east, the "Saracens" in the south, under different guises and denominations, continue to arouse fear and worry. Security policy in the Mediterranean is constructed around new figures adding to the litany of fears in the West:[16] the migrant and the terrorist. Security policy in the Mediterranean was built around several threats.[17] The migratory threat, however, was the dominant paradigm until the 11 September 2001 attacks, at which time the figure of the terrorist supplanted that of the migrant. With the Arab revolutions, the two figures have merged into a single threat: the figure of the jihadist lurks behind the migrant, driven as he is by hatred of the West and its lifestyle.

Saif al-Islam Qadhafi's Predictions

In fact, until the Arab Spring, the EU was living under the illusion that it was in control of its neighbourhood policy (ENP) in North Africa, which defined a new framework of relations with countries not eligible to join the Union. Libya's implosion turned this territory into a transit corridor toward Italy for hundreds of thousands of Africans, while the war in Syria caused millions of refugees to flee their homeland.[18] A half-million Libyans fled to Tunisia, and three million Syrians fled to Turkey and Europe. African migrants began trying to leave Libya, which had welcomed them under Qadhafi but afterward turned them into scapegoats for the country's problems.[19] Racism against Africans became rampant, and Libya's two million African residents also began trying to reach Europe. Migrant smuggling became organized, and Libya became a hub of the criminal economy.[20] The EU's entire migration control policy collapsed. Saif al-Islam Qadhafi's predictions, made on the eve of the regime's overthrow, proved accurate: "If the Europeans don't assist us, Libya could become a Mediterranean Somalia ... There will be pirates off the coast of Sicily, Crete and Lampedusa. There will be millions of migrants, terror will be at your door." In August 2017, in an interview following a meeting with the then French foreign affairs minister, Jean-Yves Le Drian, Johannes Hahn, commissioner for the

European Neighbourhood Policy and Enlargement Negotiations, pointed out, "The European Union is surrounded on its southern flank by 20 to 25 million potential migrants, 90% of them for economic reasons and therefore not eligible to seek asylum."

Throughout the entire first decade of the 2000s, the EU strove to devise a border control policy. It imploded under the battering of revolutions and wars in North Africa and the Middle East. Migrants from sub-Saharan Africa seized the opportunity of the collapse of states (and migration control policies) to leave countries at war or those considered the world's poorest. Qadhafi's Libya had previously acted as a bulwark against the tide of migration. Its good relationship with Italy prevented the more than two million Africans living in the country from migrating. Under Qadhafi, smuggler networks were controlled by the Revolutionary Committees, true pillars of the regime. The NATO-backed ouster of Colonel Qadhafi shattered a pillar in the struggle to curb migrations.[21]

The migratory threats following the Arab uprisings have actually merely accentuated the basic tendency of the EU to "militarize" the struggle against migrants. A considerable body of academic research has highlighted the security rationale underlying migration policy. The criminalization of irregular migrants has encouraged the emergence of a policy to combat migration which has resulted in the constant tightening of the border control apparatus. Anastassia Tsoukala's research shows, for instance, how public debate on immigration in Europe has often focused on the threat rather than the advantages immigrants represent for the internal security of the host country.[22] In addition to the tightening of internal border controls, there has been a toughening of external control through the militarization of frontiers. Derek Lutterbeck's research shows how the fight against illegal migrants in the Mediterranean has become a regional security issue and hence one of international cooperation (e.g. Operation Amarante, Operation Ulysses, Operation Active Endeavour, Frontex and so on).[23] As Jean-Pierre Cassarino points out, several policing and border management efforts have enabled various Mediterranean third countries, such as the Maghreb states, to become involved in a new framework of exchange and cooperation with the EU and its member states. As a consequence of these bilateral initiatives, certain Mediterranean third countries have gained not only considerable international credibility in the field of border management cooperation in the Euro-Mediterranean area, but also a strategic position which they intend to capitalize on.[24]

The migratory threat has coalesced around the demographic and economic differential between the two shores of the Mediterranean. Thus in the course of the 1980s, a Mediterranean security policy began to take shape through the "five plus five dialogue" bringing together the five Western European states and the five Arab Maghreb Union states.[25] On the premise that problems south of the Mediterranean were security issues for the north, states on either shore institutionalized the fight against transnational criminal organizations. The countries of North Africa became specialized and leveraged their expertise to enhance their special relationship with the EU. The Kingdom of Morocco came to play a pivotal role in the policy to fight illegal migration, and, along with Tunisia, it provides holding centres for expelled illegal migrants, while Algeria acts as an expert in the fight against terrorism, in which it has been participating actively since the 11 September 2001 attacks. In the early 2000s, Qadhafi's Libya exploited the migratory threat and the fight against terrorism to make a successful, though short-lived, return to grace in the international community. The countries of the Sahel were conspicuously absent from this security policy until Libya's collapse, a reversal that has turned them into central actors.

Border Control

After the Arab revolutions of 2011, the border management issue became a security issue: each country suspects its neighbour of being incapable of securing its borders.[26] The budding Tunisian democracy is the victim of attacks perpetrated by Tunisian members of AQIM hiding out in Libya, which threaten to sink into lawlessness; Algerian natural gas production sites in the Sahara have been targeted by jihadi groups also established in Libya;[27] the countries of West Africa that backed France's policy of military intervention have also been the target of terrorist attacks from jihadi groups from Libya and Mali. Throughout the entire first decade of the 2000s, Mauritania was the focus of attention and the subject of concern due to the development of jihadi groups in its territory.[28] From 2012, the securing of borders became an international problem, and a European one in particular, in view of Libya's collapse. While governments in North Africa are being threatened by revolt, revolution and insurgency, Europe pressures them to consider tightening their borders as an international security priority.

Jean-Paul Laborde, executive director of the UN Counter-Terrorism Committee, stated in an interview: "The big problem is the extreme porosity of borders. To fight an enemy on the move, it requires matériel and well-trained intelligence, customs and police officers. What is happening in the Sahel concerns all of us in Europe. The dismantling of Islamist groups in northern Mali probably helped to prevent terrorist attacks on European soil."[29] Securing borders has become a political imperative and a lucrative business. After the migratory threat, transnational organized crime has spawned a "regional security complex",[30] producing an unrealistic project of sealing borders.[31] For countries in the region, the need to secure borders has resulted in the deployment of resources in areas that were relatively abandoned until then. Investment in border security is carried out to the detriment of development assistance to the countries concerned. Moreover, the fight against jihadi groups exacerbates conflict between the state and marginalized populations such as the Fulani in central Mali, who are victims of both climate change and economic policies.[32]

In fact, pressure from the international community was intended to remind the political regimes weakened by the Arab Spring that "a border makes possible an act of real or symbolic authority that serves to consolidate state power".[33] From Tunisia to Mali, border control symbolizes the desire for the return of the state. As Michel Foucher commented, "For the state, borders are the theatre where the legitimacy of its power is closely observed. There is nothing more disastrous for a sovereign power than to be accused of losing control over its borders."[34] In answer to concerns aroused by the "loss" of border control in the region, Algeria pointed out that, since 2006, it had deployed a network of electronic surveillance in its Saharan border areas and that, since 2015, it had been installing military outposts there. For indeed, after the Arab Spring, the discourse about insecurity at the borders heightened people's fears about the regime's stability. Algeria was afraid that it was the object of a conspiracy. In Morocco, border insecurity gave rise to plans to build a barbed wire fence along its border with Algeria to highlight Morocco's exceptionality in the region. [35] As for Tunisia, beset by terrorist violence, its foreign minister, Othman Jerandi, stated during a visit to Algeria in August 2013 that "the Algerian [counterterrorism] experience is of interest to us". [36] After the spate of attacks in the Jebel Chaambi region near the Algerian border, Tunisians discovered with horror that some of their youth had fallen prey to this violent and radical ideology. [37] The Tunisian National Guard and the Algerian National Gendarmerie set up a programme to "share their experience". [38]

The overthrow of the Qadhafi regime in Libya and the French military intervention in northern Mali in 2013 drew the international community's attention to border security in the region. In the space of a few months, the southern borders of Algeria and Libya became the focus of a strategic threat likely to destabilize all the countries in the region. In terms of security risks, borders are associated with all manner of illegal trafficking: in cocaine, weapons, cigarettes and drugs. In addition to smuggling activities, the border area has become a sanctuary for terrorist groups such as AQIM, MOJWA and Ansar al-Dine. Until the Arab Spring, the Sahel was a field for anthropologists and historians. It now draws cohorts of experts funded by international security and development agencies tasked with identifying the flows and volumes of the various movements. The reports they write on the lack of security in the Sahel provide fodder for the policies devised upstream for military response and engagement. Transnational criminal organizations of smugglers and terrorists are considered vehicles for the destruction of a fragile or vulnerable state such as Mali. Among the security explanations used to account for the development of these transnational criminal organizations, the argument most often cited is the "political and security vacuum", into which the Sahel has descended because of its vast expanse and the weakness of the state. Yet, anthropologists and geographers remind us that ancient crossroads run through the Sahel, that it is an organized space in which people and goods move, and that the delimitation of borders following independence made certain exchanges unlawful. [39]

It should also be remembered that the outer limits of the Algerian Sahara stretch for over 6,000 km. The border with Libya was set for the first time by France in 1958 on the basis of an arrangement made in 1919. The frontiers with the Sahel countries were decided in an agreement concluded in 1905 between the French interior ministry, under whose jurisdiction Algeria was, and the minister of the colonies, who managed French West Africa ... The 1909 Niamey Conference included areas roamed by Adjer and Hoggar Tuareg in Algeria and territories of the Aïr and Ifora Tuareg in the former French Sudan ... Boundary conventions were concluded in 1983 with Mauritania, Mali and Niger on this basis.[40]

The End of Algerian–Libyan Joint Management of the Border

Algeria and Libya have always focused their attention on controlling their borders with the countries of the Sahel. Since their independence (1962 and 1951), officials in both countries have sought, instead of controlling these territories, to influence local actors by granting them financial and commercial advantages. Far from being an empty space where chaos rules, the borders with the Sahel have been a place where not only military might but the skills and knowledge of intelligence services are deployed. In this vast, sparsely inhabited space,[41] the Algerian and Libyan secret services encouraged an economy of contraband and smuggling that allowed the local populations to survive and permitted the security establishment to influence them. Algeria's objective, like that of Qadhafi's Libya, has always been to ensure that the vast Saharan areas do not become war zones endangering the security of their oil infrastructure, vital to the functioning of countries that are hyperdependent on hydrocarbon exports. For the Libyan and Algerian authorities, the only strategic threat—aside from Algeria's dispute with Morocco over Western Sahara—has always been located in the large, overpopulated coastal cities close to the symbolic seats of power. The insurrection in Benghazi in 2011, after the Islamist insurgency in the Mitidja region of Algeria in the 1990s, confirmed that for the powers that be the security threat came from the north and not from military surveillance of the Sahel borders. Algiers perceives the NATO-backed overthrow of the Qadhafi regime as a strategic error, because it has enabled local actors, both jihadis and those fighting for independence, to pursue their own agendas once freed of Libyan supervision. The Algiers Accords of 2006[42] were forgotten, and the

Tuareg in the National Movement for the Liberation of Azawad (MNLA) took the opportunity in January 2012 to make Amadou Toumani Touré, elected president of Mali in 2002 and re-elected in 2007, pay for his failure to honour his commitments and plunged Mali into war.[43]

Until the Arab revolts, the southern borders were under joint Algerian–Libyan management, with dramatic consequences for the stability of the Malian state. Already in July 2009, Algeria, Libya and Mali had pledged in vain to pool their military resources to combat insecurity in the Sahel–Sahara strip. Already then, regional and international cooperation appeared as a fundamental weapon to effectively combat both the AQIM threat and that of drug trafficking networks in the region. However, the Sahel remained the preserve of intelligence services for Algeria and Libya alike, which used the fight against al-Qaeda in the Islamic Maghreb to bring their countries back into favour with the international community and in particular with the United States. Furthermore, eager to keep the AQIM katibas at a distance from the capital, the Algerian security services strove to create conditions for their comfortable and lasting settlement in the Sahel. This was with the complicity of the then Malian president, Amadou Toumani Touré, who welcomed the establishment of these jihadis in the midst of Tuareg territory, as throughout the state's post-colonial history, the nomads have periodically risen up against the central Malian government.[44] Thus, fed by financial flows from smuggling and contraband, often controlled by middlemen located in Djanet, Tamanrasset and Ouargla, jihadis quickly became economic operators in the Sahel, providing sometimes vital resources to an indigent population. The Qadhafi regime used the cities of Sebha and Kufra to regulate transactions in the Sahel, enabling it to establish a large clientele there through its business connections. France's intervention in northern Mali upset the delicate balances that Algeria and Libya had carefully managed to achieve during the first decade of the 2000s. Most of all, it removed an economic actor—jihadi organizations—that had played a central role in redistributing wealth to populations abandoned by the public authorities in the two countries. It brought an end to the joint management of the Sahel by the Algerian and Libyan secret services whose objective was not to destroy these groups but to keep them as far away as possible from the urban areas in the north, hotbeds of the Islamist insurgencies in the 1990s.

The two countries had built up a policy of joint management of the border by wielding influence over local actors whom they either paid directly or permitted to make the most of their contraband activities. Algeria and Libya never had the ambition of controlling the border militarily; on the other hand, their respective security services sought to win clients that could be of use to them. Many local actors exploited the Algerian–Libyan co-management in the Sahel, not hesitating to sell their activities to the highest bidder. At the end of the first decade of the 2000s, Qadhafi's Libya was the main financier of a large number of local actors. Until Operation Serval, Algeria was convinced that it could deal with the jihadis in northern Mali because of its special relationship with Iyad Ag Ghali, leader of Ansar al-Dine. The National Movement for the Liberation of Azawad (MNLA) and Ansar al-Dine, joined by AQIM and MOJWA, drove out the Malian army and took control of northern Mali.[45] But very quickly, the MNLA "secularists" were overcome and chased out by the AQIM jihadis, who imposed their emirate in the Sahel.[46] Far from perceiving this development as a threat, Algeria hoped to recover its influence with the MNLA and Ansar al-Dine. It especially intended to prevent military intervention in a region where its secret services considered they had enough contacts (owing to a vast spy network) to maintain the status quo, even to provoke clashes between the organizations that had seized control of northern Mali. The Algerian government therefore refused to undertake a military intervention, fearing that AQIM or MOJWA would strike its oil facilities in the Sahara.

Thus, seen from Algiers, the overthrow of the Qadhafi regime torpedoed the painstaking effort of relocating jihadi groups toward the Sahel. After Qadhafi's overthrow, cities liberated in Libya soon became bastions of Salafi, Islamist and jihadi militias. It was the worst-case scenario for Algiers. With the Ennahda government in Tunisia (2012–2014) and the Muslim Brotherhood at the helm in Egypt—until President Morsi was toppled—Algeria felt surrounded. The authorities were convinced that a plot was being hatched against the country and that France had a hand in it. Instead of taking advantage of the "vacuum" in the Sahel caused by the end of the Qadhafi regime, the Algerian authorities turned their attention to the internal situation. Media hype associated the Arab Spring rebels with agents conspiring to destabilize the region. After the attack on the In Amenas gas facility, an editorial in *El Watan* dated 21 January 2013 wondered, "Is there an external threat facing the country? Who is really behind the attack on In Amenas and what is their goal?" It also noted, "Upon the fiftieth anniversary of its independence, Algeria has been put to the challenge of embarking on the path to democracy at the risk of seeing its territorial integrity damaged." The terrorist attack prompted the departure of major petroleum industry actors such as Statoil and BP as well as Japanese insurance companies involved in the energy sector.[47]

Operation Serval: An Intervention with Momentous Consequences

On 11 January 2013, French president François Hollande announced that French troops were being deployed in Mali on the grounds that "columns of hundreds of pick-up trucks out of nowhere had been detected heading toward Mali's south, putting the country, even the entire region, in danger."[48] This argument never convinced regional actors or international observers for that matter. Why did France intervene? What were the reasons behind such an operation whose consequences were incalculable? Like the US-led interventions in Afghanistan and in Iraq, to justify its action the French intervention played on the theme of the fight against transnational terrorism and the threat to the countries' stability. By deciding to expel the jihadi groups that had taken over northern Mali and providing military protection for the Malian state, did France fall into the jihadis' trap? Since their defeat in Algeria in the 1990s, these groups had indeed accused France of backing the Algerian military regime against the Armed Islamic Group (GIA). Abu Musab al-Suri, the architect of world terrorism, claimed:

> I recommended to the GIA emir at that time, Abu Abdallah Ahmad and his leadership, may God have mercy on them, that they strike deeply in France in order to deter and punish her for her war against the GIA and for the French support for the dictatorial military regime. I told them that it would be beneficial to draw France into an openly declared support for the Algerian regime, a support which existed, but only in secrecy. This will unify the Islamic nation around the jihad in Algeria as it unified the Islamic nation in Afghanistan against the Soviets.[49]

Under Jacques Chirac's presidency, the French authorities did their best never to let any support show for the "military junta" in Algiers even after the attack on the Saint-Michel railway station (RER) in Paris on 25 July 1995.

The construction of the Sahel as a source of strategic threat, due to the proliferation of Islamists groups, led to the French army intervention in northern Mali and then to a regional troop deployment. After Operation Serval, Operation Barkhane committed French troops to a permanent counterinsurgency effort against jihadi groups. But for these groups, France's intervention in the Sahel was a godsend. It enabled them to structure the jihad around a tangible, accessible, visible objective: France's departure. The goal of chasing France and the French out of the region was stated openly. After the nationalists in the 1950s and 1960s, it was now the jihadis' turn to expel the former colonizers, today called "infidels" or "invaders". Like the United States in the Middle East, France and its local allies in the Sahel have become the enemy for the "Muslims" to fight.

Driven out of their sanctuary, Islamist groups have moved into adjacent countries and are seeking to destabilize these as well, as the terrorist attacks in Côte d'Ivoire and Burkina Faso indicate. To secure their borders, the international community is promoting a policy of militarization, which is believed to be the only way to control local populations and Islamist groups hiding out among them. While countries such as Chad, Mali, Niger and Mauritania may derive diplomatic and financial benefits from their participation in this policy, it irritates others, such as Algeria, to see France return to the region. The EU and UN discourse on border security in the Sahel seems to be constructing a geopolitical space that supposedly represents values and interests common to all states facing the same threat. In short, it views North Africa and the Sahel as the South of Europe. Borders become the substance around which this discourse crystallizes, and Islamist groups become in spite of themselves the builders of the new security architecture in the Mediterranean and the Sahel. This aims to restore a political authority, the Malian state, in an environment considered lawless in which transnational criminal organizations such as AQIM and Boko Haram act with impunity.[50] From this standpoint, military intervention (be it in Afghanistan, Iraq or Mali) is a paradoxical instrument that at once pro-

143

duces violence and restores political institutions capable of buttressing a "failed state". The fact remains that this paradoxical instrument, far from restoring "societal security", causes upheaval in the region's political, ethnic and religious tectonic plates, further widening the abysses into which fall the civilian victims neglected by this strategy.

Has French military involvement contributed to enhancing the appeal of jihadism? It must be remembered that five years after Operation Serval, jihadi groups in northern Mali decided to form a united front. Worse: the peoples of northern Mali, like the Fulani in the centre, do not seem to be turning against them.[51] Perhaps this is because Operation Serval and subsequently Operation Barkhane remain misunderstood in North Africa and the states of the Sahel. After the NATO-backed overthrow of the Qadhafi regime, Operation Serval appears to have been yet another factor of regional destabilization. The failure on France's part to explain to the populations of North Africa and the Sahel the reasons and objectives of its intervention has fostered the development of conspiracy theories.

France's active military engagement against the jihadis in Iraq and in the Sahel is one of the reasons given to explain terrorist attacks on its mainland. When Bernard Cazeneuve, former French interior minister and then prime minister, was asked in May 2016 "Why is France such a target for the jihadis?" his answer was explicit: "First, because the terrorists hate what France represents: liberty, secularism, equality between men and women, the ability to live together, the values of the republic. Second, because we are resolutely engaged against terrorists abroad: against ISIS in Syria and in Iraq, but also against AQIM in Mali."[52] French interventions are part of the war against terrorism launched by the Bush administration in the wake of the 11 September 2001 attacks. And yet, jihadi groups have grown exponentially and the areas where they hold appeal stretch across continents and countries. Is the war not a losing battle? How could the French forces possibly defeat in such a vast territorial expanse an invisible enemy to whose cause the local population is sympathetic? On 13 February 2016, AQIM put online a 14-minute video entitled "From the Depths of the Sahara". The narrator boasts of AQIM's victory against France:

> Praise be to Allah, for it has been three years since the start of this criminal war, and the French media should ask their president these

questions: What has France achieved in this war after three years? Did it wipe out terrorism in northern Mali? Did it eradicate it from the Sahel region in Africa? Has it guaranteed the security of its subjects and soldiers in African countries? Has it brought security to its own capital and has it intercepted mujahideen strikes?[53]

The French authorities naturally hope to ensure and step up regional military involvement (by the G5 and Algeria) in the fight against jihadis. But isn't such a hope anachronistic? Algeria's reservations about Operation Serval illustrate the difficulties of having the former colonial power establish a military presence in the region. Faced with a sentiment of distrust, countries in the region are seeking more to benefit from the French intervention than to go off to fight an enemy with whom they will necessarily have to make peace later. The French reading of the war against terrorism out of context has led to a strategic impasse: jihadi groups in the Sahel do not bear comparison with ISIS in Syria and in Iraq. Combatants of Ansar al-Dine and MOJWA or the rebels in the Macina region come from Mali's constituent communities: Tuareg, Fulani, Songhai and so on. The jihad in the Sahel does not draw radicalized "nihilists" from the West:[54] jihadi groups espouse local causes (property rights and communal conflicts, for instance)[55] and mesh with, rather than transform, local communities, as shown in the preceding chapter. Peace will therefore require reintegrating them in the national community, as with the Algerian jihadi groups under the Civil Concord law. Moreover, the two regional powers, Morocco and Algeria, are working in the Sahel with the conviction that the longer France remains in the region, the more the populations will turn against it. Morocco is therefore developing its strategy in Africa in the guise of a benevolent power concerned with economic and religious issues. Thus, as France's image—a military one—deteriorates among the region's people, Morocco's grows more attractive.

Algeria is afraid of joining the list of countries which, like Pakistan, after having enjoyed a guaranteed income associated with the military presence of great powers in their regional environment, have wound up having to deal with an area that has been ravaged and abandoned by those same powers once their exclusively militaristic policy reaches its limits. The Moroccan monarch's attendance at President Ibrahim Boubacar Keïta's swearing in ceremony aroused worry and incomprehension in Algeria because Algeria's support for Operation Serval resulted in Morocco's bursting onto the stage in an area that Algeria believed was under its influence. Morocco is seeking to play a role from Bamako to Tripoli, as outlined in the Rabat Declaration of 14 November 2013, in which it committed itself in particular to "exchanging information related to border security between the countries of the region, and coordinating cooperation between authorities charged for border security, in order to evaluate and confront the security threats detected …; reinforcing the capacity of the countries of the region, as to new equipment and technologies …; mobilizing adequate financial resources".[56]

Subtly and cleverly, the Kingdom of Morocco has managed to reap the diplomatic benefits of Operation Serval, as these statements indicate. Morocco is intent on playing a key role in both Mali and in Libya, and the establishment of a "regional centre for training officers in charge of border security in the states of the region"[56] provides it with an instrument through which to wield its influence. Furthermore, the Moroccan kingdom's declared willingness to meet "the specific needs of the population groups in the border areas" is seen by Algeria as potentially putting "the Tuareg question" on the agenda. In the face of Algeria's unconditional support for the Sahrawi movement, Morocco now has considerable means of retaliation with "the Tuareg question". In short, if Algeria still hopes to cause Morocco to lose the territory of Western Sahara, Morocco may raise "the Tuareg question" and its claims on Azawad, which includes part of southern Algeria. Operation Serval has enabled Morocco, which already has strong influence in Mauritania and in Senegal, to expand its sectarian networks in the Sahel and throughout West Africa. Furthermore, the kingdom maintains excellent relations with the Gulf monarchies, some of which, such as Qatar, have ties with local militias in Misrata, Libya. This rivalry between Algeria and Morocco in the Sahel cripples attempts to reach a solution for Western Sahara.[58]

The Western Sahara conflict—forgotten, in limbo, at an impasse—is hostage to a clash between two powers, Algeria and Morocco, which have sought to expand their influence beyond the borders drawn during the colonial period. The Sahrawi population is caught between the Moroccan Scylla, which made the strategic decision to annex the territory ceded by Spain in 1976, and the inflexible Algerian Charybdis, which demands a referendum on self-determination, as provided by international law since the UN peace plan. With no political solution in sight, the population is left to receiving humanitarian aid, which absolves the main parties responsible for the stalemate. From the time the conflict began, Algeria under Boumediene took a stand in favour of the Sahrawi so as to prevent its neighbour from expanding its territory in the Sahara, whose economic and energy resources remain unexploited. As for the Hassan II monarchy, it considered that Algeria's territory was a gift from colonial France to Algiers, to the detriment of Rabat. It did not comprehend Algeria's aversion to seeing Morocco gain strategic depth in the Sahara, which it viewed as recovered territory after the hiatus of the Spanish protectorate (1884–1976). It felt betrayed by non-compliance with commitments made in 1961 stipulating that the Provisional Government of Algeria recognized "that the territorial dispute created by an arbitrary delineation imposed by France was ultimately to be resolved by direct negotiations between Morocco and Algeria".[59] It wasn't until Hassan II's visit to Algiers in 1968 that Morocco would relinquish its territorial claims. "Morocco's claims on Algerian and Mauritanian land were utopian and stood as an obstacle to beneficial cooperation in the region."[60] This stance paved the way for the Skhirat agreement in 1969 and a thaw in Algerian–Moroccan relations. However, the Western Sahara conflict paralyses the region and hampers any plans for economic integration. The states of North Africa have turned their backs on one another and conduct foreign policies that pull them even further apart.

North Africa: What Type of Neighbourhood Relations?

In 2006–2010, opinion polls conducted in three Maghreb countries[61] provided a snapshot of the population's expectations and frustrations prior to the Arab revolts with respect to the failure to achieve regional integration through the Arab Maghreb Union (AMU). A JDP activist said, "the Sahara problem was always a golden opportunity for the late King Hassan II to put before the people a single enemy and thus mask the country's social and economic realities so as not to deal with them". But for one Istiqlal activist, Algeria is to blame:

> Our Algerian brothers, may God guide them on the right path, have been the root of this problem since 1962. They have much greater

means than their neighbours; the Algerian military does not want a strong Morocco, it wants an agrarian Morocco and Tunisia so as to supply the Algerian market. In the mid-1970s, Algeria took in all the opponents to Hassan II's regime. It's dangerous for us that Algeria backs Polisario, it is even a danger for Algeria with the Tuareg problem. The climate between Algeria and Morocco today is highly charged.[62]

For Algeria, the major challenge since independence has been to preserve its territorial integrity. The territorial fragmentation that has affected the Arab world revives this concern: from Libya to Iraq and southern Sudan, separatist threats have become political realities. Thus, the army continues to perceive the demands of the Azawad movement and correlatively "the Tuareg question" as attempts to deprive Algeria of its Sahara. Since the creation of the Common Organization of Saharan Regions (OCRS) in 1957, the Hoggar Tuareg's refusal to take part in the war of independence (1954–1962)[63] and then the Tuareg revolts, the Algerian authorities have consistently viewed Tuareg demands as a threat to their territorial integrity. The Algerian authorities took the Azawad declaration of independence in 2012 as a declaration of war.

Political parties and representatives of civil society viewed the AMU as a necessity. "The world is tending to form economic, political and geostrategic groupings; that standpoint, it won't work if we go our own way," one socialist party (FFS) activist affirmed.[64] "With globalization," says an MSP (Hamas) activist, "we're obliged to unite. The whole world is forming groups ... the AMU countries negotiate individually ... Now, to be powerful, Algeria needs a strong AMU." For the moderate Islamist party, "The AMU is a step toward the Umma, that is what we in Hamas believe. We have to get beyond our divergences, move toward a union such as the EU."[65] A similar attitude is found in a member of JDP: "The future of Morocco is tied in with the Islamic Umma, the future of the AMU is to be apprehended within the larger entity of the third world. The future of the third world is our future. We must band together. That way the EU and the US will have more respect for us."[66] A member of Justice and Spirituality dares to go further, stating, "We are for the Islamic caliphate ... The people must unite in the name of God. We must unite and only the Muslim faith is able to bring us together, to succeed in achieving economic unity. The issue today is to come back to Allah and the right path in the framework of Islam ..."[67] This religious interpretation of unity is rejected by those who prefer the nationalist North African Star (ENA, Etoile Nord Africaine, the Algerian nationalist organization founded in 1926) organization to the AMU: "there are peoples in North Africa," says one Workers' Party activist, "and not only Muslims." Given the failure of integration, one member of FLN wanted to see it imposed by the EU: "it will take external pressure. The EU must impose this integration. People request visas to leave ... *Harragas* put their lives in danger to flee poverty, facing barbed wire fences and other dangers."[68]

In fact, between 1960 and 1980, the effect of policies to strengthen the state began to be felt. Agreements on the delimitation of land and maritime boundaries were ratified, considerably diminishing territorial disputes. There remained, however, the thorny Western Sahara problem, which became an issue of regional leadership and a stimulus for nationalism in both Morocco and Algeria. Throughout the formerly colonized territories, the state deployed its resources and its control. Some regions were favoured to the detriment of others, either for political reasons or because of economic priorities. An administration developed so as to accompany the political ambition of establishing a strong state that could control its populations. With the exception of the war of 1963, border delineation was not a factor of war or violence in North Africa. A number of bilateral accords reinforced an approach based on negotiation and warded off the spectre of clashes between neighbours. This was the period which saw the emergence of the utopia of regional integration in the context of a Maghreb united against France.

The independent states of North Africa failed to achieve Maghreb unity. The Western Sahara conflict was the main impediment to building the AMU. It illustrates Algeria's and Morocco's inability since the 1963 "sand war" to overcome a relationship based on mistrust and sometimes outright hostility. The Western Sahara conflict has proved to be mainly a tremendous political opportunity for the two countries to assert their authority. The political leaders were accused of being primarily responsible for this failure. Yet, in the 1990s, in the face of threats related to Islamist dissent, "the Moroccan and Algerian interior ministries met with a view to reinforcing their cooperation in security matters, even if not all suspicions have been lifted." Unlike Algeria,

Morocco and Libya, Ben Ali's Tunisia (1987–2011) often indicated its faith in the project. In July 1991, Ben Ali affirmed that "the AMU has a future. We believe in it and are working in this direction. The greater Maghreb is not only an ideal, it is also a requirement of our time." In the "Destour doctrine", "officials responsible for the Tunisian economy had gained the conviction since 1962 that the success of their industrialization was conditioned by a more open market: the Maghreb market." However, the creation of a greater Maghreb was quickly overshadowed by the obsession with security there due to the emergence of radical Islamism. Throughout his entire rule, Ben Ali made sure to promote Tunisia as a "haven of peace and security" in a regional environment characterized by violence and terrorism. Immune to the "diseases" that were afflicting its "powerful neighbours" in the 1990s, Ben Ali's security policy contributed to legitimating his police regime. During the 1970s, Boumediene's Algeria (1965–1979) and Qadhafi's Libya (1969–2011) were seen as two powerful neighbours driven by ambitious foreign policies. For Tunisia, they were at once poles of attraction and repulsion. Eager to maintain a balance, Tunisia sought to take advantage of the grouping while preventing its neighbours from interfering in its domestic affairs.

The Kingdom of Morocco explicitly expressed its adherence to the West. In his royal message, Mohammed VI emphasized the hierarchy of priorities for Moroccan diplomacy:

> one of the objectives of our diplomacy involves better adapting to international changes with a view to achieving greater integration in the world economy so as to serve Morocco, strengthen its structures, prepare it to face the challenges and improve Morocco's Euro-Mediterranean partnership. At the same time, our diplomacy must broaden the perspectives of our action and the circle of our economic and trade relations beyond the Euro-Med space, reaching out toward the Americas and Asia so as to diversify our ties, diminish our dependence and broaden the field of our cooperation. Morocco ... must remain true to the values and objectives of unity, solidarity, cooperation and neighbourliness with our brothers and friends in the Arab Maghreb, Africa and the Islamic world.[69]

The Maghreb was placed in various regional subgroups with which Morocco has affinities of history, religion and friendship and with which "cooperation" was desirable. But "partnership" was reserved for the Euro-Med relationship. The EU was Morocco's principal objective. The kingdom's application for membership in the EEC in 1984 was part of what Abdelkhaleq Berramdane called "Hassan II's decision to curry favour with the West". "The young king irrevocably linked the destiny of his kingdom to that of the West."[70] This was due to a legacy that dated back to the nineteenth century. Yet, since the Arab uprisings, Morocco has plainly turned its attention toward Africa.

North African states are faced with a regional security disaster that has contributed to gradually weakening them over the past several years. Engaged in costly fights against "Islamist terrorism",[71] they are squandering the meagre resources and the slender means they have available, to the detriment of economic and social development. Incapable of getting along and coming together in a framework of economic integration, they pursue bilateral strategies that sustain counterproductive rivalries and tensions. Even though the EU remains North Africa's main economic and trade partner, it is no longer a distant but desired horizon for these countries. Like Turkey, they are seeking new perspectives. While in the aftermath of independence, nationalism was a powerful ideology that was necessary to build the post-colonial states, the fact remains that sixty years later the Islamist utopia is fuelling a violent process of devaluing and deconstructing the state and its borders, raising serious concerns as to the security of populations to come and the stability of a region which the EU considers fundamental. Although in the short term states are trying to recover their sovereignty through border control policies and by combating jihadi groups, the authorities realize that in the long term these manoeuvres will not be sufficient to restore peace and confidence within their societies.

CONCLUSION

REFORGING A SENSE OF BELONGING
AND LOYALTY TO THE STATE

In this early twenty-first century, the Maghreb states are pursuing their efforts to produce national cohesion. In view of the collapse of states in the Middle East and in Libya, Maghreb leaders have realized the fragility of their political communities and the inadequacy of state instruments to sustain the nation in all its diversity and plurality. Throughout the 1980s, demands expressed by Amazigh movements to recognize the nation's plural identity came up against a monolithic definition of the nation grounded in Arabness. But from the 1990s, a transition toward the "plural nation"[1] got under way, starting with the official and institutional recognition of the Berbers. During the first decade of the 2000s, sub-Saharan migrants and students established themselves in North Africa, raising questions about the hidden dimension of Maghreb's Africanness and its structural ties with Africa through Islam. In Tunisia, the process resulted in a "redefinition of national unity" that clashed with the narrative of the "homogeneous society".[2] The collapse of post-Qadhafi Libya initiated strategic thinking about relations with sub-Saharan Africa, which for leaders in the Maghreb amounted to the intensification of military, economic and religious involvement. This has tended to renew neighbourhood relations with the countries of the Sahel. These strategic challenges are compounded by the contextual issue of ensuring law and order.

The states of North Africa have developed public policies that aim to resolve problems of law and order and "crowd control".[3] Ministries tasked with managing riots and revolts have considerably honed their skills in handling public disturbances. Governments have more or less learned to deal with social violence and urban riots, in some cases more successfully than others. The systematic crackdowns on rioters in the 1980s and 1990s gave way to a "softer" handling of unrest in the early 2000s. In Morocco as in Algeria, considerable effort was made in the handling of crackdowns on demonstrations during the Arab Spring to prevent deaths, which would very likely have provoked an outbreak of unrest. In 2012, shortly after the turmoil of the Arab Spring demonstrations, the theme of the 36th Congress of Directors-General of the Police and Security Forces was "democratic and peaceful crowd control and non-recourse to violence". "Algeria's experience in handling demonstrations is taken as a reference" in the field.[4] In Algeria as in Morocco, police forces tried to manage the Arab Spring demonstrations with greater care so as to avoid any blunder that might cause them to degenerate into riots or insurgencies. The demonstrations were controlled and "absorbed" by the authorities.[5] By comparison, crackdowns on the June 1981 riots in Casablanca left more than 600 dead, and the quashing of protest in October 1988 in Algiers claimed over 500 lives.[6]

However, these instances of protest management raise serious concerns linked to a twofold challenge: that of preserving national cohesion in a context in which it is jeopardized by jihadi violence, and that of responding to problems of social exclusion by devising an inclusive policy to promote social cohesion. Algeria, Libya and Tunisia certainly developed social welfare policies over the years, and many authors believe that social security systems are a major factor of social cohesion.[7] But it should be remembered that Algeria and Libya descended into civil war (the former in the 1990s and the latter since 2014) even though these two countries had the most generous social policies in the region. More than ever, the states of North Africa are confronted with the question of what has united and continues to unite their people despite all their differences. For decades, centralized states and authoritarian regimes produced and sustained a social order whose legitimacy rested on having restored national sovereignty after the colonial period, on social equality and the distribution of wealth. In the 1960s and 1970s, only Morocco aroused fears when the social order came under fire for being deemed illegitimate by socialist and progressive opponents of the monarchy.[8] In the 1980s, the end of Bourguiba's reign raised concerns that Islamists might come to power and the republican pact be called into question, while during the same period Algeria and Libya appeared to be strong, robust states capable of transforming their societies. However, the fact that these two "strong" states descended into civil war supports the idea that their political institutions lacked legitimacy. The implosion of Iraq, Syria and Yemen in the Middle East, and of Mali and Nigeria in Africa, were reminders to North African states of the extent to which the processes involved in producing a sense of community are fragile.

Numerous and long-standing fault lines run through the political communities of North Africa: these are regional, ethnic, social and religious.[9] While regional and social policies strive to diminish them within the framework of national solidarity, the breakdown promoted by jihadi groups stands as the greatest problem for public policy. How can social cohesion be maintained in states whose development is characterized by its "asymmetry"[10] and whose populations in marginalized or abandoned regions form potential breeding grounds for jihadi groups? Governments have indeed assessed the risks that certain regions represent because of their historical opposition to the central authorities and their economic and political marginalization in state institutions. For well over a decade, however, their primary concern has been to maintain institutional actors in a relationship of loyalty toward their political leaders. Thus, in Morocco and Algeria since the Arab revolts of 2011, armies, trade unions and political parties have been pampered by the regime out of fear of seeing them defect. On the other hand, in Tunisia the political leadership is seeking to rebuild or reinvent values and interests connected to new forms of belonging to the political community within the framework of a decentralized state.[11]

Seven years after the revolutions broke out, only Tunisia has made its exit from authoritarianism. The region seems further than ever from tilting toward democracy. The military coup in Egypt was a stark reminder of how vulnerable transition processes are and how uncertain their outcome is.[12] Libya is engulfed in civil war. In the face of such chaos, Algeria, despite anxieties about what will happen after Bouteflika, is heartened every day by the fact that it did not have to go through yet another revolution. Under Bouteflika (1999–2019), Algeria has experienced a degree of stability that it lacked for several decades. Since February 2019, hundreds of thousands of peaceful protesters have been demanding a radical change to the political system. As for its neighbour and rival, Morocco, it has undertaken beneficial reforms aimed at reducing the risk of social explosions which pose a threat to its national cohesion, as was the case of the Rif revolts.

The Arab Spring began in Tunisia. This country offers also the last, slim hope in the region. Having embarked on an adventure for which they were unprepared, soldiers, Ennahda party Islamists, human rights advocates, radicals of all stripes, young graduates or the less educated, and the unemployed are all struggling to learn to journey together toward an unknown destiny. The fear of foundering and joining the unfortunate examples of countries where civil war is raging probably makes Tunisians more reasonable and more prepared to accept compromise. The unforeseen arrival of political pluralism generated fear among many and violence among others. Surrounded by a thick political fog, the new regime appears fragile and vulnerable. Like many other regions in the world, the experience of exiting authoritarianism is here again chaotic and uncertain.

The revolutionary dynamics kept dangling for a moment the illusion of a "people united", and at one with its army. Faced with an economic and financial crisis, the countries in transition did not receive the international financial backing they had hoped for, except from Qatar and Saudi Arabia. The electoral triumph of Islamist parties thus clouded over the benign regard with which these revolutions and their potential outcome were viewed.[13] The revolutions are over, bearing in their wake a train of disillusionment and bitterness. Already in 1974, René Rémond questioned "the utility of revolutions that bring about changes which are finally more insignificant than those of progressive reformism".[14] The causes of the revolts and revolutions are still there; the governments are attempting to implement necessary reforms so that the region can finally break with the spiral of violence and preserve national unity and social cohesion.

CONCLUSION

The fact remains that while the countries of North Africa are trying to redefine a sense of community, they are confronted with jihadi violence and rejection of the state. Jihadi groups hope instead to install a new political order on the basis of identity ties to an "imaginary Islam" instead of to a homeland, a territory or a national history. In the 1960s, political leaders considered that one of the obstacles to nation-building resided in the backward, archaic mentality of their societies. Bourguiba embarked on a campaign against "bad instincts" with the hope of rectifying the deviance of a people afflicted with "historical shortcomings".[15] In this early twenty-first century, the fight against "backward mentalities" has vanished, and has now been replaced by de-radicalization policies. The involvement of thousands of young North Africans in the ranks of jihadi organizations such as al-Qaeda and ISIS represents a major challenge for the states of North Africa. Besides the devastating effects of terrorist attacks on the tourism industry, which is so vital for the region, this involvement of North African citizens in jihadism raises the problem of severing ties of allegiance to the state and erasing feelings of belonging to the nation. The realization that some youths subscribe no longer to the national narrative but instead to an "Islamic imaginary" that is destructive of the state compels the authorities in these countries to implement policies aimed at strengthening national ties and social cohesion.

As the fight against terrorism became a priority in the region, states devised strategies to prevent radicalization and violent extremism, which were considered "scourges" by international institutions.[16] The 1990s notion of "Islamist violence" has been replaced by the notions of radicalization and violent extremism.[17] Jihadis, embodying both notions, are perceived as having plans to destroy those countries that are attempting to implement counter-radicalization policies.

A number of reports underscore the need to integrate programmes to combat poverty and injustice into such counter-radicalization policies. In North Africa, the fight against terrorism now includes preventive measures which had been lacking in the past.

The 2010 revolts tested the national unity of states in the region. The disintegration of Libya is partly due to the weakness of the nation-building process under Qadhafi: once the authoritarian regime was toppled, Libya shattered into fragments centred around local powers based on tribal or regional affiliations. The Bourguiba legacy, on the other hand, probably explains the relative success of Tunisia's political transition after Ben Ali. Even though the countries of North Africa, with the exception of Libya, resisted the process of disintegration and fragmentation at work in Syria, Iraq and Yemen, over a half-century after independence the Maghreb states are still worried about preserving their national unity. The overinvestment in instruments for manufacturing national cohesion, national security and sovereignty explains their dismal economic performance in recent decades. Faced with massive youth unemployment, even among university graduates, governments are incapable of creating the conditions for economic growth that exceeds population growth. The lack of investment in the knowledge economy and in scientific research results, for instance, in the absence of North African states from the "top 500" Shanghai ranking of world universities. Yet, in recent years, Morocco and Tunisia have been striving to make up for their immense deficit in this area compared to other emerging countries.

The authoritarian design of states in North Africa reached its limit in the revolts of 2010. Demands for better governance, more justice and greater solidarity destabilized authorities who had not anticipated these citizen mobilizations. The unforeseen emergence of unrest compelled states to undertake far-reaching transformations so as to ensure national unity: the decentralization under way in Morocco and in Tunisia aims to bring the state closer to the needs of its citizens. The demands for a federal state in Libya point up the imperative of showing respect for territories and local authorities disillusioned by the authoritarian past of the Qadhafi regime. Certainly, demands for democracy reflect the people's desire to have political institutions that represent them and, especially, oversee government spending. Waste and corruption have been criticized for decades, with no improvement forthcoming. The Arab revolts challenged the states' trajectories; they drove home the need for change in the perspective of serving the general interest. Failing that, all regional and ideological political forces aimed at destroying the nation-state inherited from the colonial period will find reasons in the state's weakness to tear it down.

NOTES

INTRODUCTION: FROM COLONIAL RULE TO THE WAR ON TERROR

1. Amar Mohand-Amer, "Le 30 juin 1960, à l'indépendance du Congo-Belge, de graves troubles ont éclaté dans le pays, provoquant l'intervention des casques bleus de l'ONU," *Le Maghreb et l'indépendance de l'Algérie*, Paris: Karthala, 2012, p. 41.
2. M. Flory, "Le concept de révolution au Maroc," *Revue de l'Occident musulman et de la Méditerranée*, no. 5, 1968, p. 146.
3. Hassan II was king of Morocco from 1961 to 1999; Habib Bourguiba was president of Tunisia from 1957 to 1987; Houari Boumediene was president of Algeria from 1965 to 1978; Muammar Qadhafi was head of the Libyan state from 1969 to 2011.
4. Didier Le Saout and Marguerite Rollinde, *Emeutes et mouvements sociaux au Maghreb*, Paris, Karthala, 1999.
5. Luis Martinez, *The Algerian Civil War, 1990–1998*, London: Hurst, 2000.
6. Adeel Malik and Bassem Awadallah, "The Economics of the Arab Spring," *World Development*, vol. 45, 2013, pp. 296–313.
7. Ahmed Bouyacoub, "Croissance économique et développement 1962–2012. Quel bilan?" *Insaniyat*, no. 57–58, 2012.
8. Abderrahmane Moussaoui, "Du public au privé. La notion d'intérêt général en Algérie" in M. Kerrou (ed.), *Public et privé en Islam*, Tunisia: IRMC, 2002.
9. Amin Allal and Karine Bennafla, "Les mouvements protestataires de Gafsa (Tunisie) et Sidi Ifni (Maroc) de 2005 à 2009," *Revue du Tiers Monde*, 2011, pp. 27–45.
10. Frederick Cooper, *Africa since 1940: The Past of the Present*, New York: Cambridge University Press, 2002.

11. Daron Acemoglu and James A. Robinson, "Why is Africa Poor?", *Economic History of Developing Regions*, 25 (1 June 2010), p. 39.

12. A. el-Kenz, *L'Algérie et la modernité*, Dakar: Codesria, 1988.

13. A. Rouadjia, *Grandeur et décadence de l'état algérien*, Paris: Karthala, 1994; Jonathan N.C. Hill, *Identity in Algerian Politics: The Legacy of Colonial Rule*, Boulder: Lynne Rienner, 2009.

14. M. Ait Aoudia, *L'expérience démocratique en Algérie (1988–1992). Apprentissages politiques et changement de régime*, Paris: Les Presses de Sciences Po, 2015.

15. J.-P.Peyroulou, "Amnistie en Algérie. Quand le pouvoir se reconduit dans l'impunité," *Esprit*, no. 6, 2006; A. Moussaoui, "Algérie. La réconciliation entre espoirs et malentendus," *Politique étrangère*, no. 2, 2007.

16. John Davis, *Libyan Politics: Tribe and Revolution*, London: I.B. Tauris, 1987.

17. H. Bleuchot (ed.), *Chroniques et documents libyens, 1969–1980*, Paris, Editions du CNRS, 1983, p. 80.

18. H. Mattes, "The Rise and Fall of the Revolutionary Committees," in D. Vandewalle (ed.), *Qadhafi's Libya, 1969–1994*, New York: St Martin's Press, 1995, pp. 89–112.

19. Luis Martinez, *The Libyan Paradox* (trans. John King), London: Hurst, 2007, p. 153.

20. 2 September 2006, Jana News Agency.

21. http://edition.cnn.com/2006/WORLD/africa/02/17/libya.cartoons/.

22. "The dismissal of the Ibrahim cabinet is more than a mere crisis," interview with Ben Barka, *Le Monde*, 28 May 1960.

23. A. Yacine, "Neither the liberal reformers nor the leftwing revolutionaries are able to design the total action that would ensure our independence ... The Islamic revolution as a short-term or medium-term perspective is clearly the only alternative," in *La révolution à l'heure de l'Islam*, Imprimerie Borel et Feraud, 1979, p. 30.

24. Regarding the abduction of Mehdi Ben Barka, see M. Buttin, *Ben Barka, Hassan II, De Gaulle*, Paris: Karthala, 2015.

25. Zakya Daoud, *Maroc. Les années de plomb (1958–1988)*, Paris: Editions de la MSH, 2007.

26. Luis Martinez, "Frontières et nationalisme autour du Sahara Occidental," *CERISCOPE Frontières*, 2011, [online], accessed 5 June 2018, http://ceriscope.sciences-po.fr/content/part3/frontieres-et-nationalisme-autour-du-sahara-occidental; A. Berramdane, *Le Sahara occidental. Enjeu Maghrébin*, Paris: Karthala, 1992.

27. Abderrahmane Rachik, *Ville et pouvoirs au Maroc. Casablanca*, Casablanca:

Edition Afrique Orient, 1995 (Chapter Two, "L'état, l'émeute et la ville").

28. In his 1984 speech from the throne, the king announced that the agriculture tax would be suspended until 2000. Remy Leveau, *Le fellah défenseur du trône*, Paris: Presses de Sciences Po, 1985, p. 245.

29. Mohamed Tozy, *Monarchie et islam politique au Maroc*, Paris: Presses de Sciences Po, 1999.

30. M. Camau and V. Geisser (eds.), *Habib Bourguiba. La trace et l'héritage*, Paris: Karthala, 2004.

31. A. Chneguir, *La politique extérieure de la Tunisie (1956–1987)*, Paris: L'Harmattan, 2004, p. 227.

32. Laurence Louër and Eberhard Kienle, "Comprendre les enjeux économiques et sociaux des soulèvements arabes," *Critique internationale*, no. 61, 2013, pp. 11–17.

33. IMF Country Report no. 15/285, Tunisia, October 2015, p. 13.

34. Laurent Davezies, *Le nouvel égoïsme territorial. Le grand malaise des nations*, Paris, Seuil, 2015 ("La république des idées"), p. 29.

35. Ibid., p. 60.

36. IMF Country Report no. 15/285, p. 71.

37. Béatrice Hibou, "La formation asymétrique de l'état en Tunisie. Les territoires de l'injustice," in Irène Bono, Béatrice Hibou, Hamza Meddeb and Mohamed Tozy (eds.), *L'état d'injustice au Maghreb. Maroc et Tunisie*, Paris, Karthala, 2015, pp. 99–151.

38. L. Davezies, *Le nouvel égoïsme territorial*, p. 79.

39. "Mesure de la pauvreté, des inégalités et de la polarisation en Tunisie: 2000–2010," Rapport, Ministère du développement régional et de la planification, 2012, https://www.afdb.org/fileadmin/uploads/afdb/Documents/Project-and-Operations/Mesure_de_la_pauvret%C3%A9_des_in%C3%A9galit%C3%A9s_et_de_la_polarisation_en_Tunisie_2000–2010.PDF.

40. Pierre Lascoumes (ed.), *Gouverner par les instruments*, Paris: Presses de Sciences Po, 2005.

41. Steve Heydemann, "Social Pacts and Persistence of Authoritarianism in the Middle East," in Oliver Schlumberger (ed.), *Debating Arab Authoritarianism: Dynamics and Durability in Nondemocratic Regimes*, Stanford: Stanford University Press, 2007, p. 22.

42. Pierre Robert Baduel (ed.), *Etats, territoires et terroirs au Maghreb*, Paris: CNRS, 1985.

43. Flavient Bourrat and Amandine Gnanguenon (eds.), *Fragmentations et recompositions territoriales dans le monde arabe et en Afrique subsaharienne*, Paris, Irsem, no. 24, 2014.

44. Desmond King and Patrick Le Galès, "Sociologie de l'état en recomposition," *Revue française de sociologie*, no. 52, vol. 3, 2011.

45. Burhan Ghalioun, *L'état contre la nation*, Paris: La Découverte, 1991, p. 104.

46. Gilles Dorronsoro, Adam Baczko and Arthur Quesnay (eds.), *Syrie. Anatomie d'une guerre civile*, Paris: CNRS, 2016.

47. Laurent Bonnefoy, *Yemen and the World. Beyond Insecurity* (trans. Cynthia Schoch), London: Hurst and New York: Oxford University Press, 2018.

48. Tareq Yousfi Ismael and Jacqueline Ismael, *Iraq in the Twenty-First Century: Regime Change and the Making of a Failed State*, London: Routledge, 2015.

49. S.M. Masri, *Tunisia: An Arab Anomaly*, New York: Columbia University Press, 2017.

50. Ahmed Tlili, *Pour la démocratie. Lettre à Bourguiba, January 1966*, Tunis: Fondation Ahmet Tlili, June 2011.

51. Michel Camau, *La notion de démocratie dans la pensée des dirigeants maghrébins*, Paris: Editions du CNRS, 1971.

52. Larbi Sadiki, "Essentially, its chief premise is that post-independence Arab rulers have been paid political deference by their peoples in return for the provision of publicly subsidized services—education, health care, and a state commitment to secure employment," in "Popular Uprisings and Arab Democratization," *International Journal of Middle East Studies*, vol. 32, no. 1, 2000, p. 79.

53. Burhan Ghalioun points out that "the nationalist ideology, the myth of a centralized, strong and powerful government, the watchwords of independence that accounted for its popularity, became in the space of a few decades the cause of its unpopularity" in *L'État contre la nation*, p. 104.

54. Arjun Appadurai, "Violence et colère à l'âge de la globalisation," *Esprit*, May 2007.

55. Laurent Lacroix, "Etat plurinational et redéfinition du multiculturalisme en Bolivie," in Gros Christian and Dumoulin Kervran David (eds.), *Le multiculturalisme au concret. Un modèle latino-américain?* Paris: Presses de la Sorbonne Nouvelle, 2011, pp. 135–146.

56. C. Cambon and J. Durrieu, "Europe-Maghreb. Un partenariat stratégique à construire," *Géoéconomie*, no. 72, 2014.

57. Gérome Truc points out how "terrorist attacks call into question the ties that bind them to those who are not directly affected". "Une mise à l'épreuve du lien social," in *Sidération. Une sociologie des attentats*, Paris: PUF, 2016, p. 3.

1. THE TRIALS AND TRIBULATIONS OF NATION-BUILDING

1. Larbi Chouikha and Eric Gobe, *Histoire de la Tunisie depuis l'indépendance*, Paris: La Découverte, 2015, pp. 9–43.

2. Myriam Catusse, "Au-delà de 'l'opposition à sa Majesté'. Mobilisations, contestation et conflits politiques au Maroc," *Pouvoirs*, no. 145, 2013.

3. In Algeria, the army sees itself as the "bulwark of the Nation". See L. Addi, "L'armée, la nation et l'état en Algérie," *Confluences en Méditerranée*, 1999, pp. 39–42. The motto of the Royal Moroccan Armed Forces is "God, the Fatherland, the King". See J.C. Santucci, "Armée, pouvoir et légitimité au Maroc," in *Annuaire de l'Afrique du Nord*, 1971, vol. 2.

4. Dirk Vandewalle, *A History of Modern Libya*, Cambridge: Cambridge University Press, 2012, pp. 43–72.

5. Yves Deloye, *Sociologie historique du politique*, Paris: La Découverte, 2007, p. 54.

6. Arjun Appadurai, *Modernity at Large: Cultural Dimensions of Globalization*, Minneapolis: University of Minnesota Press, 1996, p. 165; S. Laacher and Cédric Terzi, "Comment faire peuple? Le cas des protestations publiques au Maghreb," *L'année du Maghreb*, vol. VIII, 2012, pp. 87–102.

7. Ernest Gellner, *Nations and Nationalism*, Oxford: Blackwell, 1983.

8. Victor T. Le Vine, "Nation-Building and Informal Politics," *International Social Science Journal*, no. 192, 2008, p. 156; Erik Larson and Ron Aminzade, "Les dilemmes de la construction de la nation dans les Etats-nations postcoloniaux. Les cas de la Tanzanie et des Fidji," *Revue internationale des sciences sociales*, no. 192, 2007.

9. Yâdh Ben Achour, "La réforme des mentalités. Bourguiba et le redressement moral," in Michel Camau (ed.), *Tunisie au présent*, Paris: CNRS, 1987, p. 149.

10. Cited by Michel Camau, *La notion de démocratie*, p. 171.

11. Bechir Chourou points out, "They considered that their mission did not end with the ousting of the colonial power. Rather, it extended to the eradication of poverty, ignorance and underdevelopment in general. They had achieved independence and that made them the most qualified to carry out the new task—a task so ambitious that it could not be bound by any time limit and so vital that it could not be submitted to crass political bickering." "The Challenge of Democracy in North Africa," *Democratization*, no. 9, 2002, p. 20.

12. Cited by Michel Camau, *La notion de démocratie*, pp. 232 and 238; see also Mehdi Ben Barka, *Option révolutionnaire au Maroc. Rapport au secrétariat de l'UNFP*, 1 May 1962, https://www.almounadila.info/ (last accessed 29 January 2019).

13. Manfred Halpern, *The Politics of Social Change in the Middle East and North Africa*, Princeton: Princeton University Press, 1963; Elbaki Hermassi, *Leadership and National Development in North Africa*, Berkeley: University of California Press, 1972.

14. O. Debbasch, "La formation des partis uniques africains," *RMMM*, no. 2, 1966, p. 57.

15. Charles Issawi, "The Economic and Social Foundations of Democracy in the Middle East," *International Affairs*, vol. 32, no. 1, 1956.

16. P.R. Baduel (ed.), *Etats, territoires et terroirs au Maghreb*, p. 23.

17. Amar Mohand-Amer and Belkacem Benzenine (eds.), *Le Maghreb et l'indépendance de l'Algérie*, Paris: Karthala, 2012.

18. Cited in Michel Camau (ed.), *Tunisie au présent*, p. 145.

19. Ahmed Mahiou (ed.), *L'état de droit dans le monde arabe*, Paris: CNRS, 1997, p. 402.

20. Khalifa Chater, "Ben Dhiaf et l'idéaltype des Lumières dans la régence de Tunis au XIX siècle," in *Entre Orient et Occident. Juifs et musulmans en Tunisie*, Paris: Eclat, 2007, p. 2.

21. Ibid., p. 4.

22. Ibid., p. 3.

23. Ibid., p. 4. Ahmed Ben Dhiaf was a nineteenth-century Tunisian historian and politician.

24. Raberh Achi, "A deeply rooted view that Islam is a religion incapable of reform and unable to bring about any form of secularism dominated among the political and intellectual spheres where colonial and religious matters were decided, making null and void any proposal that aimed to separate the Muslim faith and the state." "Les apories d'une projection républicaine en situation colonial. La dépolitisation de la séparation du culte musulman et de l'état en Algérie," in Pierre-Jean Luizard (ed.), *Le choc colonial et l'islam*, Paris: La Découverte, 2006, p. 242.

25. Julia Clancy-Smith, "Islam, Gender and the Making of French Algeria, 1830–1962," in Julia Clancy-Smith and Frances Gouda (eds.), *Domesticating the Empire: Languages of Gender, Race, and Family Life in French and Dutch Colonialism, 1830–1962*, Charlottesville: University Press of Virginia, 1998, p. 173.

26. Giovanni Sartori, *Democratic Theory*, New York: Praeger, 1965, p. 264.

27. Bruce Maddy-Weitzman, *The Berber Identity Movement and the Challenge to North African States*, Austin: University of Texas Press, 2011; Malika Reba Maamri, "The Imazighen's Quest for Inclusion," in *The State of Algeria: The Politics of a Post-Colonial Legacy*, London: I.B. Tauris, 2015, Chapter 6; Salem Chaker and Masin Ferkal, "Berbères de Libye. Un

paramètre méconnu, une irruption politiques inattendue," *Politiques africaine*, no. 125, 2012.

28. P.R. Baduel (ed.), *Etats, territoires et terroirs au Maghreb*, p. 24.

29. Yâdh Ben Achour, "La réforme des mentalités. Bourguiba et le redressement moral," in Michel Camau (ed.), *Tunisie au présent*, p. 149.

30. Soukaina Bouraoui, "Ordre masculin et fait féminin," in Michel Camau (ed.), *La notion de démocratie*.

31. Clement Henry Moore, "De Bourguiba à Ben Ali. Modernisation et dictature éducative," in M. Camau and V. Geisser (eds.), *Habib Bourguiba*, p. 194.

32. *La Charte Nationale de 1976*, p. 31.

33. Cited by Michel Camau, *La notion de démocratie*, p. 256.

34. Tahar Saoud, "La place de l'islam dans l'Algérie indépendante," in Amar Mohand-Amer and Belkacem Benzenine, *Le Maghreb et l'indépendance de l'Algérie*, p. 120; Oissila Saaidia, "L'invention du culte musulman dans l'Algérie coloniale du XIXe siècle," *L'année du Maghreb*, 2016, pp. 115–132.

35. Mohammed Arkoun, "Islam et développement dans le Maghreb indépendant," *Arabica*, vol. 29, 1982, p. 126; F. Frégosi, "Islam et état en Algérie. Du gallicanisme au fondamentalisme d'état," *RMMM*, vol. 65, no. 1, 1992.

36. For Ben Bella the ideal Algerian was a "Muslim Arab socialist". See J.N.C. Hill, "Independence and the Challenges of Nation Building" in *Identity in Algerian Politics*, p. 79.

37. Cited by Michel Camau, *La notion de démocratie*, p. 193.

38. The Istiqlal party (Independence Party) was founded in 1943. It was the main nationalist political force opposing the French protectorate until independence in 1956. Allal al-Fassi (1910–1974) was the party's figurehead. See G. Attilio, *Allal el-Fassi ou l'histoire de l'Istiqlal*, Paris: Ed. Moreau, 1972.

39. Cited by Michel Camau, *La notion de démocratie*, p. 235.

40. Cited ibid., p. 236.

41. Remi Leveau, *Le fellah marocain défenseur du trône*, Paris: Presses de Sciences Po, 1985.

42. Abdallah Laroui, *L'état dans le monde arabe contemporain. Eléments d'une problématique*, Cermac, Cahiers no. 3, 1980, p. 25.

43. Cited by François Burgat, in *L'islamisme au Maghreb*, Paris, Karthala, 1988.

44. He returned to Tunisia in 2011 and his party, Ennahda, won the elections to the Constituent Assembly.

45. Leyla Dakhli, "Arabisme, nationalisme arabe et identifications transna-

tionales arabes au 20ᵉ siècle," *Vingtième siècle. Revue d'histoire*, no. 103, 2009, p. 19.

46. Mohamed Chekroun, "Islamisme, messianisme et utopie au Maghreb," *Archives des sciences sociales et des religions*, no. 75, 1991, pp. 127–152.

47. Michael Willis, *The Islamist Challenge in Algeria: A Political History*, Reading: Ithaca Press, 1996; Moncef Djaziri, *Etat et société en Libye*, Paris: Karthala, 1996.

48. Isabelle Werenfels, *Managing Instability in Algeria: Elites and the Political Change since 1995*, London: Routledge, 2007.

49. Article 41 of the Constitution stipulates, "The King, Commander of the Faithful [Emir el-Mu'minin], ensures respect for Islam. He guarantees freedom of worship. He presides over the High Council of Ulemas. The Council is the only authority empowered to issue officially approved religious consultations (Fatwas)."

50. Malika Zeghal, *Les islamistes marocains. Le défi à la monarchie*, Paris: La Découverte, 2005.

51. Francesco Cavatorta and Vincent Durac (eds.), *Civil Society and Democratization in the Arab World: The Dynamics of Activism*, New York: Routledge, 2011.

52. Ernest Gellner, *Nations and Nationalism*.

53. Paul du Gay and Alan Scott, "State Transformation or Regime Shift?", *Sociologica*, vol. 2, 2010, p. 8.

2. INJUSTICE, A CHALLENGE TO SOCIAL COHESION

1. Jean-Pierre Filiu, *The Arab Revolution*, London: Hurst, 2011 and *From Deep State to Islamic State: The Arab Counter-Revolution and Its Jihadist Legacy*, London: Hurst, 2015.

2. Hamit Bozarslan, *Révolution et état de violence. Moyen-Orient 2011–2015*, Paris: CNRS, 2015.

3. Sarah ben Nafissa, "Révolution arabes. Les angles morts de l'analyse politique des sociétés de la région," *Confluences méditerranée*, no. 77, 2011, p. 87; Philippe Droz-Vincent, "Quel avenir pour l'autoritarisme dans le monde arabe?", *Revue française de science politique*, vol. 54, 2004.

4. Steven Heydemann, "Explaining the Arab Uprising: Transformations in Comparative Perspective," *Middle East Studies*, October 2015.

5. "La Tunisie et l'intégration régionale," Euromesco paper no. 78, January 2009.

6. Jean-Noël Ferrié and Jean-Claude Santucci (eds.), *Dispositifs de démocratisation et dispositifs autoritaires en Afrique du Nord*, Paris: CNRS, 2006, p. 11.

7. Speech on 5 February 1960 in Tunis, quoted by Frank Frégosi, "La

régulation institutionnelle de l'islam en Tunisie. Entre audace modern-
iste et tutelle étatique," http://www.ceri-sciences-po.org, May 2004,
p. 9.

8. Gilbert Rist, *Le développement. Histoire d'une croyance occidentale*, Paris:
Presses de Sciences Po, 2001.

9. "'The bread riot' broke out in Tunisia even before the decision came
into effect to raise the price of pasta and semolina by 70% and double the price of bread. On 29 December 1983, revolts had already
broken out in southern Tunisia, affecting the most underprivileged
areas in Tunisia. From Kebili, Douz, Souk El Ahad, El Hamma, Gabes,
and Gafsa, they spread to the capital, Tunis," explains Olfa Lamloum.
"Janvier 84 en Tunisie ou le symbole d'une transition," in Didier Le
Saout and Marguerite Rollinde (eds.), *Emeutes et mouvements sociaux au
Maghreb*, p. 232.

10. Ibid., p. 231.

11. Khadija Abada points out that between 1980 and 1987, several protest movements took place: "In 1980, the events in Tizi Ouzou were
sparked when a conference on Berber poetry was banned.
Demonstrators called for freedom of speech and criticized the state's
authoritarianism. On 19 May 1981, during 'student day', violence
broke out in the cities (Constantine, Bejaia, Annaba, Algiers). Rioters
attacked public buildings, which were symbols of preferential treat-
ment and favouritism. In 1982, in Oran, for lack of a partner to dialogue with, a protest of secondary school students turned into a riot.
In 1986, due to the introduction of new subjects of study in school,
high school students went on strike. This too degenerated into rioting. Protesters denounced the abuse of power by the wali (prefect),
President Chadli's brother." "La crise économique et la mobilisation
en October 1988," in Didier Le Saout and Marguerite Rollinde (eds.)
Emeutes et mouvements sociaux au Maghreb, p. 241.

12. Daniel Brumberg, "The Trap of Liberalized Autocracy," *Journal of
Democracy*, no. 13, 2002, pp. 56–68.

13. George Joffé, "Civil Activism and the Roots of the 2011 Uprisings" in
Jason Pack (ed.), *The 2011 Libyan Uprisings and the Struggle for the Post-
Qadhafi Future*, New York: Palgrave Macmillan, 2013.

14. Saad Eddin Ibrahim, *Egypt, Islam and Democracy: Critical Essays*, Cairo:
American University in Cairo Press, 1996, 2002.

15. *Egypt's Social Contract: The Role of Civil Society*, UNPD: Egypt Human
Development Report, 2008.

16. Myriam Catusse, "Les réinventions du social dans le Maroc 'ajusté',"
Revue des mondes musulmans et de la Méditerranée, no. 105–106, June

2005, pp. 221–246; Younes Abouyoub, "Peut-on parler d'exception marocaine?" *Tumultes*, 2012, p. 100.

17. Francesco Cavatorta, "Le printemps arabe: le réveil de la société civile. Aperçu général," *Annuaire IEMed de la Méditerranée*, 2012, pp. 83–91. See Laith Kubba, "The Awakening of Civil Society," *Journal of Democracy*, no. 11, 2000, pp. 84–90.

18. Larry Diamond, "Rethinking Civil Society," *Journal of Democracy*, vol. 3, 1994, pp. 5–17.

19. Michel Camau, "Globalisation démocratique et exception autoritaire arabe," *Critique Internationale*, no. 30, January–March 2006, pp. 59–83.

20. Abdelkader Zghal, "Le concept de société civile et la transition vers le multipartisme," *Annuaire de l'Afrique du Nord*, vol. XXVIII, 1989.

21. Sarah ben Nafissa (ed.), *ONG et governance dans le monde arabe*, Paris: Karthala, 2004.

22. Interview, Rabat, 2008, cited in Luis Martinez, Euromesco Paper no. 67, "Le Maroc, l'UMA et l'intégration régionale," May 2008.

23. Ibid.

24. Frédéric Vairel, *Politique et mouvements sociaux au Maroc. La révolution désamorcée?* Paris: Presses de Sciences Po, 2014.

25. Interview, Tunis, 2008, Luis Martinez, Euromesco Paper no. 78, p. 10.

26. Michael Bechir Ayari, "La révolution tunisienne, une émeute qui a réussi?" in Amin Allal and Thomas Pierret (eds.), *Devenir révolutionnaire. Au cœur des révoltes arabes*, Paris: Armand Colin, 2013.

27. Rémy Leveau, "Crise des états et transitions incertaines," in *Le Maghreb en suspens. Les cahiers du CERI*, no. 8, 1994.

28. Youssef Courbage, *A Convergence of Civilizations: The Transformation of Muslim Societies*, New York: Columbia University Press, 2014.

29. Kamel Kateb, "A qui profitera la 'fenêtre démographique' des pays du Maghreb," *Insaniyat*, no. 39, 2008.

30. Jean-Marc Dupuis, Claire el-Moudden and Anne Petron, "Les systèmes de retraite du Maghreb face au vieillissement démographique," *Revue française d'économie*, vol. XXV, 2010, p. 109.

31. Zahia Ouadah-Bedidi, "Maghreb. La chute irrésistible de la fécondité," *Médecines et sciences*, 2001. On the social effects of such a drop in the fertility rate, see Kamel Kateb, "A qui profitera la 'fenêtre démographique' au Maghreb," *Insaniyat*, no. 39–40, 2008.

32. Maurice Catin and Mouhoub el-Mouhoub write, "The population growth rate in Arab countries is between one 1 and 2% on average, whereas the working age population increases by about 3% per year, job-seekers by 4% per year and the number of graduates by 6% to 8%. In the Maghreb, university graduates thus have a higher unem-

ployment rate than non-graduates." "Inégalités et pauvreté dans les pays arabes," *Région et développement*, no. 35, 2012, p. 6.

33. This figure was originally published in Luis Martinez, "Injustices sociales et contestations politiques au Maghreb," *CERISCOPE Pauvreté*, 2012, [online], accessed 7 June 2018, http://ceriscope.sciences-po.fr/pauvrete/content/part3/injustices-sociales-et-contestations-politiques-aumaghreb.

34. Omar Bessaoud, "Aux origines paysannes et rurales des bouleversements politiques en Afrique du Nord. L'exception algérienne," *Maghreb-Machrek*, no. 215, 2013.

35. Véronique Alary and Mohammed el Mourid, "Les politiques alimentaires au Maghreb et leurs conséquences sur les sociétés agropastorales," *Revue du Tiers Monde*, no. 4, 2005; Jacek Henryk Schirmer, "L'agriculture des pays arabes. Entre le désert et le pétrole," *Bulletin de la Société géographique*, vol. 33, 1997.

36. This figure was originally published in Luis Martinez, "Injustices sociales et contestations politiques au Maghreb," *CERISCOPE Pauvreté*, 2012, [online], accessed 7 June 2018, http://ceriscope.sciences-po.fr/pauvrete/content/part3/injustices-sociales-et-contestations-politiques-aumaghreb.

37. http://www.unodc.org/pdf/publications/morocco_cannabis_survey_2003_fr.pdf.

38. Kenza Afsahi, *Les producteurs de cannabis dans le Rif-Maroc. Etude d'une activité économie à risque*, PhD thesis, Université de Lille 1, 2009.

39. This figure was originally published in Luis Martinez, "Injustices sociales et contestations politiques au Maghreb," *CERISCOPE Pauvreté*, 2012, [online], accessed 7 June 2018, http://ceriscope.sciences-po.fr/pauvrete/content/part3/injustices-sociales-et-contestations-politiques-aumaghreb.

40. See Chapter 5 on the Hirak Movement in Morocco.

41. This figure was originally published in Luis Martinez, "Injustices sociales et contestations politiques au Maghreb," *CERISCOPE Pauvreté*, 2012, [online], accessed 7 June 2018, http://ceriscope.sciences-po.fr/pauvrete/content/part3/injustices-sociales-et-contestations-politiques-aumaghreb.

42. ILO, Algiers, "Marché du travail et emploi en Algérie," October 2003, p. 43.

43. Mohammed Hachmaoui, "Institutions autoritaires et corruption politique. L'Algérie et le Maroc en perspective comparée," *Revue internationale de politique comparée*, vol. 19, 2012.

44. "WikiLeaks: Le regard clinique des diplomates yankee sur les écono-

mies du Maghreb," *Maghreb Emergent*, 14 December 2013; "WikiLeaks: Petits secrets du grand Maghreb," *Jeune Afrique*, 13 December 2010.

45. Emad el-Din Shahin, "The February 17th: Intifada in Libya," in Ricardo Laremont (ed.), *Revolution, Revolt and Reform in North Africa: The Arab Spring and Beyond*, New York: Routledge, 2014.
46. Sarah ben Nafissa, *ONG et governance dans le monde arabe*.
47. Luis Martinez, "La Libye à l'épreuve du legs de la Jamahiriyya," *Les Etudes du CERI*, 2013.
48. *Le Figaro*, 8 December 2007.
49. "Socialist People's Libyan Arab Jamahiriyya," *Country Economic Report*, July 2006, https://www.imf.org/external/pubs/ft/scr/2006/cr06137.pdf.
50. Luis Martinez, *The Violence of Petro-Dollar Regimes: Algeria, Iraq and Libya* (trans. Cynthia Schoch), London: Hurst, 2012.

3. TUNISIA: FROM THE SPECTRE OF CIVIL WAR TO DEMOCRATIC COMPROMISE

1. Guilain Denoeux, "La Tunisie de Ben Ali et ses paradoxes", *Maghreb-Machrek*, no. 166, 1999.
2. Béatrice Hibou, *The Force of Obedience: The Political Economy of Repression in Tunisia* (trans. Andrew Brown), Cambridge: Polity Press, 2011.
3. Mohamed Bouazizi was a young street vendor whose suicide by immolation is considered one of the events that triggered the rioting that led to Tunisia's Arab Spring.
4. Frédéric Volpi, *Revolution and Authoritarianism in North Africa*. London: Hurst, 2017; F. Cavatorta and V. Durac (eds.), *Civil Society and Democratization in the Arab World: The Dynamics of Activism*, New York: Routledge, 2011.
5. Nizar Messari, "A propos de la complexité des révoltes dans les pays arabes," *Cultures et conflits*, no. 85–86, 2012, p. 193.
6. Eva Bellin, "Reconsidering the Robustness of Authoritarianism in the Middle East: Lessons from the Arab Spring," *Comparative Politics*, vol. 44, no. 2, 2012.
7. T. Kuran, "Sparks and Prairie Fires: A Theory of Unanticipated Political Revolution," *Public Choice*, no. 61, 1989; François Chazel, "De la question de l'imprévisibilité des révolutions et des bonnes (et moins bonnes) manières d'y répondre," *Revue européenne des sciences sociales*, no. 123, 2003.
8. Interview with a human rights activist, Tunis, 2008 cited in Luis Martinez, "La Tunisie, l'Union du Maghreb Arabe et l'intégration régionale," Euromesco Paper, no. 78, January 2009, p. 8.

9. Ibid., p. 10.

10. Ibid., p. 9.

11. Landry Signé and Remy Smida point out that "This aspect is too often neglected by observers and analysts in explaining the Tunisian transition. Even if we in no way dispute the necessary role played by the demonstrators to initiate regime change, this popular uprising does not suffice to explain the speed with which the transition came about." "Les actions de l'armée tunisienne à Gafsa in 2008 et lors du soulèvement protestataire de 2011," *ASPJ Afrique et Francophonie*, 2016, p. 42; see also James Gelvin, *The Arab Uprisings: What Everyone Needs to Know*, Oxford: Oxford University Press, 2012.

12. Doubts have been expressed as to whether General Rashid Ammar was really given this order. On 17 July 2011, blogger and cyberactivist Yassine Ayari claimed that "the army never received orders to shoot," *Slate Afrique*, 20 July 2011. On 12 June 2014, during a programme on Ettounsiyya television, Ben Ali's general, Ahmed Chabir, former head of military intelligence, claimed that "Ben Ali had never given orders to fire on the crowd."

13. AFP, 24 January 2011.

14. Sadri Khiari and Olfa Lamloum, "Le Zaïm et l'artisan de Bourguiba à Ben Ali," *Annuaire de l'Afrique du Nord*, vol. XXXVII, CNRS, 1998, p. 377.

15. Michel Camau and Vincent Geisser point out, "the Neo-Destour party, unlike the Baath in Syria and Iraq and the FLN in Algeria, never had direct ties with a military force. The fellaga movement was neither the core nor the legendary reference for the new state." *Le syndrome autoritaire. Politique en Tunisie de Bourguiba à Ben Ali*, Paris: Presses de Sciences Po, 2003, p. 164.

16. Landry Signé and Remy Smida, "Les actions de l'armée tunisienne à Gafsa in 2008," p. 45.

17. Sadri Khiari, *Le délitement de la cité*, Paris: Karthala, 2003.

18. Larbi Sadiki, "The Search for Citizenship in Bin Ali's Tunisia: Democracy versus Unity," *Political Studies*, vol. 50, 2002, p. 498.

19. Sadri Khiari, *Le délitement de la cité*, p. 49.

20. Rasmus Boserup Alenius and Luis Martinez (eds.), *Algeria Modern: From Opacity to Complexity*, London: Hurst, 2016.

21. Y. Brissette, L. Dupont and M. Guitouni, *La Tunisie de Ben Ali. Les défis de l'émergence*, Paris: Ed. Carte Blanche, 2003.

22. "Tunisie. L'empire économique des Trabelsi et Ben Ali menacé," *La Tribune*, 18 January 2011.

23. Sadri Khiari, *Le délitement de la cité*, p. 142.

24. Ibid., p. 145.

25. Ibid., p. 194.
26. Ali Mezghani, "Tunisie. Une révolution, une élection et des malenten-dus," *Le débat*, no. 168, 2012; Habib Ayeb, "Tunisie. Les islamistes à l'épreuve du pouvoir," *Tumultes*, no. 38, 2012.
27. Jean-Philippe Bras, "Le Maghreb dans la 'guerre contre le terrorisme'. Enjeux juridique et politiques des législations 'anti-terroristes'," *L'année du Maghreb*, 2005–2006; Jean-Philippe Bras, "Tunisie. L'élaboration de la loi anti-terroriste de 2015 ou les paradoxes de la démocratie sécu-ritaire," *L'année du Maghreb*, 2016.
28. Regarding the history and ideology of the group, see M. Béchir Ayari and F. Merone, "Ansar al-Charia Tunisie. Une institutionnalisation à la croisée des chemins," in M. Camau and F. Vairel (eds.), *Soulèvements et recompositions politiques dans le monde arabe*, Montreal: PUM, 2014.
29. F. Cavatorta, "Salafism, Liberalism and Democratic Learning in Tunisia," *Journal of North African Studies*, no. 20, 2015.
30. N. Grimaud, *La Tunisie à la recherche de sa sécurité*, Paris: PUF, 1995.
31. See "Tunisia: Violence and the Salafi Challenge," *ICG*, no. 137, 13 February 2013, p. 3.
32. Henda Cherni, "Salafistes en Tunisie. Faudra-t-il nous défendre nous-mêmes?" *Outre-terre*, no. 33–34, 2012.
33. Interview with *Politique internationale*, no. 137, 2012.
34. "Average poverty rates remained three times as high in the interior of the country than in richer coastal 'offshore' areas; unemployment rates in the interior regions were double those of coastal areas; and only 13 percent of foreign firms were created in the interior regions." IMF Country Report no. 15/285, Tunisia, October 2015, p. 22.
35. Wolfgang Muhlberger, "La transition en Tunisie. La délicate éclosion d'un compromis politique," *Annuaire IEMed*, 2016, p. 219.
36. IMF Country Report no. 15/285, Tunisia, October 2015, p. 17.
37. "Tunisie. La bataille de Ben Gardane," *Jeune Afrique*, 17 March 2016.
38. Hassan Boubakri, "Echanges transfrontaliers et commerces parallèles aux frontières tuniso-libyenne," *Revue européenne des migrations interna-tionales*, no. 2, 1991, and Hassan Boubakri and Moustapha Chandoul, "Migrations clandestines et contrebandes à la frontière tuniso-libyenne," *Revue européenne des migrations internationales*, no. 2, 1991.
39. Mourad Ben Jelloul, "La réhabilitation du quartier Ourasnia à Ben Gardane," *La revue géographie et développement au Maroc*, vol. 1, 2013, p. 17.
40. H. Mzabi, "Frontière et croissance urbaine. Le cas de Ben Gardane dans le sud tunisien," *Revue tunisienne de géographie*, no. 25, 1994, p. 129.
41. "Foreign Fighters: An Updated Assessment of the Flow of Foreign Fighters into Syria and Irak," Soufan Group, December 2015, p. 11.

42. A.Y. Zelin, "The Others: Foreign Fighters in Libya," *The Washington Institute*, Policy note no. 45, January 2018.

43. Hedi Mejdoub, "Le traitement sécuritaire de la lutte contre le terrorisme," *La Majalla*, 31 January 2017.

44. Lisa Watanabe, "La gestion des jihadistes de retour en Afrique du Nord," *Politique de sécurité. Analyses du CSS*, no. 222, March 2018.

45. Committee for the Respect of Freedom and Human Rights in Tunisia and the International Federation for Human Rights (https://www.fidh.org/IMG/pdf/crldht-altt-torture-en-tunisie-rapport.pdf).

46. "Tunisie. L'impérative réforme de la police," Nawaat (https://nawaat.org/portail/?p), 16 May 2001.

47. "Genèse et réforme de la loi antiterroriste en Tunisie," https://inkyfada.com/2014/.

48. International Crisis Group, "Reform and Security Strategy in Tunisia," ICG Report no. 161, 23 July 2015, p. 23.

49. "The budget of the ministry of interior has grown by 60 per cent between 2011 and 2015. Its staff's base salary has increased by one-third. ISF employees have the right to join professional unions and can express themselves in the media. Nevertheless, agents report that their psychological state has suffered and their sense of insecurity increased." ICG Report no. 161, p. 4.

50. Refurbishment of 12 F-5E and F-5F fighter-bombers, purchase of drones, transport vehicles and night-flying helicopters. The army received $160 million in aid from the United States. See *Jeune Afrique*, 1 July 2017.

51. Fabio Merone, "Between Social Contention and Takfirism: The Evolution of the Salafi-Jihadi movement in Tunisia," *Mediterranean Politics*, vol. 22, no. 1, 2017.

52. A. Dworkin and Fatim-Zohra el-Malki, "The Southern Front Line: EU Counter-terrorism Cooperation with Tunisia and Morocco," Policy Brief, European Council on Foreign Relations, 15 February 2018.

53. Béatrice Hibou, "La formation asymétrique de l'état en Tunisie" in Béatrice Hibou, Mohamed Tozy, Irène Bono and Hamza Meddeb (eds.), *L'état d'injustice au Maghreb. Maroc et Tunisie*, p. 103.

54. Intissar Kheriji, PhD student at Sciences-Po, in her thesis (forthcoming) on decentralization in Tunisia entitled "Why decentralization could be the key to saving the Arab world" (http://www.middleeasteye.net/topics/arabspring). She also points out, "In Tunisia's case, centralization was a double curse—not only was power centralised politically, but also geographically on the country's coast. Ben Ali's last budget in 2011 allocated 82% of public expenditure to the 11 coastal regions while a paltry 18% went to the 13 interior regions."

55. Jean-Philippe Bras and Aude Signoles, "Etats et territoires du politique. La décentralisation en débat," *L'Année du Maghreb*, no. 16, 2017, p.7.

56. As Ines Labiadh points out, "Article 131 of the 2014 Constitution stipulates the generalization of the decentralization process, entailing the presence of all categories of local authorities in all territories. This fact is especially important when one notes that 50% of Tunisia had no municipal governments, thereby depriving over one-third of the population from choosing their representatives at the municipal level … In rural areas there was no elected representative body; members of rural councils were appointed by the governor." "Décentralisation et renforcement du pouvoir local. La Tunisie à l'épreuve des réformes institutionnelles," January 2016, p. 3 (https://halshs.archives-ouvertes.fr/halshs-01293413).

57. Amin Allal and Vincent Geisser (eds.), *Tunisie. Une démocratisation au-dessus de tout soupçon?* Paris: CNRS, 2018.

4. LIBYA, A MULTINATIONAL STATE?

1. I refer here to Alain Dieckhoff, *Nationalism and the Multinational State* (trans. Cynthia Schoch), London: Hurst, 2016.

2. *Le Monde*, 18 July 2017.

3. Wolfram Lacher, "Families, Tribes and Cities in the Libyan Revolution," *Middle East Policy*, no. 4, vol. 18, 2012.

4. M. Ouannes, *Militaires, élites et modernisation dans la Libye contemporaine*, Paris, L'Harmattan, 2009; Luis Martinez; *The Libyan Paradox* (trans. John King), London: Hurst, 2007; Moncef Djaziri, *Etat et société en Libye*, Paris, L'Harmattan, 1996; Dirk Vandewalle, *Libya since Independence: Oil and State-Building*, London: Cornell University Press, 1998; John Davis, *Libyan Politics: Tribe and Revolution*, London, Tauris, 1987.

5. Luis Martinez, "Libye. Une transition à l'épreuve du legs de la Jamahiriyya," *Les études du CERI*, no. 195, 2013; W. Lacher and Alaa al-Idrissi, "Capital of Militias: Tripoli's Armed Groups Capture the Libyan State," *Small Arms Survey*, June 2018, available at http://www.smallarmssurvey.org/fileadmin/docs/T-Briefing-Papers/SAS-SANA-BP-Tripoli-armed-groups.pdf.

6. J. Scheele, "The Libyan Connection: Settlement, War, and Other Entanglements in Northern Chad," *Journal of African History*, no. 57, 2016.

7. A. Quesnay, "Renégocier l'espace politique libyen. Du local au national," *Noria*, September 2012.

8. Rafaa Tabib and Jean-Yves Moisseron, "Daech dans la Libye fragmentée," *Hérodote*, no. 160–161, 2016.

9. D. Vandewalle, "After Qadhafi: The Surprising Success of the New

Libya," *Foreign Affairs*, 1 November, 2012; H. Salam Marjan; *Libye, de la dictature à la liberté*, 2012 (in Arabic); A. Wahab Mahmoud Zintani. *La révolution populaire libyenne*, 2012 (in Arabic).

10. Between 31 March and 31 October, NATO flew 17,939 armed sorties over Libya: 17,314 were flown by fighter aircraft, 375 by helicopter, 250 by drones. In May 2012, a Human Rights Council Commission report concluded that NATO took important steps to minimize civilian casualties. See https://www.ohchr.org/Documents/HRBodies/HRCouncil/RegularSession/Session19/A.HRC.19.68.pdf.

11. A. Bensaâd, "Changement social et contestation en Libye," *Politique africaine*, no. 125, March 2012.

12. W. Lacher, "Was Libya's Collapse Predictable?" *Survival*, no. 59, 2017; Mohamed Faraj Ben Lamma, "The Responsibility to Protect in Libya: Back to Square One?" *Revue internationale stratégique*, no. 101, 2016, pp. 14–24.

13. P. Cole and B. MacQuin (eds.), *The Libyan Revolution and Its Aftermath*, London: Hurst, 2013; J. Mundy, *Libya*, Cambridge: Polity Press, 2018.

14. V. Collombier, "Make Politics, Not War: Armed Groups and Political Competition in Post-Qadhafi Libya," in B. Kodmani and Nayla Moussa (eds.), *Out of the Inferno? Rebuilding Security in Iraq, Libya, Syria and Yemen*, Arab Reform Initiative, 2017.

15. "Tawergha. Le martyre des Libyens noirs," *Jeune Afrique*, February 2014.

16. Human Rights Watch, *Libya Report 2018*, https://www.hrw.org/world-report/2018/country-chapters/libya#.

17. See the United Nations Human Rights Commission report, *Report of the International Commission of Inquiry on Libya*, 2 March 2012. Available at http://www.refworld.org/docid/4ffd19532.html.

18. *Al Khabar*, 3 September 2011.

19. P. Boiley, "Géopolitique africaine et rébellions touarègues. Approches locales, approches globales (1960–2011), *Année du Maghreb*, CNRS, 2011.

20. Interview, Tripoli, November 2012.

21. M. Grifa, "Libya: Establishing a New Political System and the Transition to Statehood," *Arab Reform Initiative*, September 2012, p. 3.

22. In August 2011, the NTC prepared a constitutional charter laying down the constitutional basis for Libya pending the drafting of the new Constitution by the new Assembly. Article 1 stipulates, "Libya is an independent democratic state wherein the people are the source of authority. The city of Tripoli shall be the capital of the State. Islam is the religion of the state and the principal source of legislation is Islamic jurisprudence (sharia)."

23. The same number as those who had drafted the Constitution of 1951.

24. *The Libya Herald*, 5 January 2013.
25. Z. al-Ali, "International Assistance to Arab Spring Transitions," in S. Lacroix and J.-P. Filiu (eds.), *Revisiting the Arab Uprisings*, London: Hurst, 2018.
26. F. Gaub, "Libye. Le rêve de Qadhafi devient-il réalité?" *Politique étrangère*, no. 3, 2012.
27. *La Presse*, 14 April 2012.
28. W. Lacher, "Libya's Local Elites and the Politics of Alliance Building," *Mediterranean Politics*, vol. 21, no. 1 (2016), pp. 64–84.
29. Interview, Tripoli, November 2012.
30. Interview with Saif al-Islam, broadcast on France 2 television, 5 March 2011.
31. Diane Ethier, "Réflexions sur les causes et l'issue des rebellions arabes," 22 November 2011. www.dandurand.uqam.
32. Libyan foreign affairs minister Mohamed Abdelaziz stated that "after 42 years of dictatorship, everything must be rebuilt. Among our many challenges, it is essential to manage to change Libyan mentalities and educate them to democracy, to make them realize that the rule of law is stronger than arms, which they must lay down and surrender." *Jeune Afrique*, 5 December 2013.
33. J. Linz and A. Stepan, *Problems of Democratic Transition and Consolidation*, Baltimore: Johns Hopkins University Press, 1996, p. 17.
34. In 2012, out of an electorate 2 million strong, 1.7 million people cast their vote; in 2014, fewer than 500,000 voters went to the polls.
35. Wolfram Lacher, "Supporting Stabilization in Libya: The Challenges of Finalizing and Implementing the Skhirat Agreement," *SWP Comments*, July 2015.
36. Interview, Tripoli, November 2012.
37. Interview, Tripoli, November 2012.
38. Interview with Hakim, veterinarian, Tripoli, November 2012.
39. M. Djaziri, "Tribus et état dans le système politique libyen," *Outre-terre*, no. 23, 2009; M. Faraj ben Lamma, "The Tribal Structure in Libya: Factor for Fragmentation or Cohesion?" FRS, July 2017. Available at https://www.frstrategie.org/en/programmes/observatoire-du-monde-arabo-musulman-et-du-sahel/the-tribal-structure-in-libya-factor-for-fragmentation-or-cohesion-14.
40. *Explication of the Green Book*, vol. 1, Tripoli: World Center for Research and Study on the Green Book, p. 274.
41. Remarks from Qadhafi's Green Book, cited by J. Davis, *Libyan Politics*, pp. 211–12.
42. A.A. Ahmida, *The Making of Modern Libya: State Formation, Colonization*

and Resistance, 1830–1932, New York: State University of New York Press, 1994.

43. E. Picard, "Armée et sécurité au cœur de l'autoritarisme," in O. Dabène, *Autoritarismes démocratiques. Démocraties autoritaires au XXI siè-cle*, Paris: La Découverte, 2008.

44. "Libya: Oil and Gas Report Q1 2013," *Business Monitor International*, January, 2013, p. 9, see www.businessmonitor.com.

45. E.E. Evans-Pritchard, "The Sanusi of Cyrenaica," *Africa: Journal of the International African Institute*, vol. 15, no. 2, 1945.

46. A. Martel, *La Libye (1835–1990). Essai de géopolitique historique*, Paris: PUF, 1991, p. 152.

47. H. Bleuchot, *Chroniques et documents libyens (1969–1980)*, Paris: CNRS, 1983.

48. During a debate in 1998, in answer to a sheikh who asked him to clarify whether his interpretation of Islam contradicted the Quran, Qadhafi replied, "If one of you were to say to me, for example, 'the Green Book is against the faith,' then I would behave like Ataturk did." Cited by M. Djaziri, *Etat et société en Libye*, p. 85.

49. J. Oakes, "Libya: The Zawiya Tribe," Berenice Stories, http://libyasto-ries.com/2013/01/06.

50. A. Quesnay, "Renégocier l'espace politique libyen. Du local au national," *Noria*, September 2012.

51. Arturo Varvelli, "La diplomatie internationale va-t-elle surmonter l'impasse en Libye," *IEMed*, 2016.

52. Italian giant ENI seems to have been the hardest hit by the political transition: on 2 March 2013, the natural gas production facility in Mellitah, near Tripoli, inaugurated in 2004 at a cost of $9 billion, was partly destroyed in the course of clashes between the Zintan and Zuwara militias, both of which claim a monopoly over its protection and payment for this service. These local clashes between militias made Italy nervous: 12% of the natural gas imported by Italy comes from this facility. On 4 March 2013, the Libyan army brokered a ceasefire between the two militias, and as a result the army was put in charge of security for the gas production facility.

53. "The Libyan Political Agreement: Time for a Reset," *ICG*, 4 November 2016.

54. https://www.un.org/press/fr/2017/cs12860.doc.htm.

55. *Final Report of the Panel of Experts on Libya established pursuant to Resolution 1973*, 1 June 2017, p. 3.

56. Jalel Harchaoui, "Libye. Quand Haftar saccage des années de diploma-tie," *Orient XXI*, 26 April 2019.

57. There were 700 dead and 3,000 wounded among the Misrata military coalition that back the Presidential Council.

58. According to M. Djaziri, "holding these elections at all costs in 2018 seems like a reckless endeavour ... that can only worsen the situation." "Libye. Propositions pour sortir de la crise," *Politique internationale*, no. 159, 2018, p. 320; Jalel Harchaoui, "La Libye depuis 2015. Entre morcelleemnt et interferences," *Politique étrangère*, no. 4, 2018.

59. "Report of the Secretary-General on the United Nations Support Mission in Libya," http://www.un.org/en/sc/documents/sgreports/2017.shtml, p. 17.

60. Ibid., p. 11.

5. MOROCCO: BENEFICIAL REFORMS

1. Pierre Vermeren, *Le Maroc en transition*. Paris: La Découverte, 2001, p. 71.

2. Mounia Bennani-Chraibi and Mohamed Jeghllaly, "La dynamique protestataire du Mouvement du 20 February à Casablanca," *Revue française de science politique*, no. 62, 2012, pp. 867–893; Karine Benafla and Haoues Seniguer, "Le Maroc à l'épreuve du printemps arabe. Une contestation désamorcée?" *Outre-terre*, no. 29, 2011.

3. Frédéric Vairel, *Politique et mouvements sociaux au Maroc. La révolution désarmorçée?*, Paris: Presses de Sciences Po, 2014.

4. In an article published in *Le Monde diplomatique* in January 1960 ("Les revendications marocaines sur les territoires sahariens. Le point de vue de M. Allal el-Fassi"), Allal El Fassi explained, "well before Islam, Mauritania included the Sahara, Northern Morocco and the region around Oran. Since time immemorial and up until the French (military) occupation, the land of Chenguitt, today known as Mauritania, as well as the lands that naturally link it to Tarfaya and Souss, were part of the Moroccan provinces. Since the time of the Almoravid dynasty (1053), its history, its religious events, and its political and social transformations have always been associated with the events that all of Morocco experienced during this period." See https://www.monde-diplomatique.fr/1960/01/ALLAL_EL_FASSI/23406.

5. A. Dialmy writes, "Yassin advocates the prophetic method, based on gentleness and wisdom, in order to organize and spread the *da'wa*. To bring an end to moral degeneracy, heresies and political and administrative decay, such are the objectives of the *jihad* he suggests. Political contestation, of course, but without resorting to violence. Islamism should strive to produce an Islamic public opinion by rehabilitating primitive Islam as Islam's only historical achievement, and the only

normative model for the state. The major motivation that pushes Islamism to rise to power in order to restore the califat." "L'islamisme marocain. Entre révolution et intégration," *Archives de sciences sociales des réligions*, no. 110, 2000, p. 11.

6. UNDP, Human Development Report 2016, http://www.undp.org/content/undp/en/home/librarypage/hdr/2016-human-development-report.html.

7. Haut-commissariat au Plan (Rabat)), https://www.hcp.ma/attachment/840964/.

8. "Le Maroc à la veille des élections législatives. Les islamistes en embuscade," *Médiarabe*, 5 September 2007.

9. Ahmed Benchemsi, "Mohammed VI, despote malgré lui," *Pouvoirs*, no. 145, 2013.

10. In March 2018, SNI, the royal family holding company, was renamed Al Mada: "As a long-term pan-African private investment fund, Al Mada means to assert its mission as a leading partner in the economic development of the African continent, while SNI has pursued an 'African strategy' for many years, relying on flagships of its economy," *La Tribune Afrique*, 28 March 2018.

11. Eric Laurent and Catherine Graciet, *Le roi prédateur*, Paris: Seuil, 2012.

12. Pascal Croset, *La transformation de l'Office Chérifien des Phosphates*, Paris: Dunod, 2012.

13. Michel Abitbol, *Histoire du Maroc*, Paris: Ed. Perrin, 2009, p. 675.

14. J.-N. Ferrié and B. Dupret, "La nouvelle architecture constitutionnelle et les trois désamorçages de la vie politique marocaine," *Confluences méditerranée*, no. 77, 2011, pp. 25–34.

15. Driss el-Yazami, "Transition politique, histoire et mémoire," *Confluences méditerranée*, no. 62, 2007.

16. Rabéa Naciri, "Le mouvement des femmes au Maroc," *Nouvelles questions féminines*, vol. 33, 2014.

17. Rapport Haut-Commissariat au Plan, Kingdom of Morocco, October 2016, p. 3.

18. Claude de Miras, "Initiative nationale pour le développement humain et économie solidaire au Maroc," *Revue du Tiers Monde*, no. 190, 2007.

19. E. Rozca and A. Belhaj, "Ceuta et Melilla. Risques et gestion des risques," *Euromesco Papers*, no. 75, 2008.

20. Kenza Afsahi, "Pas de culture de cannabis sans les femmes. Le cas du Rif au Maroc," *Déviance et société*, vol. 39, 2015.

21. Romain Caillet, "L'influence de la guerre en Syrie sur le courant jihadiste marocain," *Religionscopes. Etudes et analyses*, no. 33, April 2014.

22. On 18 and 19 January 2016, ISIS issued two videos calling on Muslims in Maghreb to combat the "apostate" regimes in Morocco and Tunisia.

Morocco is a member of the international coalition along with the Saudis and is very active in the Sahel region.

23. Iraqi Fahd, "Sécurité. Comment le Maroc est devenu une référence en matière antiterroriste," *Jeune Afrique*, 7 July 2016. Available at http://www.jeuneafrique.com/mag/336594/politique/securite-maroc-devenu-reference-matiere-dantiterrorisme/.

24. In 2015, Morocco created the Central Bureau of Judicial Investigation (BCIJ), similar to the United States FBI.

25. Abdellah Tourabi, "Les attentats du 16 May 2003 à Casablanca. L'émergence du salafisme jihadiste," in Bernard Rougier (ed.), *Qu'est-ce que le salafisme?* Paris: PUF, 2008, pp. 211–228.

26. "O Islamic nations of resistance and jihad in the Maghreb, see how your children are uniting under the banner of Islam and jihad against the United States, France and Spain." Al-Qaeda leader Ayman al-Zawahiri's call to jihad in the Maghreb, 3 November 2007. "Le Maroc à la veille des élections législatives. Les islamistes en embuscade," *Médiarabe*, 5 September 2007.

27. Regelio Alonso and Marcos Garcia Rey, "The Evolution of Jihadist Terrorism in Morocco," *Terrorism and Political Violence*, vol. 19, 2007. The authors ask the following: "Morocco: A Producer of Terrorists?" p. 579. R. Ilhem, "La tentation jihadiste des salafistes marocains," *Mediapart*, 19 June 2016.

28. The council listed the many kinds of legitimate jihad, the most important of them being jihad of the soul, which comes to shape, tame and cultivate the soul and prepare it to bear responsibility. Next comes jihad of the mind, which is performed by training and polishing the mind and using it in a way that benefits humanity; jihad of the pen, performed by writing books and essays that enlighten the mind and confront doubts and false accusations directed at Islam and the Muslims; jihad of money, [performed] by making generous donations, which is one of the 'gates of good' [leading to Paradise], and also by contributing to social and economic development." See *Tel Quel*, 14 November 2015, https://www.memri.org/reports/moroccos-high-council-ulema-fatwa-following-paris-attacks-terror-forbidden-islam-only-ruler.

29. K. Benafla and Seniguer Haoues, "Le Maroc à l'épreuve du printemps arabe. Une contestation désarmorcée," *Outre-terre*, vol. 29, no. 3, 2011.

30. The Mohamed VI Institute trained over 450 foreign imams between 2014 and 2015: 212 Malians, 100 Guineans, 75 Ivoirians, 53 Nigerians and 37 Tunisians. On 25 and 27 January 2016, a forum to promote peace in Muslim societies was organized in Marrakech by the ministry of habous and religious affairs. More than 300 religious figures

from 60 countries took part. See also Bakary Sambe, *Islam et diplomatie. La politique africaine du Maroc*, Washington DC: Phoenix Press International, 2011.

31. Foreign affairs ministry of the Kingdom of Morocco, "Questions globales. Luttes antiterroriste", https:www.diplomatie.ma/Actiondu Maroc/Lesquestionsglobales/Luttecontreleterrorisme/tabid/210/language/en-US/default.aspx.

32. Jean Noël Ferrié and Baudoin Dupret, "La nouvelle architecture constitutionnelle et les trois désamorçages de la vie politique marocaine," *Confluences méditerranée*, no. 78, 2011.

33. On 28 October 2016, Mohsen Fikri, a young fishmonger, was crushed to death by a garbage truck as he was trying to recover produce a police officer had confiscated and thrown into the truck. A popular uprising broke out (*Hirak*), demanding freedom, dignity and social justice. The ensuing crackdown on the movement was fierce, and raised concerns about the stability of a region that had a long history of rebelling against the central authorities.

34. Pierre Vermeren, *Le Maroc en transition*, p. 240.

35. Omar Bendjelloun, "Le Rif, un 'volcan' méditerranéen," *Les cahiers de l'Orient*, no. 129, 2018.

36. Ibid.

37. "Pourquoi le Rif marocain s'est–il soulevé?" *Orient XXI*, available at https://orientxxi.info/va-comprendre/pourquoi-le-rif-marocain-s-est-il-souleve,2217.

38. Aboubakr Jamaï, "Au Maroc, le Rif défie le roi," *Le Monde diplomatique*, July 2017.

39. According to Michel Abitbol, more than 100,000 civilians were killed during the war. See *Histoire du Maroc*, Paris: Ed. Perrin, 2009, p. 513.

40. Hisham Aidi, "Les blessures ouvertes du Rif," *Multitudes*, no. 68, 2017.

41. M'hamed Lazaar, "Conséquences de l'émigration dans les montagnes du Rif central," *Revue européenne des migrations internationales*, vol. 3, nos. 1–2, 1987.

42. Evelyne Gauché, "Le désenclavement des territoires ruraux marginalisés du Nord du Maroc," *Norois*, no. 214, 2010, p. 7 (https: journals.openedition.org/norois/3142).

43. Ibid., p. 7.

44. See Khalid Mouna, "Les nouvelles figures du pouvoir dans le Rif central du Maroc." The author points out that "800,000 people are involved in the cannabis economy, and cultivation covers an area of 134,000 hectares. Resin production is estimated at 3,080 metric tons for a total income of 214 million US dollars." *Anthropologie et sociétés*, vol. 35, nos. 1–2, 2011, p. 231.

45. The geographer Saïd Boujrouf emphasizes that "Morocco's mountain massifs have remained fairly neglected by the central authorities … marginal territories compared to useful parts of the national territory." "La montagne dans la politique d'aménagement du territoire du Maroc," *Revue de géographie alpine*, vol. 84, no. 4, 1996, p. 42.

46. Fact File (Association de Défense des Droits de l'Homme in Morocco; Collectif d'Associations de Solidarité et des Droits de l'Homme en Hollande; Coordination Maghrébine des Organisations des Droits Humains), *Le Hirak du RIF. Revendications légitimes et pacifiques*, European Parliament, Brussels, 9 October 2017.

6. ALGERIA: A SOCIETY ON THE BRINK

1. Fatma Oussédik, "L'Algérie, une société en guerre contre elle-même," *Naqd*, no. 32, 2015.

2. Lahouari Addi, "Le régime algérien après les révoltes arabes," *Mouvements*, no. 66, 2011.

3. Luis Martinez and Rasmus Alenius Boserup (eds.), *Algeria Modern*, op. cit.

4. Louisa Driss-Ait Hamadouche, "L'Algérie face au printemps arabe," *Confluences mediterranée*, no. 81, 2012.

5. The FCE is an organization founded in October 2000 and it currently boasts 4,000 members. "The main sectors covered (18 out of the 22 listed in the national classification) are in particular the agrifood industries, construction materials, electricity and electronic industries, mechanical industries, pharmaceuticals, paper goods and packaging, lumber, public works and construction, and large retail chains." See http://www.fce.dz/presentation/.

6. See the special issue of *Politique africaine*: "L'Algérie aux marges de l'état," no. 137, 2015.

7. *Le matin d'Algérie*, 22 February 2018.

8. Michael Bonner emphasizes to what extent, in the Middle East, in North Africa and in Central Asia, "the triumph (in the 1990s) over the Islamists in Egypt, Algeria and elsewhere has proven costly. The nation-state seems vulnerable indeed." *Le Jihad. Origines, interprétations, combats*, Paris: Téraèdre, 2004, p. 200.

9. Djallil Lounnas, "The Moderate Islamist Parties," in Rasmus Alenius Boserup and Luis Martinez (eds.), *Algeria Modern*, pp. 77–93; Amel Boubekeur, "The Future of Algerian Islamist Parties," *Maghreb Center Journal*, no. 1, 2010.

10. M. Hafez Mohammed, "Armed Islamist Movement and Political Violence in Algeria," *Middle East Journal*, vol. 54, no. 4, 2000.

11. Nicknamed "the Brain" due to his influence on the army's strategy during the war against the Islamists in the 1990s.
12. "Terrorisme et guerre des chiffres," *Algeria Watch*, 27 November 2002.
13. *Le jeune indépendant*, 4 May 2002.
14. In favour of suspending the electoral process in 1991, General Belkheir was considered the all-powerful embodiment of the Algerian system until his death in 2010.
15. A member of President Bouteflika's inner circle, he was in favour of amnestying members of the GIA in the framework of a national reconciliation policy. He died in 2017.
16. Transcription of Bouteflika's radio address in *Algeria Watch*, 10 July 1999. Translation from *The Civil Concord: A Peace Initiative Wasted*, ICG Africa Report no. 31, 9 July 2001.
17. The decree stipulated that "people belonging to organizations who voluntarily and spontaneously decided to stop acts of violence and who placed themselves completely at the disposal of the state and whose names are listed in appendix to the original of this decree ... shall be entitled to all their civic rights and have been granted immunity from prosecution."
18. *Amnesty International*, 8 November 2000.
19. Regarding the Ghardaïa riots, see Fatma Oussédik, "L'Algérie, une société en guerre contre elle-même," *Naqd*, no. 32, 2015.
20. Mohamed Elshimin points out, "De-radicalization is an instrument of counterterrorism policy that, in theory, is designed to provide the police and the policy makers with a more selective, targeted and structural approach to tackling the threat of terrorism." "Prevent 2011 and Counter-Radicalisation: What Is De-radicalisation?" in Christopher Baker-Beall, Charlotte Heath-Kelly and Lee Jarvis (eds.), *Counter-Radicalisation: Critical Perspectives*, New York: Routledge, 2005, p. 216.
21. O. Ashour, *The De-radicalization of Jihadists: Transforming Armed Islamist Movements*, New York: Routledge, 2009; T. Bjorgo and J. Horgan, *Leaving Terrorism Behind: Disengagement from Political Violence*, New York: Routledge, 2008.
22. See also Farid Bencheikh, "Comprendre pour combattre. Salafisme armé, les fondamentaux," *Sécurité globale*, no. 7, 2016.
23. Document from the Ministry of Foreign Affairs, "Algeria and Deradicalization: An Experience to Share," September 2015. Translation taken from the Algerian Embassy in Pretoria website.
24. Ibid.
25. Ibid.
26. Ibid.
27. Ibid.

28. This quote and those preceding are taken from ibid.
29. Camille Lacoste-Dujardin, "Géographie culturelle et géopolitique en Kabylie. La révolte de la jeunesse kabyle pour une Algérie démocratique," *Hérodote*, no. 103, 2001.
30. Alain Mahé, *Histoire de la Grande Kabylie*, Algiers: E. Bouchène, 2001, p. 506.
31. Historian Karima Dirèche-Slimani points out that Christians in Kabylie number only a few thousand. See *Chrétiens de Kabylie 1873–1954. Une action missionnaire dans l'Algérie coloniale*, Algiers: Bouchène, 2004.
32. *El Watan*, 4 August 2004.
33. Kamel Chachoua inventories the clichés about Kabyle religiosity. He quotes Alfred Rambaud, author of a book in the nineteenth century on Greater Kabylie, who wrote, "After having been rather doubtful Christians, they have become Muslims of a peculiar sort." Or again Father Dugas, "They say that Kabylie is Algeria's Switzerland, but for the Archbishop of Algiers, it is Africa's Lebanon." See K. Chachoua, *L'islam kabyle*, Paris: Maisonneuve et Larose, 2001.
34. Jérémy Guedj, "Juifs et musulmans d'Algérie en France," *Hommes et migrations*, no. 1295, 2012.
35. Ali Mérad, *Le réformisme musulman en Algérie de 1925 à 1960*, Paris: MSH, 1967.
36. Sossie Andezian, "Mysticisme extatique dans le champ religieux algérien contemporain," in S. Ferchiou (ed.), *Islam pluriel au Maghreb*, Paris: CNRS, 1996, p. 325.
37. *Sans frontière. Le magazine de la solidarité internationale*, 9 March 2018; Plateforme Migration Algérie brings together some 20 associations working in favour of respect for human dignity.
38. Mohamed Said Musette states, "Algeria has changed ... In the 1960s–1970s, it welcomed lots of black African students ... Today there is more reluctance to accept the presence of foreigners. Black foreigners, I mean, because "whites" have no problem! In Algeria the victims of xenophobia are mainly the blacks." *Algeria Watch*, January 2018.
39. *Le Quotidien d'Oran*, 28 April 2018.
40. "Rapport Algérie," International Monetary Fund, 1 June 2017.
41. *TSA*, 18 November 2017.
42. Former FLN legislator, he left the party to found al-Moustakbal in February 2012. He was a candidate in the 2014 presidential election.
43. Close to the Muslim Brotherhood, he is the founder of the Justice and Development Front.
44. Former prime minister (December 1999 to August 2000), minister

on several occasions and an economist, he regularly sounds warnings in the media as to the impending "catastrophe" in Algeria.

45. Former prime minister (2000–2003), candidate in the 2004 and 2014 presidential elections. In 2015, he founded the Talaie el-Houriat political party.

46. Prime minister since 2017, he has held this post on several occasions in the past two decades. He was also director of the president's office from 2014 to 2017.

47. Prime minister from 2012 to 2017.

48. Special adviser to the president, his brother Saïd is considered a potential successor. The media describe his influence in all domains (political, economic, security). See "Quel est le pouvoir de Saïd Bouteflika, le très influent frère du président?" *Jeune Afrique*, 26 June 2017.

49. "Algeria's Choice: Reform or Collapse," available at www.aei.org/publication/algerias-choice-reform-or-collapse.

50. Algeria exports 54 billion cubic metres of gas and 1.02 million barrels of oil per day. Hydrocarbons represent 94.5% of its total exports.

51. The African Union commissioner for peace and security, Smail Chergui, stated, "There are reports of 6,000 African fighters among the 30,000 foreign elements who joined this terrorist group in the Middle East." *El Moudjahid*, 11 December 2017.

52. "L'Algérie cherche activement un successeur à Abdelaziz Bouteflika," *Le Monde Afrique*, 18 February 2018.

53. "When Bouteflika goes, Algeria will probably implode. The Islamists who have been kept at bay by his iron hand will exploit the vacuum. Tensions that have been buried since the civil war will re-emerge. And then Europe could be overwhelmed by another great wave of refugees from North Africa," announced *The Spectator*. "How Algeria could destroy the EU," 3 December 2016, available at https://www.spectator.co.uk/2016/12/how-algeria-could-destroy-the-eu/.

54. "Algérie, une capitale interdite de manifestation," *Orient XXI*, 15 January 2018.

55. The Confederation of Independent Unions (CSA); the Civil Forum for Change; Collective for Civil Society (NGO), Algerian League for Human Rights.

7. THE DECONSTRUCTION OF NATION-STATES: THE JIHADIS' REVENGE

1. Luc-Willy Deheuvels, *Islam et pensée contemporaine en Algérie*, Paris: CNRS, 1991.

2. An estimated 500 Libyans joined the Arab combatants against the Soviets after the USSR invaded Afghanistan in 1979. Alison Pargeter, "Localism and Radicalization in North Africa: Local Factors and the Development of Political Islam in Morocco, Tunisia and Libya," *International Affairs*, vol. 85, no. 5, 2009, p. 1031; Mustapha Hamid and Farrall Leah, *The Arabs at War in Afghanistan*, London: Hurst, 2015; Mohamed Mokeddem, *Les Afghans algériens*, Algiers: Anep, 2002.

3. Bernard Rougier (ed.), *Qu'est-ce que le salafisme?* Paris: PUF, 2008; Francesco Cavatorta and Fabio Merone (eds.), *Salafism after the Arab Awakening: Contending with People's Power*, London: Hurst, 2016.

4. Brynjar Lia points out, "In the five-year period between 2011 and 2016, jihadis created more territorial proto-states than they had done over the more than 20 years since al-Qaeda's foundations in 1988." "Jihadism in the Arab World after 2011: Explaining Its Expansion," *Middle East Policy*, vol. XXIII, no. 4, 2016, p. 81.

5. Henrik Gratud and Vidar Benjamin Skretting, "Ansar al-Sharia in Libya: An Enduring Threat," *Perspectives on Terrorism*, vol. 11, no. 1, 2017, p. 2.

6. Aaron Y. Zelin explains that "the formation of Ansar al-Sharia in Libya is likely a logical conclusion and implementation of Maqdisi's ideas, changing emphasis on the groups' actions ... One of the main critiques Maqdisi presents, and hopes to create a course correction within the jihadi movement, is his differentiation between the idea of *qital al-nikayya* (fighting to hurt or damage the enemy) and *qital al-tamkin* (fighting to consolidate one's power), which he expounds upon in his book *Waqafat ma Thamrat al-Jihad* (Stances on the Fruit of Jihad) in 2004. Maqdisi argues the former provides only short-term tactical victories that in many cases do not amount to much in the long term whereas the latter provides a framework for consolidating an Islamic state. In this way, Maqdisi highlights the importance of planning organization, education, as well as *dawa* (calling individuals to Islam) activities." "The Terrorist Threat in North Africa," Testimony before the House Committee on Foreign Affairs, Subcommittee on Terrorism, Nonproliferation, and Trade, and the Subcommittee on the Middle East and North Africa, 10 July 2013.

7. Frederic Wehrey, "The Struggle for Security in Eastern Libya," *Carnegie Papers*, September 2012.

8. http://www.jadaliyya;com/pages/index/7514/libyan-eastern.

9. Geoff D. Porter, "The Islamic State in Libya," *CTC Sentinel*, vol. 9, no. 3, March 2016.

10. ISIS set up a vice squad, an Islamic tribunal, a tax collection office, media outlets, radio and TV. A charter was issued, stipulating that Islamic law would be imposed on the city; alcohol, cigarettes and

drug-use were forbidden; women were obligated to wear traditional muslim dress (hijab) and remain at home; money in the coffers of the infidel would be returned to Muslims; the Caliph would decide how to distribute the funds; residents were forbidden to have relations with infidel governments (in Tobruk and Tripoli). See *ISIS in Libya: A Major Regional and International Threat*, January 2016, Meir Amit Intelligence and Terrorism Information Center, p. 44.

11. Emigration of a Muslim from a non-Muslim country to a Muslim country is considered "salutary migration" by the Salafis. Mohamed Ali Adraoui, "La hijra au service d'un projet intégral dans le salafisme français," *Ethnologie française*, no. 168, 2017, p. 5.
12. *Dabiq*, no. 11, September 2015, p. 60.
13. Geoff D. Porter, "The Islamic State in Libya," p. 2.
14. http://www.slateafrique.com/660889/sadio-gassam.
15. Charlie Winter, "Libya: The Strategic Gateway for the ISIS," Quilliam, February 2015. http://www;quilliamfoundation.org/wp/wp-content/uploads/publications.free/libya-the-strategic-gateway-for-is.pdf.
16. Jason Pack, Rhiannon Smith and Karim Mezran, *The Origins and Evolution of ISIS in Libya*, Atlantic Council, Rafik Hariri Center for the Middle East, June 2017.
17. According to Nabil Mouline, "this book has become essential reading for two reasons. For one, it offers a clear synthesis of the main jihadi ideologues as well as one of the greatest modern strategists in Latin America, the Far East and Europe. Furthermore, the strategy outlined and especially the terminology, have been adopted by the Islamic State organization … unlike Al-Qaeda, Abû Bakr Nâji wants to re-territorialize jihadist action … he advises jihadis to settle in a certain number of areas and make them sanctuaries … These relocation areas should meet various objective conditions such as a rugged terrain, a weak regime, a predisposed population, the existence of a local jihadi movement and an abundance of weapons." *Le califat. Histoire politique de l'islam*, Paris: Flammarion, 2016, p. 254.
18. Grand Mufti Al-Ghariani regularly criticized France's presence in Libya, which he described as aggression and an act of war. Ansar al-Sharia called for retaliation against France. See Henrik Gratud and Vidar Benjamin Skretting, "Ansar al-Sharia in Libya: An Enduring Threat," p. 6.
19. Luis Martinez, *The Libyan Paradox*, p. 68.
20. http://www.tsa-algerie.com/20160319/aqmi-devoile-details-lattaque-site-gazier-menace-multinationales-exploitant-gaz-de-schiste/.
21. Moncef Ouannes, "Islamistes en Libye. Itinéraires idéologiques et con-

frontation avec le pouvoir," *Revue d'histoire maghrebine*, no. 146, May 2004.

22. Jean-Pierre Filiu, "The Local and Global Jihad of al-Qa'ida in the Islamic Maghrib," *Middle East Journal*, vol. 63, no. 2, Spring 2009, pp. 213–226.

23. Serge Daniel, *AQMI, l'industrie de l'enlèvement*, Paris: Fayard, 2012.

24. A. Antil, "Trafic de cocaïne au Sahel," *Etudes*, no. 417, October 2012, p. 312.

25. Sergio Altuna Galan, "JNIM : A propaganda analysis of al Qaeda's project for the Sahel", ARI 72, 20 June 2019.

26. A UNDP report estimates that between 2011 and 2016, 35,000 people were victims of terrorist attacks in sub-Saharan Africa. "Journey to Extremism in Africa," *UNDP*, 2017, p. 10; see also "Terrorism and Violent Extremism in Africa," Congressional Research Service, 14 July 2016.

27. "Islamist Terrorism in the Sahel: Fact or Fiction?" ICG Report, no. 92, 41 March 2005.

28. Solomon Hussein, *Terrorism and Counter-Terrorism in Africa: Fighting Insurgency from al-Shabaab, Ansar Dine and Boko Haram*, Basingstoke: Palgrave Macmillan, 2015; Marc-Antoine Pérouse de Montclos, *L'Afrique. Nouvelle frontière du djihad?* Paris: La Découverte, 2018.

29. Axel Augé and Patrick Klaousen (eds.), *Reformer les armées africaines*, Paris: Karthala, 2010; Lassina Diarra, *La Cédéao face au terrorisme transnational*, Paris: L'Harmattan, 2016.

30. Emmanuel Grégoire and André Bourgeot, "Désordre, pouvoirs et recompositions territoriales au Sahara," *Hérodote*, no. 142, 2011.

31. "L'Afrique, le spectre d'un djihad peul," *Le Monde diplomatique*, May 2017; B. Haidara, "Conflits armés aux relents de guerre civile dans le centre du Mali," https://lamenparle.hypotheses.org/606; A. Thiam, "Centre du Mali. Enjeux et dangers d'une crise négligée," Institut du Macina, Centre pour le dialogue humanitaire, March 2017, available at https://www.hdcentre.org/fr/updates/nouvelle-publication-centre-du-mali-enjeux-et-dangers-dune-crise-negligee/.

32. "Situation dans le Nord-Tillaberi"; "Situation dans l'est du Burkina Faso," November 2018, Promediation.

33. M. Goita, "Nouvelle menace terroriste en Afrique de l'Ouest. Contrecarrer la stratégie d'AQIM au Sahel," Centre d'études stratégiques de l'Afrique (CESA), *Bulletin de la sécurité africaine*, no.11, February 2011, p. 2.

34. Adib Benchérif, "Al-Qaïda au Maghreb islamique. Une hiérarchie en redéfinition sous fond de crise," *Chronique du Moyen-Orient et de l'Afrique du Nord*, 11 December 2012.

35. Anouar Boukhars, "The Potential Jihadi Windfall from the Militarization of Tunisia's Border Region with Libya," *CTC Sentinel*, January 2018; Anouar Boukhars and Frederic Wehrey (eds.), *Perilous Desert: Insecurity in the Sahara*, Carnegie Endowment for International Peace, 2013.

36. A. Thurston, *Boko Haram: The History of an African Jihadist Movement*, Princeton: Princeton University Press, 2017.

37. Regarding terrorist attacks in the region, see the press review compiled by the African Union's African Centre for the Study and Research on Terrorism, CAERT, Algiers.

38. *La Nouvelle Tribune*, 4 March 2018.

39. *The Social Roots of Jihadist Violence in Burkina Faso's North*, ICG Report no. 254, 12 October 2017.

40. "Note d'analyse sur la situation dans l'est du Burkina Faso," November 2018, Promediation.

41. Ibid.; *The Social Roots of Jihadist Violence in Burkina Faso's North*, ICG Report, no. 254, 12 October 2017; *Journey to Extremism in Africa*, UNDP, 2017 (http://journey-to-extremism.undp.org/en/reports); *La violence des jeunes et les enjeux de l'extrémisme violent à Zinder*, OIM, 2017 (http://base.afrique-gouvernance.net/docs/youth-violence-fr.pdf).

42. *Boko Haram: From Local Grievances to Violent Insurgency*, DIIS Report, 21, 2015.

43. A. Benjaminsen, "Does Climate Change Drive Land-use Conflicts in the Sahel?" *Journal of Peace Research*, no. 49, 2012; N. Bagayoko, B. Ba, B. Sangaré and K. Sidibé (eds.), *Gestion des ressources naturelles et configuration des relations de pouvoir dans le centre du Mali*, June 2017 (http://africansecuritynetwork.org/assn/wp-content/uploads/2017/06/Gestion-des-ressources-naturelles-et-configuration-des-pouvoirs-dans-le-centre-du-Mali.pdf).

44. R. Otayek and B. Soares (eds.), *Islam and Muslim Politics in Africa*, New York: Palgrave Macmillan, 2007; M. Gomez-Perez, *L'islam politique au sud du Sahara*, Paris: Karthala, 2005; R. Otayek, "Religion et globalisation. L'islam subsaharien à la conquête de nouveaux territoires," *Revue internationale et stratégique*, no. 52, 2003.

45. Rodrigue Nana Ngassam, "Le Cameroun sous la menace de Boko Haram," *Le Monde diplomatique*, January 2015; Sambé Bakary, *Boko Haram. Du problème nigérian à la menace régionale*. Montreal: Presses Panafricaines, 2015,

46. G. Abdoulaye, "Les diplômés béninois des universités arabo-islamiques. Une élite moderne, déclassée en quête de légitimité socioreligieuse et politique," Working Papers, Department of Anthropology and African Studies, no. 18, 2003.

47. M. Fall Ould Bah, "Les réseaux de la finance islamique en Afrique," *Politique étrangère*, no. 4, 2010.

48. According to ICG, Wahhabism is the largest fundamentalist sect in Cameroon. It makes up 10% of the population. These tensions were illustrated in exchanges between Imam Mahmoud Dicko of the Wahhabi-leaning High Islamic Council and the Group of Muslim Spiritual Leaders presided over by Sherif Ousmane Madani Haïdara. *ICG*, no. 229, September 2015; G. Holder, "Chérif Ousmane Madani Haïdara et l'association islamique Ançar Dine," *Cahiers d'études africaines*, no. 206, 2012.

49. Abdoulaye Sounaye, "Salafi revolution in West Africa," Working paper, no. 19, Berlin, 2017 (www.ssoar.info).

50. Christian Seignobos and Olivier Iyebi-Mandjek, *Atlas de la province extrême-Nord Cameroun*, Marseille: IRD, e-book, 2017, p. 768.

51. Marie Miran-Guyon, "Le wahhabisme à Abiddjan. Dynamisme urbain d'un islam réformiste en Côte d'Ivoire contemporaine," *Islam et société au sud du Sahara*, no. 12, 1998.

52. Marie Miran-Guyon, *Guerres mystiques en Côte d'Ivoire. Religion, patriotisme et violence*, Paris: Karthala, 2015.

53. Thomas J. Basset, "Nord musulman et sud Chrétiens. Les moules médiatiques de la crise," *Afrique contemporaine*, no. 206, 2003, p. 15.

54. Lassina Diarra, "Terrorisme. Man, foyer de radicalisation en Côte d'Ivoire?" http://www.centre4s.org/index.php?option=com_content&view=article&id=221:terrorisme-man-foyer-de-radicalisation-en-cote-divoire-&catid=45:articles&Itemid=63.

55. L. Diarra, *Terrorisme international. La réponse de la Côte d'Ivoire*, Paris: L'Harmatan, 2016.

56. "Is Côte d'Ivoire Facing Religious Radicalism?" *ISS*, no. 13, July 2015. In 2019, *La lettre du continent*, dated 12 June, mentioned that large-scale terrorist attacks have been thwarted in Abijan.

57. Christian Seignobos, "Boko Haram. Innovations guerrières depuis les monts Mandara," *Afrique contemporaine*, no. 252, 2014; Comolli Virginia, *Boko Haram: Nigeria's Islamist Insurgency*, London: Hurst, 2015; Marc-Antoine Pérouse de Montclos (ed.), *Boko Haram: Islamism, Politics, Security and the State of Nigeria*, Los Angeles: Tsehai, 2015.

58. "The Islamic utopia is alive and well, with the inevitable consequence of devaluing the very idea of the state," Abdallah Laroui wrote in "L'état et le monde arabe. Eléments d'une problématique," *Cermac*, Cahiers no. 3, Université de Louvain, p. 26.

59. Ali Bensaad, "Le Sahara et la transition migratoire entre Sahel, Maghreb, Europe," *Outre-mer*, no. 23, 2009.

60. Gillian Weiss, *Captives and Corsairs: France and Slavery in the Early Modern Mediterranean*, Stanford: Stanford University Press, 2011.

8. SECURITY BREAKDOWN AND REGIONAL DISINTEGRATION

1. David Nievas, "Rebellion and Sharia in the Sahel: An Analysis of the Tuareg Rebellion and the Occupation of Northern Mali by Armed Jihadist and Islamist Groups," Unisci Discussion Papers, January 2014, issue 34. See F. Wehrey and A. Boukhars, *Perilous Desert Insecurity in the Sahara*, Washington: Carnegie Foundation, 2013.

2. Luis Martinez, "L'Afrique du Nord en 2013, à l'aune de la crise au Mali," in F. Charillon and A. Dieckhoff, *Afrique du Nord et Moyen-Orient. L'échec du rêve démocratique*, Paris: La Documentation Française, 2014.

3. Jean-Yves Le Drian, *Qui est l'ennemi?* Paris: Editions du Cerf, 2016. See Jean Fleury (former chief of staff of the French air force), *La France en guerre au Mali. Les combats d'Aqmi et la révolte des Touaregs*, Paris: Jean Picollec, 2013.

4. Frédéric Volpi, *Islam and Democracy: The Failure of Dialogue in Algeria*, London: Pluto, 2002.

5. Jalel Harchaoui, "La Libye depuis 2015 : entre morcellement et interférences". Politique étrangères, no. 4, 2018.

6. Mohamed Faraj Ben Lamma, "L'application de la responsabilité de protéger en Libye. Retour à la case départ?" *Revue internationale et stratégique*, no. 101, 2016.

7. Rasmus A. Boserup and Luis Martinez (eds.), *Europe and the Sahel-Maghreb Crisis*, DIIS report, no. 3, 2018.

8. Lelia Rousselet, *La stratégie africaine du Maroc. Un nouveau rôle pour la politique étrangère marocaine?* Master's thesis: Paris, Institut d'études politiques, 2015.

9. René Otayek, *La politique africaine de la Libye*, Paris: Karthala, 1987.

10. *L'Autre Afrique*, 18–24 March 1998. See Luis Martinez, "Nouvelle Libye?" *Outre-terre*, no. 20, 2008.

11. *Revue arabies*, February 2003.

12. "Overview: Terrorism in 2016," Start (Study of Terrorism and Responses to Terrorism), http://www.start.umd.edu/publication/overview-terrorism-2016.

13. Thomas Hegghammer, "The Future of Jihadism in Europe: A Pessimistic View," *Perspective on Terrorism*, vol. 10, no. 6, 2016.

14. Michel Hastings, "Dieu est-il Scandinave?" *Revue internationale de politique comparée*, vol. 13, 2006.

15. Antonela Capelle-Pogacean, "Hybris et incertitude dans la Hongrie de Victor Orban," *Dossier du CERI*, 2011, http://www.sciencespo;fr/ceri/sites/sciencespo;fr/files/art_AC.pdf.

16. Jean Delumeau, *La peur en Occident*, Paris: Hachette, 1999.

17. Taoufik Bourgou and Frédéric Ramel, "Les perceptions de la menace en Méditerranée dans l'après-guerre froide. Regards croisés," in M.

Bacot-Décriaud, J.-P. Joubert and M.-C. Plantin (eds.), *La sécurité inter-nationale d'un siècle à l'autre*, Paris: L'Harmattan, 2002.

18. Catherine Wihtol de Wenden, *Migrations. Une nouvelle donne*, Paris: MSCH, 2016. See Peter Seeberg, "The Arab Uprisings and the EU's Migration Policies: The Cases of Egypt, Libya and Syria," *Democracy and Security*, no. 9, 2013.

19. According to the director of Frontex, "In 2016, detection of African migrants reached 180,000—a record figure—compared to approxi-mately 40,000 between 2009 and 2013." *Politique internationale*, no. 155, 2017.

20. "The high number of migrants along the North African coast has enabled the development of a far more lucrative coastal migrant trade, valued now at US$255–323 million per year in Libya alone … The Colombian drug trade via Guinea-Bissau produces drugs with a street value of some US$1.25 billion in Europe and US$150 million in West Africa, generating local incomes of at most US$10–20 million for operatives in the Sahel, Algeria and Libya … The full value of the Libyan arms trade in the post-Qadhafi era is probably in the range of US$15–30 million annually." "Libya: A Growing Hub for Criminal Economies and Terrorist Financing in the Trans-Sahara," *Policy Brief. The Global Initiative Against Transnational Organised Crime*, May 2015.

21. Emanuela Paoletti, *The Migration of Power and North-South Inequalities: The Case of Italy and Libya*, Basingstoke: Palgrave Macmillan, 2010.

22. Anastassia Tsoukala, "La criminalisation des immigrés en Europe," in Laurent Bonelli and Gilles Sainati (eds.), *La machine à punir*, Paris: L'esprit frappeur, 2004; Anastassia Tsoukala, "Looking at Migrants as Enemies," in Didier Bigo and Elspeth Guild (eds.), *Controlling Frontiers*, Aldershot: Ashgate, 2005.

23. Derek Lutterbeck, "Policing Migration in the Mediterranean," *Mediterranean Politics*, vol. 11, no. 1, 2006.

24. Jean-Pierre Cassarino, "Migration and Border Management in the Euro-Mediterranean Area: Heading towards New Forms of Interconnectedness," in *Med 2005*, IEMed, 2005.

25. Abdennour Benantar, "NATO, Maghreb and Europe," *Mediterranean Politics*, vol. 11, no. 2, July 2006.

26. In the framework of a programme for the Instrument for Peace and Stability in Sub-Saharan Africa, coordinated by Civipol, the author con-ducted research on border security in 2016 in Mali, Burkina Faso, Côte d'Ivoire, Guinea and Tunisia and in 2018 in Benin, Cameroon, Chad and Niger.

27. On the night of 15 to 16 January 2013, the katibas, "those who signed in blood," took over the Tiguentourine natural gas production facility near In Amenas. The Algerian army stormed the site and freed the

hostages: 37 hostages and 29 terrorists were killed. It was the largest-scale attack on a natural gas and oil facility in Algeria.

28. Cédric Jourde, "Politique des récits de l'islamisme en Mauritanie," *Politique africaine*, no.114, 2009; Zekeria Ould Ahmed Salem, *Prêcher dans le désert. Islam politique et changement social en Mauritanie*, Paris: Karthala, 2013.

29. "Sahel. L'extrême porosité des frontières demeure le grand problème," *Le Figaro*, 26 July 2013.

30. Abdennour Benantar, "Complexe de sécurité Ouest-méditerranéen. Externalisation et sécurisation de la migration," *Année du Maghreb*, no. 9, 2013.

31. Philippe Beaulieu-Brossard and Charles-Philippe David, "Le blindage des frontières selon les théories des relations internationales. Contribution et dialogue," *L'espace politique*, no. 20, 2013.

32. Remi Carayol, "En Afrique, le spectre d'un jihad peul," *Le Monde diplomatique*, May 2017; Adam Thiam, *Centre du Mali: enjeux et dangers d'une crise négligée*, Centre pour le dialogue humanitaire, March 2017.

33. Hélène Pellerin, "Une nouvelle économie politique de la frontière," *A contrario*, vol. 2, no. 2, 2004.

34. Michel Foucher, *L'obsession des frontières*, p. 26.

35. "Algérie-Maroc. Bientôt une frontière de barbelés?" http://www.algerie-focus.com/blog/2013/1é/algerie-maroc-bientot-une-frontière-en-barbeles/.

36. See www.icilome.com/nouvelles/news.asp?id=888&idnews=760093.

37. Meryem Sellami and Jihed Haj Salem, "Conversion djihadiste des jeunes en Tunisie post révolutionnaire: altérité, corporalité et spatialité," in Denis Jeffrey (ed.), *Jeunes et djihadisme*, Montreal: PUL, 2016, pp. 115–155.

38. See Abdennour Benantar, "Sécurité aux frontières. Portée et limites de la stratégie algérienne," *L'année du Maghreb*, 2016.

39. Ali Bensaad, "Agadez, carrefour migratoire sahélo-maghrébin," *Revue européenne des migrations internationales*, vol. 19, no. 1, March 2013.

40. Michel Foucher, *L'obsession des frontières*, p. 80.

41. "The space of the Sahel is vast, nearly 5.3 million km^2, or almost 10 times the size of France, but sparsely populated. It has fewer than 80 million inhabitants. There are very strong population density contrasts between the Saharan zone (fewer than 1/km^2) and the tropical Sahel zone (50 to 100/km^2) ... The Tuaregs number about two million, spread over Niger (1.5), Mali (0.6), Burkina Faso (0.3) and Algeria and Libya (a few dozen thousands)." Jacques Fontaine, "Crise malienne. Quelques clefs pour comprendre," *Confluences méditerranée*, vol. 2, no. 85, 2013.

42. The Algiers Accords of 2006 were concluded on 4 July 2006 between representatives of the Malian state and representatives of the 23 May Democratic Alliance for Change. Their aim was to "restore peace, security and development in the region of Kidal."

43. A. Bencherif, "De la 'question touareg' aux mémoires du conflit. Pour une réconciliation malienne," Centre Francopaix Report, February 2018. Available at https://issat.dcaf.ch/Learn/Resource-Library/Policy-and-Research-Papers/De-la-question-touaregue-aux-memoires-du-conflit-pour-une-reconciliation-malienne.

44. Hervé Beugeot, "Révoltes et rebelles en pays touareg," *Afrique contemporaine*, no. 170, 1994; Clotilde Barbet, *Les rébellions touaregs au Nord Mali. Entre idées reçues et réalités*, Paris: L'Harmattan, 2016.

45. Fatouma Keïta, *Crise sécuritaire et violences au Nord du Mali*, Bamako: La Sahélienne, 2014.

46. The newspaper *Libération* published an 80-page document found on 16 February 2012 in Timbuktu and signed by the leader of AQIM, A. Droukbal. This document revealed the organization's strategy, and its leader urged his men to "build bridges between the various strata and components of Arab, Tuareg and Black societies of Azawad" and consider "our Islamic project in the region of Azawad as a newborn ... If we really want it to stand on its own two feet in this world full of enemies waiting to pounce, we must ease its burden, take it by the hand, help it and support it until it stands." Such advice was not followed by all, as evident in the formation of Islamic courts and the "extreme speed with which [they] applied the sharia".

47. See the Statoil report, "The In Amenas Attack: Report of the Investigation into the Terrorist Attack on In Amenas." Available at https://www.equinor.com/en/news/archive/2013/09/12/12SepInAmenasreport.html.

48. Jean-Christophe Notin, *La guerre de la France au Mali*, Paris: Tallandier, 2014, p. 149.

49. Lia Brynjar, *Architect of Global Jihad: The Life of Al-Qaida Strategist Abu Mus'ab al Suri*, London: Hurst, 2007.

50. Beatriz Mesa, "Le rôle transformateur des groupes armés du Nord du Mali", PhD Thesis, Université de Grenoble, 2017.

51. Boukary Sangaré, *Le centre du Mali. Epicentre du djihadisme*, Rapport GRIP, May 2016.

52. Thomas Hofnung, "Entretien avec Bernard Cazeneuve, ministre français délégué aux affaires européennes depuis juin 2012," *Politiques internationales*, no. 152, 2016. Available at http://www.politiqueinternationale.com/revue/print_article.php?id=1503&id_revue=152&content=texte.

53. Regarding the use of videos, see Elodie Apard, "Boko Haram, le jihad en vidéo," *Politique africaine*, no. 138, 2015, pp. 135–162.

54. Olivier Roy, *Jihad and Death* (trans. Cynthia Schoch), London: Hurst, and New York: Oxford University Press, 2017.

55. Serigne Bamba Gaye, "Conflicts between Farmers and Herders against a Backdrop of Asymmetric Threats in Mali and Burkina Faso," Friedrich-Ebert-Stiftung Peace and Security, 2018; Boubacar Ba and Morten Boas, "Mali: A Political Economy Analysis," NUPI (Norwegian Institute of International Affairs), 2017, available at http://hdl.handle.net/11250/2468085.

56. 2nd Regional Ministerial Conference on Border Security (Rabat, 14 November 2013), Declaration of Rabat, https://www.icao.int/Security/FAL/TRIP/Documents/14%20NOV%202013%20D%C3%A9claration%20de%20RABAT.pdf.

57. Ibid.

58. Luis Martinez and Rasmus Alenius Boserup, "Beyond Western Sahara, the Sahel-Maghreb Axis Looms," in Raquel Ojeda-Garcia, Irene Fernandez-Molina and Victoria Veguilla (eds.), *Global, Regional and Local Dimensions of Western Sahara's Protracted Decolonization*, Basingstoke: Palgrave Macmillan, 2017.

59. Protocol on reciprocal Morocco–Algeria commitments signed in Rabat on 6 July 1961.

60. Khadija Mohsen Finan, *Sahara occidental. Les enjeux d'un conflit régional*, Paris: CNRS, 1997.

61. Euromesco Papers, "Algérie, Maroc, Tunisie et l'intégration régionale" (2006, 2008, 2009).

62. Interview, Rabat, 2008, cited in Luis Martinez, Euormesco Paper, "Le Maroc, l'UMA et l'intégration régionale," no. 67, May 2008.

63. Michel Vallet, "Les Touaregs du Hoggar entre décolonisation et indépendance (1954–1974)," *Revue du monde musulman et de la Méditerranée*, no. 57, 1990.

64. Interview, Algiers, 2006.

65. Interview, Algiers, 2006. See also Luis Martinez, "L'Algérie, l'UMA et l'intégration régionale," Euromesco paper, no. 59, October 2006.

66. Interview, Rabat, 2008. See also Luis Martinez, "Le Maroc, l'UMA et l'intégration régionale," Euromesco paper, no. 67, May 2008

67. Interview, Rabat, 2008.

68. Interview, Algiers, 2006.

69. Royal message to the participants of a colloquium held in Rabat, 28 April 2006.

70. Abdelkhaleq Berramdane, *Le Maroc et l'Europe. Un destin commun*, *AAN*, no. XXVIII, 1990, p. 41.

71. In Tunisia, one estimate considers that the fight against terrorism costs the state budget 0.67% of GDP per year, or 3.3% of GDP in 2020. Report: http://www.iac.tn/articles/1–8-dupib-par-an-est-le-prix-a-payer-pour-la-guerre-contre-le-terrorisme.

CONCLUSION: REFORGING A SENSE OF BELONGING AND LOYALTY TO THE STATE

1. Hassan Rachik, "Nation, nationalisme et citoyenneté," *Les Cahiers bleus*, no. 8, 2007.
2. Stéphanie Pouessel, "L'islam au Nord," *Cahiers d'etudes africaines*, no. 211, 2013.
3. Aissa Kasmi, *La police algérienne, une institution pas comme les autres*, Algiers: Anep, 2002; René Gallisot, "Emeutes. Ordre étatique et désordre social," in D. Le Saout and M. Rollinde (eds.), *Emeutes et mouvements sociaux au Maghreb*, p. 25 ("Comment l'état se prépare à l'émeute").
4. *Horizons*, 10 December 2012.
5. Mekouar Merouan, *Protest and Mass Mobilisation: Authoritarian Collapse and Political Change in North Africa*, New York: Ashgate, 2016.
6. Didier Le Saout and Marguerite Rollinde (eds.), *Emeutes et mouvements sociaux au Maghreb*, p. 261.
7. Myriam Catusse, Blandine Destremau and Eric Verdier (eds.), *L'état face aux débordements du social au Maghreb. Formation, travail et protection sociale*, Paris: Karthala, 2009.
8. Mehdi Ben Barka, "Option révolutionnaire au Maroc," Rapport au secrétariat de l'UNFP, avant le 2° congrès, Rabat, 1 May 1962, http://www.al-mounadhil-a.info.
9. Michael Willis, *Politics and Power in the Maghreb: Algeria, Tunisia and Morocco from Independence to the Arab Spring*, Oxford: Oxford University Press, 2014. See the chapter "The Berber Question," p. 203; Yousra Aboubari, "La réapparition du drapeau de la république du riff lors du printemps arabe," in Baudoin Dupret, Zakaria Rhani, Assia Boutaleb and Jean-Noël Ferrié (eds.), *Le Maroc au Présent*, pp. 617–626; Karima Dirèche-Slimani, "Nation algérienne ou nation musulmane?" *Naqd*, 2014, pp. 19–44.
10. Béatrice Hibou, "La formation asymétrique de l'état en Tunisie," pp. 99–151.
11. Souhail Belhadj, "De la centralisation autoritaire à la naissance de 'pouvoir local'. Transition politique et recomposition institutionnelle en Tunisie, *Social Science Information*, no. 4, 2016.

12. Bernard Rougier and Stéphane Lacroix (eds.), *Egypt's Revolutions* (trans. Cynthia Schoch), New York: Palgrave Macmillan, 2016.

13. Vincent Geisser and Michael Béchir Ayari, *Renaissances arabes*.

14. René Remond, *Introduction à l'histoire de notre temps. Le XIX siècle (1815– 1914)*. Paris: Seuil, 1974.

15. Yâdh ben Achour, "La réforme des mentalités. Bourguiba et le redressement moral," in Michel Camau (ed.), *Tunisie au présent*, p. 148.

16. The UN secretary-general, in the "Plan of Action to Prevent Violent Extremism", stated that the plan "considers and addresses violent extremism as, and when, conducive to terrorism" and described violent extremism as "a diverse phenomenon, without clear definition. It is neither new nor exclusive to any region, nationality or system of belief." In Resolution 2178 (2014), the Security Council explicitly links "violent extremism" and "terrorism". Analysis of the "Plan of Action to Prevent Violent Extremism" (December 2015) shows that the notion has no clear definition: violent extremism is the label assigned to practices by "terrorist and violent extremist groups" such as Islamic State, AQIM and Boko Haram.

17. A notion has emerged: "Before the September 11, 2001 attacks, radicalization was a marginal notion … Since the September 11 attacks, the United States has attempted to promote research on terrorism and the factors that might encourage it, and radicalization has become a key notion for explaining the genesis of groups that embrace violent action," writes the sociologist Farhad Khosrokhavar, in his book *Radicalization*. The year 2004 has been identified as the moment when the notion of radicalization became the focus of discourse on terrorism and counterterrorism in the Anglo-Saxon countries. The vocabulary of radicalization began to be used to discuss Islam and terrorism, and the attacks perpetrated by al-Qaeda gave rise to a correlation between the notion of radicalization and Islamist terrorist groups.

BIBLIOGRAPHY

Books

Abidi, Hasni (ed.), *Où va le monde arabe?*, Paris: Editions Erik Bonnier, 2012.

Abitbol, Michel, *Histoire du Maroc*, Paris: Editions Perrin, 2009.

Ahmida, Ali Abdullah, *The Making of Modern Libya: State Formation, Colonization and Resistance, 1830–1932*, Albany: State University of New York Press, 1994.

Ait Aoudia, Myriam, *L'expérience démocratique en Algérie*, Paris: Presses de Sciences Po, 2015.

Allal, Amin and Thomas Pierret (eds.), *Devenir révolutionnaire. Au cœur des révoltes arabes*, Paris: Armand Colin, 2013.

Allal, Amin and Vincent Geisser (eds.), *Tunisie. Une démocratisation au-dessus de tout soupçon?*, Paris: CNRS, 2018.

Amer, Mohand and Belkacem Benzenine (eds.), *Le Maghreb et l'indépendance de l'Algérie*, Paris: Karthala, 2012.

Appadurai, Arjun, *Modernity at Large: Cultural Dimensions of Globalization*, Minneapolis: University of Minnesota Press, 1996.

Ashour, Omar, *The De-radicalization of Jihadists: Transforming Armed Islamist Movements*, New York: Routledge, 2009.

Augé, Axel Eric and Patrick Klaousen (eds.), *Reformer les armées africaines*, Paris: Karthala, 2010.

Baduel, Pierre-Robert (ed.), *Etats, territoires et terroirs au Maghreb*, Paris: CNRS Editions, 1985.

Baker-Beall, Christopher, Charlotte Heath-Kelly and Lee Jarvis (eds.), *Counter-radicalisation: Critical Perspectives*, New York: Routledge, 2005.

Barbet, Clotilde, *Les rébellions touaregs au Nord Mali. Entre idées reçues et réalités*, Paris: L'Harmatan, 2016.

Bayart, Jean-François, *Violence et religion en Afrique*. Paris: Karthala, 2018.

Ben Nafissa, Sarah (ed.), *ONG et gouvernance dans le monde arabe*, Paris: Karthala, 2004.

BIBLIOGRAPHY

Bjorgo, T. and J. Horgan, *Leaving Terrorism Behind: Disengagement from Political Violence*, New York: Routledge, 2008.

Bleuchot, Henry (ed.), *Chroniques et documents libyens, 1969–1980*, Paris: Editions du CNRS, 1983.

Bonnefoy, Laurent, *Yemen and the World: Beyond Insecurity* (trans. Cynthia Schoch), London: Hurst and New York: Oxford University Press, 2018.

Boserup, Rasmus Alenius and Martinez, Luis (eds.), *Algeria Modern: From Opacity to Complexity*, London: Hurst and New York: Oxford University Press, 2016.

Bozarslan, Hamit, *Révolution et état de violence. Moyen-Orient 2011–2015*, Paris: CNRS Editions, 2015.

Brownlee, Jason, Masoud Tarek and Andrew Reynolds, *The Arab Spring: Pathways of Repression and Reform*, New York: Oxford University Press, 2015.

Brynjar, Lia, *Architect of Global Jihad: The Life of al-Qaeda Strategist Abu Mus'ab al Suri*, London: Hurst, 2007.

Burgat, François, *L'islamisme au Maghreb*, Paris: Karthala, 1988.

Buttin, Maurice, *Ben Barka, Hassan II, De Gaulle*, Paris: Karthala, 2015.

Camau, Michel, *La notion de démocratie dans la pensée des dirigeants maghrébins*, Paris: CNRS, 1971.

Camau, Michel and Vincent Geisser, *Le syndrome autoritaire. Politique en Tunisie de Bourguiba à Ben Ali*, Paris: Presses de Sciences Po, 2003.

———— (eds.), *Habib Bourguiba. La trace et l'héritage*, Paris: Karthala, 2004.

Camau, Michel and Frédéric Vairel (eds.), *Soulèvements et recompositions politiques dans le monde arabe*, Montreal: PUM, 2014.

Catusse, Myriam, Blandine Destremau and Eric Verdier (eds.), *L'état face aux débordements du social au Maghreb. Formation, travail et protection sociale*, Paris: Karthala, 2009.

Cavatorta, Francesco and Vincent Durac (eds.), *Civil Society and Democratization in the Arar World: The Dynamics of Activism*, New York: Routledge, 2011.

Chacoua, Kamel, *L'islam kabyle*, Paris: Maisonneuve et Larose, 2001.

Chouikha, Larbi and Eric Gobe, *Histoire de la Tunisie depuis l'indépendance*, Paris: La Découverte, 2015.

Cole, Peter, and Brian MacQuin (eds.), *The Libyan Revolution and Its Aftermath*, London: Hurst, 2013.

Cooper, Frederick, *Africa since 1940: The Past of the Present*, New York: Cambridge University Press, 2002.

Courbage, Youssef and Emmanuel Todd, *Le rendez-vous des civilisations*, Paris: Seuil, 2007.

————, *A Convergence of Civilizations: The Transformation of Muslim Societies*, New York: Columbia University Press, 2014.

Daoud, Zakya, *Maroc. Les années de plomb (1958–1988)*, Paris: Editions de la MSH, 2007.

BIBLIOGRAPHY

Davezies, Laurent, *Le nouvel égoïsme territorial. Le grand malaise des nations*, Paris: Seuil, 2015.

Davis, John, *Libyan Politics: Tribe and Revolution*, London: I.B. Tauris, 1987.

Deheuvels, Luc-Willy, *Islam et pensée contemporaine en Algérie*, Paris: CNRS, 1991.

Deloye, Yves, *Sociologie historique du politique*, Paris: La Découverte, 2007.

Dieckhoff, Alain, *Nationalism and the Multinational State* (trans. Cynthia Schoch), London: Hurst and New York: Oxford University Press, 2016.

Dirèche-Slimani, Karima, *Chrétiens de Kabylie 1873–1954. Une action missionnaire dans l'Algérie coloniale*, Algiers: Bouchène, 2004.

Djaziri, Moncef, *Etat et société en Libye*, Paris: Karthala, 1996.

Dorronsoro, Gilles, Adam Baczko and Arthur Quesnay (eds.), *Syrie. Anatomie d'une guerre civile*, Paris: CNRS, 2016.

Ferrié, Jean-Noël and Jean-Claude Santucci (eds.), *Dispositifs de démocratisation et dispositifs autoritaires en Afrique du Nord*, Paris: CNRS, 2006.

Filiu, Jean-Pierre, *The Arab Revolution*, London: Hurst, 2011.

———, *From Deep State to Islamic State: The Arab Counter-Revolution and Its Jihadist Legacy*, London: Hurst, 2015.

Foucher, Michel, *L'obsession des frontières*, Paris: Perrin, 2007.

Geisser, Vincent and Michael Béchir Ayari, *Renaissances arabes*, Ivry sur Seine: Editions de l'Atelier, 2011.

Gellner, Ernest, *Nations and Nationalism*, Oxford: Blackwell, 1983.

Gelvin, James, *The Arab Uprisings: What Everyone Needs to Know*, New York: Oxford University Press, 2012.

Ghalioun, Burhan, *L'état contre la nation*, Paris: La Découverte, 1991.

Gomez-Perez, Muriel (ed.), *L'islam politique au sud du Sahara*, Paris: Karthala, 2005.

Grimaud, Nicole, *La Tunisie à la recherche de sa sécurité*, Paris: PUF, 1995.

Gros, Christian and David Dumoulin Kervran (eds.), *Le multiculturalisme au concret. Un modèle latino-américain?*, Paris: Presses de la Sorbonne Nouvelle, 2011.

Halpern, Manfred, *The Politics of Social Change in the Middle East and North Africa*, Princeton: Princeton University Press, 1963.

Hamid, Mustapha and Leah Farrall, *The Arabs at War in Afghanistan*, London: Hurst, 2015.

Hermassi, Elbaki, *Leadership and National Development in North Africa*, Berkeley: University of California Press, 1972.

Hibou, Béatrice, *The Force of Obedience: The Political Economy of Repression in Tunisia* (trans. Andrew Brown), Cambridge: Polity, 2011.

———, Hamza Meddeb and Mohamed Tozy (eds.), *L'état d'injustice au Maghreb. Maroc et Tunisie*, Paris: Karthala, 2015.

201

Hill, Jonathan N.C., *Identity in Algerian Politics: The Legacy of Colonial Rule*, Lynne Rienner: Boulder, 2009.

Ismael, Tareq Yousfi and Jacqueline Ismael, *Iraq in the Twenty-First Century: Regime Change and the Making of a Failed State*, London: Routledge, 2015.

Jeffrey, Denis, Jocelyn Lachance, David Le Breton, Meryem Sellami and Jihed Haj Salem, *Jeunes et djihadisme*, Montreal: PUL, 2016.

Joffé, George (ed.), *North Africa's Arab Spring*, London: Routledge, 2013.

Kasmi, Aissa, *La police algérienne, une institution pas comme les autres*, Algiers: Anep, 2002.

Kenz, Ali el-, *L'Algérie et la modernité*, Dakar: Codesria, 1988.

Khiari, Sadri, *Le délitement de la cité*, Paris: Karthala, 2003.

Khosrokhavar, Farhad, *Radicalization.Why Some People Choose the Path of Violence* (trans. Jane Marie Todd), New York: The New Press, 2017.

Laroui, Abdallah, *L'état dans le monde arabe contemporain. Eléments d'une problématique*, Cermac, Cahiers no. 3, 1980.

Larramendi, Miguel and Thierry Desrues (eds.), *Mohamed VI. Politica y cambio social en Marruecos*, Madrid: Almuzara, 2011.

Lascoumes, Pierre (ed.), *Gouverner par les instruments*, Paris: Presses de Sciences Po, 2005.

Le Drian, Jean-Yves, *Qui est l'ennemi?*, Paris: Editions du Cerf, 2016.

Le Saout, Didier and Marguerite Rollinde (eds.), *Emeutes et mouvements sociaux au Maghreb*, Paris, Karthala, 1999.

Leveau, Rémy, *Le fellah défenseur du trône*, Paris: Presses de Sciences Po, 1985.

Luizard, Pierre-Jean (ed.), *Le choc colonial et l'islam*, Paris: La Découverte, 2006.

Mahé, Alain, *Histoire de la Grande Kabylie*, Algiers: E. Bouchène, 2001.

Mahiou, Ahmed (ed.), *L'état de droit dans le monde arabe*, Paris: CNRS, 1997.

Martel, André, *La Libye (1835–1990). Essai de géopolitique historique*, Paris: PUF, 1991.

Martinez, Luis, *The Algerian Civil War, 1990–1998* (trans. Jonathan Derrick), London: Hurst, 2000.

———, *The Libyan Paradox* (trans. John King), London: Hurst, 2007.

———, *The Violence of Petro-Dollar Regimes: Algeria, Iraq and Libya* (trans. Cynthia Schoch), London: Hurst, 2012.

Masri, Safwan, *Tunisia: An Arab Anomaly*, New York: Columbia University Press, 2017.

Mekouar, Merouan, *Protest and Mass Mobilisation: Authoritarian Collapse and Political Change in North Africa*, Farnham: Ashgate, 2016.

Mérad, Ali, *Le réformisme musulman en Algérie de 1925 à 1960*, Paris: Editions de la MSH, 1967.

Miran-Guyon, Marie, *Guerres mystiques en Côte d'Ivoire. Religion, patriotisme et violence*, Paris: Karthala, 2015.

BIBLIOGRAPHY

Mohsen Finan, Khadija, *Sahara Occidental. Les enjeux d'un conflit régional*, Paris: CNRS, 1997.

Mokeddem, Mohamed, *Les Afghans algériens*, Algiers: Anep, 2002.

Mouline, Nabil, *Le califat. Histoire politique de l'islam*, Paris: Flammarion, 2016.

Mundy, Jacob, *Libya*, Cambridge: Polity Press, 2018.

Notin, Jean-Christophe, *La guerre de la France au Mali*, Paris: Tallandier, 2014.

Ojeda-Garcia, Raquel, Irene Fernández-Molina and Victoria Veguilla (eds.), *Global, Regional and Local Dimensions of Western Sahara's Protracted Decolonization*, New York: Palgrave Macmillan, 2017.

Otayek, René, *La politique africaine de la Libye*, Paris: Karthala, 1987.

Otayek, René and Benjamin Soares (eds.), *Islam and Muslim Politics in Africa*, New York: Palgrave Macmillan, 2007.

Ouannes, Moncef, *Militaires, élites et modernisation dans la Libye contemporaine*, Paris: L'Harmatan, 2009.

Ould Ahmed Salem, Zekeria, *Prêcher dans le désert. Islam politique et changement social en Mauritanie*, Paris: Karthala, 2013.

Pack, Jason (ed.), *The 2011 Libyan Uprisings and the Struggle for the Post-Qadhafi Future*, New York: Palgrave Macmillan, 2013.

Paoletti, Emanuela, *The Migration of Power and North-South Inequalities: The Case of Italy and Libya*, New York: Palgrave Macmillan, 2010.

Pérouse de Montclos, Marc-Antoine, *L'Afrique. Nouvelle frontière du djihad?*, Paris: La Découverte, 2018.

Rachik, Abderahmane, *Ville et pouvoirs au Maroc. Casablanca*, Casablanca: Edition Afrique Orient, 1995.

Rist, Gilbert, *Le développement. Histoire d'une croyance occidentale*, Paris: Presses de Sciences Po, 2001.

Rouadjia, Ahmed, *Grandeur et décadence de l'état algérien*, Paris: Karthala, 1994.

Rougier, Bernard (ed.), *Qu'est-ce que le salafisme?*, Paris: PUF, 2008.

Rougier, Bernard, and Stéphane Lacroix (eds.), *Egypt's Revolutions* (trans. Cynthia Schoch), New York: Palgrave, 2016.

Roy, Olivier, *Jihad and Death* (trans. Cynthia Schoch), London: Hurst, 2017.

Schlumberger, Oliver (ed.), *Debating Arab Authoritarianism: Dynamics and Durability in Nondemocratic Regimes*, Palo Alto: Stanford University Press, 2007.

Thurston, Alexander, *Boko Haram: The History of an African Jihadist Movement*, Princeton: Princeton University Press, 2018.

Tozy, Mohamed, *Monarchie et islam politique au Maroc*, Paris: Presses de Sciences Po, 1999.

Triaud, Jean-Louis, *Islam, sociétés et politiques en Afrique subsaharienne. Les exemples du Sénégal, du Niger et du Nigéria*, Paris: Les Indes Savantes, 2007.

Truc, Gérone, *Sidération. Une sociologie des attentats*, Paris: PUF, 2016.

BIBLIOGRAPHY

Vairel, Frédéric, *Politique et mouvements sociaux au Maroc. La révolution désamor-cée?*, Paris: Presses de Sciences Po, 2014.

Vandewalle, Dirk, *A History of Modern Libya*, Cambridge: Cambridge University Press, 2012.

Vermeren, Pierre, *Le Maroc en transition*, Paris: La Découverte, 2001.

Volpi, Frédéric, *Revolution and Authoritarianism in North Africa*, London: Hurst, 2017.

Volpi, Frédéric, *Islam and Democracy: The Failure of Dialogue in Algeria*, London: Pluto Press, 2002.

Weiss, Gillian, *Captives and Corsairs: France and Slavery in the Early Modern Mediterranean*, Stanford: Stanford University Press, 2011.

Werenfels, Isabelle, *Managing Instability in Algeria: Elites and the Political Change since 1995*, London: Routledge, 2007.

Willis, Michael, *The Islamist Challenge in Algeria: A Political History*, Reading: Ithaca Press, 1996.

————, *Politics and Power in the Maghreb: Algeria, Tunisia and Morocco from Independence to the Arab Spring*, Oxford: Oxford University Press, 2014.

Zeghal, Malika, *Les islamistes marocains. Le défi à la monarchie*, Paris: La Découverte, 2005.

Articles and Book Chapters

Acemoglu, Daron, and James A. Robinson, "Why is Africa Poor?", *Economic History of Developing Regions*, no. 25 (2010), pp. 21–50.

Alary, Véronique and Mohammed el Mourid, "Les politiques alimentaires au Maghreb et leurs conséquences sur les sociétés agropastorales," *Revue du Tiers Monde*, no. 4 (2005), pp. 785–810.

Ali, Zaid al-, "International Assistance to Arab Spring Transitions," in Stéphane Lacroix and Jean-Pierre Filiu (eds.), *Revisiting the Arab Uprisings*, London: Hurst, 2018.

Allal, Amin and Karine Bennafla, "Les mouvements protestataires de Gafsa (Tunisie) et Sidi Ifni (Maroc) de 2005 à 2009," *Revue du Tiers Monde*, no. 5 (HS) (2011), pp. 27–45.

Andezian, Sossie, "Mysticisme extatique dans le champ religieux algérien contemporain," in S. Ferchiou (ed.), *Islam pluriel au Maghreb*, Paris: CNRS, 1996.

Apard, Elodie, "Les mots de Boko Haram. Décryptages de discours de Mohammed Yusuf et d'Abubakar Shekau," *Afrique contemporaine*, no. 255 (2015), pp. 43–74.

Appadurai, Arjun, "Entretien. Violence et colère à l'âge de la globalisation," *Esprit*, May 2007, pp. 75–89.

Bechir Ayari, Michael, "La révolution tunisienne, une émeute qui a réussi?" in Amin Allal and Thomas Pierret (eds.), *Devenir révolutionnaire. Au cœur des révoltes arabes*, Paris, Armand Colin, 2013.

BIBLIOGRAPHY

Béchir Ayari, Michael and F. Merone, "Ansar al-Charia Tunisie. Une institutionnalisation à la croisée des chemins," in M. Camau and Frédéric Vairel (eds.), *Soulèvements et recompositions politiques dans le monde arabe*, Montreal: PUM, 2014.

Belhadj, Souhail, "De la centralisation autoritaire à la naissance de 'pouvoir local'. Transition politique et recomposition institutionnelle en Tunisie," *Social Science Information*, no. 4 (2016), pp. 479–494.

Bellin, Eva, "Reconsidering the Robustness of Authoritarianism in the Middle East: Lessons from the Arab Spring," *Comparative Politics*, vol. 44, no. 2 (2012), pp. 127–149.

Benafla, Karine and Haoues Seniguer, "Le Maroc à l'épreuve du printemps arabe. Une contestation désamorcée?", *Outre-terre*, no. 29 (2011), pp. 143–158.

Ben Lamma, Mohamed Faraj, "The Responsibility to Protect in Libya: Back to Square One?", *Revue internationale et stratégique*, no. 101 (2016), pp. 14–24.

————, "L'application de la responsabilité de protéger en Libye. Retour à la case départ?", *Revue internationale et stratégique*, no. 101 (2016), pp. 14–24.

Ben Nafissa, Sarah, "Révolution arabes. Les angles morts de l'analyse politique des sociétés de la région," *Confluences Méditerranée*, no. 77 (2011), pp. 75–90.

Bennani-Chraibi, Mounia and Mohamed Jeghllaly, "La dynamique protestataire du Mouvement du 20 February à Casablanca," *Revue française de science politique*, no. 62 (2012), pp. 867–893.

Benantar, Abdennour, "Complexe de sécurité Ouest-méditerranéen. Externalisation et sécurisation de la migration," *Année du Maghreb*, no. 9 (2013), pp. 55–75.

————, "NATO, Maghreb and Europe," *Mediterranean Politics*, vol. 11, no. 2 (2006), pp. 167–188.

————, "Sécurité aux frontières. Portée et limites de la stratégie algérienne," *L'Année du Maghreb*, 2016, pp. 147–163.

Bensaâd, Ali, "Changement social et contestation en Libye," *Politique africaine*, no. 125 (March 2012), pp. 5–22.

Boiley, Pierre, "Géopolitique africaine et rébellions touarègues. Approches locales, approches globales (1960–2011)," *L'Année du Maghreb*, CNRS, 2011, pp. 151–162.

Boserup, Rasmus Alenius and Martinez, Luis, "Beyond Western Sahara, the Sahel-Maghreb Axis Looms," in Raquel Ojeda-Garcia, Irene Fernadez-Molina and Victoria Veguilla (eds.), *Global, Regional and Local Dimensions of Western Sahara's Protracted Decolonization*, New York: Palgrave Macmillan, 2017, pp. 143–165.

Bouyacoub, Ahmed, "Croissance économique et développement 1962–2012: Quel bilan?", *Insaniyat*, no. 57–58 (2012), pp. 91–113.

BIBLIOGRAPHY

Bras, Jean-Philippe, "Le Maghreb dans la 'guerre contre le terrorisme'. Enjeux juridique et politiques des législations 'anti-terroristes'," *L'Année du Maghreb 2005–2006*, CNRS Editions, pp. 447–467.

————, "Tunisie. L'élaboration de la loi anti-terroriste de 2015 ou les paradoxes de la démocratie sécuritaire," *L'Année du Maghreb 2016*, CNRS Editions, pp. 309–323.

Bras, Jean-Philippe and Aude Signoles, "Etats et territoires du politique. La décentralisation en débat," *L'Année du Maghreb 2017*, pp. 9–25.

Brumberg, Daniel, "The Trap of Liberalized Autocracy," *Journal of Democracy*, no. 13 (2002), pp. 56–68.

Brynjar, Lia, "Jihadism in the Arab World after 2011: Explaining Its Expansion," *Middle East Policy*, vol. XXIII, no. 4 (2016), pp. 74–91.

Camau, Michel, "Globalisation démocratique et exception autoritaire arabe," *Critique internationale*, no. 30 (2006), pp. 59–81.

Catin, Maurice and Mouhoub el-Mouhoub, "Inégalités et pauvreté dans les pays arabes," *Région et développement*, no. 35 (2012), pp. 5–10.

Catusse, Myriam, "Au-delà de 'l'opposition à sa Majesté'. Mobilisations, contestation et conflits politiques au Maroc," *Pouvoirs*, no. 145 (2013), pp. 31–46.

Cavatorta, Francesco, "Le printemps arabe: le réveil de la société civile. Aperçu général," *Annuaire IEMed de la Méditerranée*, 2012, pp. 83–91.

————, "Salafism, Liberalism and Democracy Learning in Tunisia," *Journal of North African Studies*, no. 20 (2015), pp. 770–783.

Chaker, Salem and Masin Ferkal, "Berbères de Libye. Un paramètre méconnu, une irruption politiques inattendue," *Politique africaine*, no. 125 (2012), pp. 105–126.

Chekroun, Mohamed, "Islamisme, messianisme et utopie au Maghreb," *Archives des sciences sociales et des religions*, no. 75 (1991), pp. 127–152.

Chourou, Béchir, "The Challenge of Democracy in North Africa," *Democratization*, no. 9 (2002), pp. 17–39.

Clancy-Smith, Julia, "Islam, Gender and the Making of French Algeria, 1830–1962," in Julia Clancy-Smith and Frances Gouda (eds.), *Domesticating the Empire: Languages of Gender, Race, and Family Life in French and Dutch Colonialism, 1830–1962*, Charlottesville: University Press of Virginia, 1998, pp. 154–174.

Djaziri, Moncef, "Tribus et état dans le système politique libyen," *Outre-terre*, no. 23 (2009), pp. 127–134.

Driss-Aït Hamadouche, Louisa, "L'Algérie face au printemps arabe," *Confluences mediterranée*, no. 81 (2012–2), pp. 55–67.

Droz-Vincent, Philippe, "Quel avenir pour l'autoritarisme dans le monde arabe?", *Revue française de science politique*, vol. 54 (2004), pp. 945–979.

Dupuis, Jean-Marc, Claire el-Moudden and Anne Petron, "Les systèmes de retraite du Maghreb face au vieillissement démographique," *Revue française d'économie*, vol. XXV (2010), pp. 79–116.

Ferrié, Jean-Noël and Baudouin Dupret, "La nouvelle architecture constitutionnelle et les trois désamorçages de la vie politique marocaine," *Confluences méditerranée*, no. 78 (2011), pp. 25–34.

Flory, Maurice, "Le concept de révolution au Maroc," *Revue de l'Occident musulman et de la Méditerranée*, no. 5 (1968), pp. 145–152.

Gay, Paul and Alan Scott, "State Transformation or Regime Shift?", *Sociologica: Italian Journal of Sociology Online*, vol. 2 (2010), available at https://www.rivisteweb.it/issn/1971–8853/issue/3216.

Gratud, Henrik and Vidar Benjamin Skretting, "Ansar al-Sharia in Libya: An Enduring Threat," *Perspectives on Terrorism*, vol. 11, no. 1 (2017), pp. 40–53.

Grégoire, Emmanuel and André Bourgeot, "Désordre, pouvoirs et recompositions territoriales au Sahara," *Hérodote*, no. 142 (2011), pp. 3–11.

Hachmaoui, Mohmamed, "Institutions autoritaires et corruption politique. L'Algérie et le Maroc en perspective comparée," *Revue internationale de politique comparée*, vol. 19 (2012), pp. 141–164.

Hafez, M. Mohammed, "Armed Islamist Movement and Political Violence in Algeria," *Middle East Journal*, vol. 54, no. 4 (2000), pp. 572–591.

Hegghammer, Thomas, "The Future of Jihadism in Europe: A Pessimistic View," *Perspectives on Terrorism*, vol. 10, no. 6 (2016), available at http://www.terrorismanalysts.com/pt/index.php/pot/issue/view/61.

Heydemann, Steven, "Explaining the Arab Uprising: Transformations in Comparative Perspective," *Middle East Studies*, October 2015, pp. 192–204.

Heydemann, Steve, "Social Pacts and Persistence of Authoritarianism in the Middle East," in Oliver Schlumberger (ed.), *Debating Arab Authoritarianism: Dynamics and Durability in Nondemocratic Regimes*, Stanford: Stanford University Press, 2007.

Issawi, Charles, "The Economic and Social Foundations of Democracy in the Middle East," *International Affairs*, vol. 32, no. 1 (1956), pp. 27–42.

Joffé, George, "Civil Activism and the Roots of the 2011 Uprisings," in Jason Pack (ed.), *The 2011 Libyan Uprisings and the Struggle for the Post-Qadhafi Future*, New York: Palgrave Macmillan, 2013.

Jourde, Cédric, "Politique des récits de l'islamisme en Mauritanie," *Politique africaine*, no. 114 (2009), pp. 67–86.

Kateb, Kamel, "A qui profiterala 'fenêtre démographique' des pays du Maghreb," *Insaniyat*, no. 39 (2008), pp. 139–153.

Khiari, Sadri and Olfa Lamloum, "Le Zaïm et l'artisan de Bourguiba à Ben Ali," *Annuaire de l'Afrique du Nord*, vol. XXXVII, CNRS Editions, 1998.

King, Desmond and Patrick Le Galès, "Sociologie de l'état en recomposition," *Revue française de sociologie*, no. 52, vol. 3 (2011), pp. 453–480.

BIBLIOGRAPHY

Kubba, Laith, "The Awakening of Civil Society," *Journal of Democracy*, no. 11 (2000), pp. 84–90.

Laacher, Smain and Cédric Terzi, "Comment faire peuple? Le cas des protestations publiques au Maghreb," *L'Année du Maghreb*, vol. VIII (2012), pp. 87–102.

Lacher, Wolfram, "Libya's Local Elites and the Politics of Alliance Building," *Mediterranean Politics*, vol. 21, no. 1 (2016), pp. 64–84.

————, "Families, Tribes and Cities in the Libyan Revolution," *Middle East Policy*, no. 4, vol. 18 (2012), pp. 140–154.

————, "Supporting Stabilization in Libya: The Challenges of Finalizing and Implementing the Skhirat Agreement," *SWP Comments*, July 2015, available at https://www.swp-berlin.org/en/publication/supporting-stabilization-in-libya/.

————, "Was Libya's Collapse Predictable," *Survival*, no. 59 (2017), pp. 139–152.

Lacoste-Dujardin, Camille, "Géographie culturelle et géopolitique en Kabylie. La révolte de la jeunesse kabyle pour une Algérie démocratique," *Hérodote*, no. 103 (2001), pp. 57–90.

Lacroix, Laurent, "Etat plurinational et redéfinition du multiculturalisme en Bolivie," in Christian Gros and David Dumoulin Kervran (eds.), *Le multiculturalisme au concret. Un modèle latino-américain?*, Paris: Presses de la Sorbonne Nouvelle, 2011.

Larson, Erik and Ron Aminzade, "Les dilemmes de la construction de la nation dans les Etats-nations postcoloniaux. Les cas de la Tanzanie et des Fidji," *Revue internationale des sciences sociales*, no. 192 (2007), pp. 187–201.

Leveau, Rémy, "Crise des états et transitions incertaines," in *Le Maghreb en suspens. Les Cahiers du CERI*, no. 8, 1994, available at https://www.sciencespo.fr/ceri/fr/cahier?page=1.

Le Vine, Victor T., "Nation Building and Informal Politics," *International Social Science Journal*, no. 192 (2007), pp. 173–186.

Louër, Laurence and Eberhard Kienle, "Comprendre les enjeux économiques et sociaux des soulèvements arabes," *Critique internationale*, no. 61 (2013), pp. 11–17.

Malik, Adeel and Bassem Awadallah, "The Economics of the Arab Spring," *World Development*, vol. 45 (2013), pp. 296–313.

Miras, Claude de, "Initiative nationale pour le développement humain et économie solidaire au Maroc," *Revue du Tiers Monde*, no. 190, 2007.

Moussaoui, Abderrahmane, "Du public au privé. La notion d'intérêt général en Algérie," in Mohammed Kerrou (ed.), *Public et privé en Islam*, IRMC, Maisonneuve et Larose, 2002.

Nievas, David, "Rebellion and Sharia in the Sahel: An Analysis of the Tuareg

BIBLIOGRAPHY

Rebellion and the Occupation of Northern Mali by Armed Jihadist and Islamist Groups," *Unisci Discussion papers*, January 2014.

Otayek, René, "Religion et globalisation. L'islam subsaharien à la conquête de nouveaux territoires," *Revue internationale et stratégique*, no. 52 (2003), pp. 56–65.

Ouannes, Moncef, "Islamistes en Libye. Itinéraires idéologiques et confrontation avec le pouvoir," *Revue d'histoire maghrebine*, vol. 31, no. 116 (2004), pp. 137–149.

Oussédik, Fatma, "L'Algérie, une société en guerre contre elle-même," *Naqd*, no. 32 (2015), pp. 105–134.

Picard, Elisabeth, "Armée et sécurité au cœur de l'autoritarisme," in Olivier Dabène (ed.), *Autoritarismes démocratiques. Démocraties autoritaires au XXI siècle*, Paris: La Découverte, 2008.

Pouessel, Stéphanie, "L'Islam au Nord," *Cahiers d'études africaines*, no. 211 (2013), pp. 571–594.

Quesnay, A, "Renégocier l'espace politique libyen. Du local au national," *Noria*, September 2012, available at https://www.noria-research.com/fr/renegocier-lespace-politique-libyen-du-local-au-national/.

Reba Maamri, Malika, "The Imazighen's Quest for Inclusion," in *The State of Algeria: The Politics of a Post-Colonial Legacy*, London: I.B. Tauris, 2015.

Saaidia, Oissila, "L'invention du culte musulman dans l'Algérie coloniale du XIXᵉ siècle," *L'Année du Maghreb*, 2016, pp. 115–132.

Sadiki, Larbi, "Popular Uprisings and Arab Democratization," *International Journal of Middle East Studies*, vol. 32, no. 1 (2000), pp. 71–95.

———, "The Search for Citizenship in Bin Ali's Tunisia: Democracy versus Unity," *Political Studies*, vol. 50 (2002), pp. 497–513.

Santucci, Jean-Claude, "Armée, pouvoir et légitimité au Maroc," in *Annuaire de l'Afrique du Nord*, vol. 2 (1971), pp. 137–178, available at http://aan.mmsh.univ-aix.fr/volumes/1971/Pages/AAN-1971-10_02.aspx.

Scheele, Judith, "The Libyan Connection: Settlement, War, and Other Entanglements in Northern Chad," *Journal of African History*, no. 57 (2016), pp. 115–134.

Seignobos, Christian, "Boko Haram. Innovations guerrières depuis les monts Mandara," *Afrique contemporaine*, no. 252 (2014), pp. 149–169.

Sellami, Meryem and Jihed Haj Salem, "Conversion djihadiste des jeunes en Tunisie post révolutionnaire. Altérité, corporalité et spatialité," in Denis Jeffrey (ed.), *Jeunes et djihadisme*, Montreal: PUL, 2016, pp. 115–155.

Shahin, Emad el-Din, "The February 17th Intifada in Libya," in Ricardo Laremont (ed.), *Revolution, Revolt and Reform in North Africa: The Arab Spring and Beyond*, New York: Routledge, 2014.

Reports and Research Documents

Ba, Boubacar and Morten Boas, "Mali: A Political Economy Analysis", NUPI

(Norwegian Institute of International Affairs), 2017, available at http://hdl.handle.net/11250/2468085.

Ben Lamma, Mohamed Faraj, "The Tribal Structure in Libya: Factor for Fragmentation or Cohesion?", Fondation pour la recherche stratégique, July 2017, available at https://www.frstrategie.org/en/programmes/observatoire-du-monde-arabo-musulman-et-du-sahel/the-tribal-structure-in-libya-factor-for-fragmentation-or-cohesion-14.

Bencherif, Adil, "De la 'question touareg' aux mémoires du conflit. Pour une réconciliation malienne," Centre Francopaix, February 2018, available at https://dandurand.uqam.ca/centre-francopaix/.

Boserup, Rasmus Alenius and Luis Martinez (eds.), *Europe and the Sahel-Maghreb Crisis*, DIIS report, no. 3, 2018, available at https://www.diis.dk/en/research/the-european-powers-and-the-sahel-maghreb-crisis.

Cold-Ravnkilde, Signe Marie and Sine Plambech, "Boko Haram: From Local Grievances to Violent Insurgency, DIIS Report 2015, available at https://www.diis.dk/.../avoiding-past-mistakes-in-the-fight-against-....

Collombier, Virginie, "Make Politics, Not War: Armed Groups and Political Competition in Post Qadhafi Libya," in B. Kodmani and Nayla Moussa (eds.), *Out of the Inferno? Rebuilding Security in Iraq, Libya, Syria and Yemen*, Arab Reform Initiative, 2017, available at https://www.arab-reform.net/en/node/1090.

Congressional Research Service, "Terrorism and Violent Extremism in Africa," 14 July 2016, available at https://www.everycrsreport.com/.../20160714_R44563_044e4e8d...

Dworkin, Anthony and Fatim-Zohra el Malki, "The Southern Front Line: EU Counter-terrorism Cooperation with Tunisia and Morocco," Policy Brief, European Council on Foreign Relations, 15 February 2018, available at https://www.edfr.eu/publications/summary/the_southern_front_line_eu_counter_terrorism_cooperation.

Friedrich Ebert Stiftung, "Islamist Movements in Libya: Chances and Challenges of Political Power," FES Libya Office, 2015, available at https://www.fes.org.ma/.../FES%20Libya%20English%20DEF.pdf.

Gaye, Serigne Bamba, "Conflits between Farmers and Herders against a Backdrop of Asymmetric Threats in Mali and Burkina Faso," Friedrich-Ebert-Stiftung Peace and Security, 2018, available at https://library.fes.de/pdf-files/bueros/fes-pscc/14174.pdf.

Global Initiative Against Transnational Organized Crime (GITNOC), "Libya: A Growing Hub for Criminal Economies and Terrorist Financing in the Trans-Sahara," May 2015, available at http://globalinitiative.net/wp-content/uploads/2015/05/2015–1.pdf.

Grifa, Mohhamed, "Libya: Establishing Political System and the Transition to

Statehood," Arab Reform Initiative, September 2012, available at https://www.arab-reform.net/en/node/449.

Human Rights Watch, *Libya Report 2018*, available at https://www.hrw.org/world-report/2018/country-chapters/libya#.

ICG, "Islamist Terrorism in the Sahel: Fact or Fiction?", no. 92, March 2005, available at https://www.crisisgroup.org/africa/central-africa/chad/islamist-terrorism-sahel-fact-or-fiction.

———, "Reform and Security Strategy in Tunisia," Report no. 161, Middle East and North Africa, 23 July 2015, available at https://www.crisisgroup.org/middle-east-north-africa/north-africa/tunisia/reform-and-security-strategy-tunisia.

———, "The Libyan Political Agreement: Time for a Reset," Report no. 170, Middle East and North Africa, 4 November 2016, available at https://www.crisisgroup.org/middle-east-north-africa/north-africa/libya/libyan-political-agreement-time-reset.

———, "The Social Roots of Jihadist Violence in Burkina Faso's North," Report no. 170, Middle East and North Africa, no. 254, 12 October 2017, available at https://www.crisisgroup.org/africa/west-africa/burkina-faso/254-social-roots-jihadist-violence-burkina-fasos-north.

Lacher, Wolfram and Alaa al-Idrissi, "Capital of Militias: Tripoli's Armed Groups Capture the Libyan State," *Small Arms Survey*, June 2018, available at http://www.smallarmssurvey.org/fileadmin/docs/T-Briefing-Papers/SAS-SANA-BP-Tripoli-armed-groups.pdf.

Martinez, Luis, "Libye. Une transition à l'épreuve du legs de la Jamahiriyya," *Les Etudes du CERI*, no. 195, 2013, available at www.sciencespo.fr/ceri/fr/papier/etude.

Pack, Jason, Rhiannon Smith and Karim Mezran, *The Origins and Evolution of ISIS in Libya*, Atlantic Council, Rafik Hariri Center for the Middle East, June 2017, available at https://www.atlanticcouncil.org/publications/reports/the-origins-and-evolution-of-isis-in-libya.

Sangaré, Boukary, "Le centre du Mali. Epicentre du djihadisme," GRIP Report, May 2016, available at https://www.grip.org/fr/node/2008.

Statoil, "The In Amenas Attack: Report of the Investigation into the Terrorist Attack on In Amenas," available at https://www.equinor.com/en/news/archive/2013/09/12/12SepInAmenasreport.html.

Thiam, Adam, "Centre du Mali. Enjeux et dangers d'une crise négligée," Institut du Macina, Centre pour le dialogue humanitaire, March 2017, available at https://www.hdcentre.org/fr/updates/nouvelle-publication-centre-du-mali-enjeux-et-dangers-dune-crise-negligee/.

United Nations, Human Rights Council, *Report of the International Commission of Inquiry on Libya*, 2 March 2012, available at https://www.ohchr.org/documents/hrbodies/hrcouncil/.../a_hrc_19_68_en.doc.

BIBLIOGRAPHY

————, *Final Report of the Panel of Experts on Libya Established Pursuant to Resolution 1973 (2011) (S/2017/466)*, available at http://undocs.org/S/2017/466.

United Nations Development Programme, "Journey to Extremism in Africa," 2017, available at http://journey-to-extremism.undp.org/en/reports.

Watanabe, Lisa, "La gestion des djihadistes de retour en Afrique du Nord," *Politique de sécurité: analyses du CSS*, no. 222, March 2018, available at www. css.ethz.ch/content/dam/ethz/special-interest/gess/.../CSSAnalyse222-FR.pdf.

Wehrey, Frederick, "The Struggle for Security in Eastern Libya," Carnegie Endowment for International Peace, September 2012, available at http://carnegieendowment.org/2012/09/19/struggle-for-security-in-eastern-libya-pub-49425.

Winter, Charlie, "Libya: The Strategic Gateway for the Islamic State," Quilliam Foundation, February 2015, available at http://www.quilliamfoundation. org/wp/wp-content/uploads/publications.free/libya-the-strategic-gateway-for-is.pdf.

Zelin, Aaron Y., "The Terrorist Threat in North Africa, before and after Benghazi," Testimony before the House Committee on Foreign Affairs, Subcommittee on Terrorism, Nonproliferation, and Trade and the Subcommittee on the Middle East and North Africa, The Washington Institute, 10 July 2013, available at https://www.washingtoninstitute. org/.../ZelinTestimony20130710-...

————, "The Others: Foreign Fighters in Libya," The Washington Institute, Policy Note no. 45, January 2018, available at https://www.washingtoninstitute.org/policy-analysis/view/the-others-foreign-fighters-in-libya-and-the-islamic-state.

INDEX

213

INDEX

INDEX

INDEX